A
TEXTBOOK OF
FOODS, NUTRITION
AND
DIETETICS
(Second Revised Edition)

A
TEXTBOOK OF
FOODS, NUTRITION
AND
DIETETICS

(Second Revised Edition)

Raheena Begum

STERLING PUBLISHERS PRIVATE LIMITED

STERLING PUBLISHERS PRIVATE LIMITED
A-59 Okhla Industrial Area, Phase-II, New Delhi-110020.
Tel: 6916165, 6916209, 6912677
Fax: 91-11-6331241 E-mail: ghai@nde.vsnl.net.in
www.sterlingpublishers.com

A Textbook of Foods, Nutrition and Dietetics
© 1991, Raheena Begum
ISBN 81 207 0932 2
First Edition 1989
Second Revised Edition 1991
Reprint 1992, 1994, 1995, 1996, 1997, 1999, 2000, 2001, 2002

PRINTED IN INDIA

Published by Sterling Publishers Pvt. Ltd., New Delhi-110 020.
Printed at Ram Printograph (India), Delhi-110051.

PREFACE TO THE SECOND EDITION

An attempt is made to elaborate the first edition of this book based on the suggestions received from various sources. More chapters on dietetics, sample diets for various groups, diets for patients and more low-cost recipes are the new additions in this edition.

Within a short period a second edition of this book was made possible by the Home Scientists and students of Home Science and B.Sc Nursing. I thank them all, along with all wishers.

I am indebted to Mr. S.K. Ghai, Managing Director, Sterling Publishers (Pvt.) Ltd. for encouraging me to elaborate the book and also for bringing out the second edition so soon.

With pleasure I acknowledge the understanding and help offered to me by family members without which I would not have finished this book.

Raheena Begum

PREFACE TO THE SECOND EDITION

An attempt is made to elaborate the first edition of this book based on the suggestions received from various sources. More chapters on dietetics, sample diets for various groups, diets for patients and more low-cost recipes are the new additions in this edition.

Within a short period a second edition of this book was made possible by the Home Scientists and students of Home Science and B.Sc. Nursing. I thank them all, along with all wishers.

I am indebted to Mr. S.K. Ghai, Managing Director, Sterling Publishers (Pvt.) Ltd. for encouraging me to elaborate the book and also for bringing out the second edition so soon.

With pleasure I acknowledge the understanding and help offered to me by family members without which I would not have finished this book.

Rabeya Begum

TO THE FIRST EDITION PREFACE

From my twenty years of experience in teaching Foods, Nutrition and Dietetics to Graduates and Post-graduates and B.Sc. Nursing students, I felt the need for a reference book that deals with all the three subjects. This prompted me to write a book and my efforts materialised into this: *A Textbook of Foods, Nutrition and Dietetics*. Every effort has been made to make it a useful reference book for B.Sc. Home Science, B.Sc. Nursing and Food Science students.

This book is divided into four parts. Part I consists of chapters on Nutrition. In Part II chapters on Foods are included. Part III has chapters on Nutrition in Health and in Part IV Nutrition in Diseases are included.

Four more chapters of Applied Nutrition, Diet Surveys, Anthropometric Measurements and Food Adulteration are included for the benefit of extension students. My practical experience in Applied Nutrition, Extension and Dietetics provided me opportunities to transfer theoretical knowledge into practical work and I have tried to incorporate that in this book.

The tables of Recommended Dietary intake for various groups were derived from *Recommended Dietary Intake for Indians*, Indian Council of Medical Research (1984) and *The Nutritive Value of Indian Foods and Planning Satisfactory Diets* (6th edn-revised) by Gopalan, C., and Balasubramanian, S.C. (1963), Indian Council of Medical Research, New Delhi. I am thankful to the Indian Council of Medical Research for permission to draw from their material.

My sincere gratitude goes to my family members who patiently endured me throughout the work without which I would not have finished this book so soon.

I must also express my appreciation of the service rendered by Shri P. Thomas who happily helped me to prepare the script of the book.

Above all, the services rendered by Sterling Publishers in getting this book printed and published are invaluable, for without their kind interest this book would not have seen the light of day. I do heartily thank them all.

Raheena Begum

TO THE FIRST EDITION PREFACE

From my twenty years of experience in teaching Foods, Nutrition and Dietetics to Graduates and Post-graduates and B.Sc. Nursing students, I felt the need for a reference book that deals with all the three subjects. This prompted me to write a book and my efforts materialised into this: A Textbook of Foods, Nutrition and Dietetics. Every effort has been made to make it a useful reference book for B.Sc. Home Science, B.Sc. Nursing and Food Science students.

This book is divided into four parts. Part I consists of chapters on Nutrition. In Part II chapters on Foods are included. Part III has chapters on Nutrition in Health and in Part IV Nutrition in Diseases are included.

Four more chapters of Applied Nutrition, Diet Surveys, Anthropometric Measurements and Food Adulteration are included for the benefit of extension students. My practical experience in Applied Nutrition, Extension and Dietetics provided me opportunities to transfer theoretical knowledge into practical work and I have tried to incorporate that in this book.

The tables of Recommended Dietary intake for various groups were derived from Recommended Dietary Intake for Indians, Indian Council of Medical Research (1984) and The Nutritive Value of Indian Foods and Planning Satisfactory Diets (6th edn-revised) by Gopalan, C., and Balasubramanian, S.C. (1963), Indian Council of Medical Research, New Delhi. I am thankful to the Indian Council of Medical Research for permission to draw from their material.

My sincere gratitude goes to my family members who patiently endured me throughout the work without which I would not have finished this book so soon.

I must also express my appreciation of the service rendered by Shri P. Thomas who happily helped me to prepare the script of the book.

Above all, the services rendered by Sterling Publishers in getting this book printed and published are invaluable, for without their kind interest this book would not have seen the light of day. I do heartily thank them all.

Raheena Begum

CONTENTS

PART III: NUTRITION IN HEALTH

PART IV: NUTRITION IN DISEASES

Part I
NUTRITION

Part 1
NUTRITION

RELATION OF FOOD TO HEALTH

Food is essential for human existence just like the air we breathe or the water we drink. The food that we eat is utilised in the body and the assimilated substances are used for the growth and maintenance of tissues. A living organism is the product of nutrition. The human being requires more than 45 different nutrients for its well-being. Food materials ingested by the body are digested, absorbed and metabolised. Useful chemical substances derived from food by the body are called nutrients. A number of foodstuffs have to be selected to get all the nutrients. The health of a person depends on the type and quantity of foodstuff he chooses to make his diet. For sustaining healthy and vigorous life, diet should be planned according to the principles of nutrition. Extensive research work carried out on human beings and on experimental animals throughout the world has provided us with sufficient knowledge on nutrition and health. World Health Organisation defines health as "the state of complete physical, mental and social well being and not merely the absence of disease or infirmity".

Nutrition is the science of food values. It is relatively a new science which was evolved from chemistry and physiology. Nutrition is often mentioned as a branch of chemical science or biochemistry. The effect of food on our body is explained in nutrition. In other words, nutrition is defined as food at work in the body. In a broader sense nutrition is defined as the combination of process by which the living organism receives and utilises the materials necessary for the maintenance of its functions and for the growth and renewal of its components. Nutrients are defined as the constituents of food which help us to maintain our body functions, to grow and to protect our organs. There are six major nutrients in our body. They are carbohydrates, proteins, lipids, vitamins and minerals. The human body requires 17 vitamins and 24 mineral elements for various day-to-day activities. The composition of human body is 60-62 per cent water, 17 per cent proteins, 14 per cent fat, 6 per cent minerals and 1 per cent carbohydrates. In infants the percentage of water is more as compared to an adult. In women water content is slightly lower whereas fat content is more than in men. Fat deposition in the body increases with age.

Percentage Composition of Human Body

Nutrients	Man	Woman
Water	60-62	54
Protein	17	15
Fat	14	25
Minerals	6	5
Carbohydrates	1	1

Vitamins are present in negligible amounts.

Relationships of food to health have been made from the research conducted by chemists, microbiologists, pathologists and nutritionist from the past two centuries.

Human nutrition is governed by many factors like food habits and behaviour, food beliefs, ethnic influences, geographic influences, religious and sociological factors, psychological factors, food and production, income, national and international food policies, food technology, processing, fisheries, transportation, marketing, educational status and other mass media facilities.

The benefits of good nutrition are health, happiness, efficiency and longevity.

Optimum or Adequate Nutrition

When all the essential nutrients are present in a correct proportion as required by our body, it is called optimum nutrition or adequate nutrition. Optimum nutrition is required to maintain good health.

There are certain signs of good nutrition. They are height and weight for the age, clear complexion, fresh and lively skin and hair, healthy pink nails, correct posture and gait, inquisitive and alert eyes, good appetite and bowel evacuation, emotional maturity and confident deeds and pleasing personality and optimism in life and overall health.

Undernourishment

When almost all nutritions are below the requirement, the condition is known as undernourishment. Undernourishment may be defined as a state of partial starvation. An undernourished person manifests symptoms of deficiencies and feels unwell. Poor body weight, poor resistance to infection, weakness, apathy and general ill-health are symptoms of undernourishment.

Malnutrition

Malnutrition is an impairment of health either from a deficiency or excess or imbalance of nutrients. Malnutrition is a condition when one or two nutrients are less or are in excess in the body. This again manifests in disorders and discomforts. Severe malnutrition in certain phases of life can do irreparable damage to the body. Physical, mental and intellectual well-being in a person is affected due to malnourishment. Emotional upset and intellectual dwarfism create personality problems in later life. Impaired functional ability and deficient structural integrity result from malnutrition. Marasmus, kwashiorkor, xerophthalmia, scurvy, rickets, osteomalacia, beri-beri, pellagra and anaemia result from the deficiencies of protein, calories, vitamin A, vitamin C, vitamin D, B-complex vitamins and minerals, respectively. Malnutrition creates lasting effect on the growth and development of a person. Permanent retardation of the central nervous system occurs due to protein calorie malnutrition in early life. Thus nutrients from food sources enable one to keep fit and maintain health. These substances include energy which gives the capacity to work, proteins which form our body muscles, bones, blood, body fluids, enzymes, hormones, antibodies, organs, skin, hair and nervous tissues. Food also supplies minerals and vitamins which protect our organs and regulate their functions and other physiological processes.

Classification of Foods

Based on these functions, foods are grouped into energy-yielding foods, body-building foods and protective foods. Nutrients which engage in these activities are known as energy-yielding nutrients, body-building nutrients and protective nutrients. Carbohydrates, fats and proteins release energy on metabolism in our body.

1 gm of carbohydrates provides   - 4 kcals
1 gm of proteins provides   - 4 kcals
1 gm of fat provides   - 9 kcals

Cereal grains like rice, wheat, ragi and maize, roots and tubers like potato, sweet potato and tapioca are good sources of carbohydrates. Fats are considered the concentrated source of energy as they supply more than double the quantity of carlories compared to carbohydrates and proteins. Though proteins yield energy, normally they are considered body-building foods. Nutrients like proteins, mineral salts like calcium, phosphorus, iron and water are body-building nutrients. Their sources are body-building foods. Just like a house is built from wood, brick, cement, sand, iron rods, nails and other materials our organs in the body are built from the substances derived from food.

Protein foods like milk, meat, fish, eggs, pulses, grams and nuts are essential to build our tissues and to form blood.

Our body functions are regulated by water, certain minerals and vitamins. They are essential for the well-being and working of the body. They are called protective foods. Foods rich in protein, minerals, vitamins and water are termed as protective foods. Water is necessary for various body processes.

Minerals like calcium help in controlling blood clotting, muscular contraction and for the efficiency of heart muscles. Iron is essential for blood formation and iodine is necessary for regulating body function through the thyroid gland.

Vitamins are essential for regulating the body process such as growth, muscular coordination of various organs and functions of several organs like eyes, ears, nose and skin.

Thus foods play a prominent role in providing physical, mental and social well-being which is otherwise known as health to the people. Health is reflected in a person's nutritional status. Nutritional status is the condition of the individual as influenced by the utilisation of the nutrients. Dietary history, physical examination and laboratory examinations reveal it.

2

CARBOHYDRATES

Carbohydrates àre compounds which contain carbon, hydrogen and oxygen. Oxygen and hydrogen are present in carbohydrates in the same proportion as in water. They are the main sources of energy for our body and the only source of energy for our nervous tissues.

Carbohydrates are mainly distributed among plant foods with few exceptions like glycogen, lactose and ribose which are present in muscles or in liver, human milk and animal cells, respectively.

In various parts of the plants like leaves, stems, fruits, seeds and roots, carbohydrate is stored as starches and sugars. And the plant sources supply about 45 to 80 per cent of the energy requirement of the people throughout the world. Plants through the process of photosynthesis manufacture carbohydrate and after its use store them as polysaccharides.

Chemistry

Carbohydrates are chemically known as saccharides, as carbon, hydrogen and oxygen form saccharide groups. Carbohydrates are classified, based on the number of saccharide groups in them:

a. Monosaccharides
b. Disaccharides, and
c. Polysaccharides.

Monosaccharides

On hydrolysis or by digestion, monosaccharides cannot be simplified as they are the simple form of carbohydrates. This is the absorbable form of carbohydrate in our body. Based on the number of carbon atoms present in them, monosaccharides are grouped into triose (3 carbons), tetrose (4 carbons), pentose (5 carbons), and hexose (6 carbons).

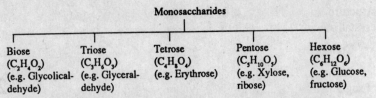

Biose, triose and tetrose are not nutritionally significant.

Pentoses like ribose, xylose and arabinose are of little dietary significance, xylose and arabinose are widely distributed in many root vegetables and in many vegetables. Ribose is part of riboflavin and DNA and RNA Body can synthesise it and so it is not a dietary essential.

Xylose and Arabinose are not present in free state in nature. Both of them are present in gums of various origins like woodgum, cherry gum or gum arabic.

In human nutrition only hexoses are of importance. Commonly found hexoses are aldose and ketose. The three monosaccharides of hexose group are glucose or dextrose, fructose or levulose and galactose and mannose.

Glucose: Also known as grape sugar, glucose is an aldose sugar. It is a white crystalline substance easily soluble in water with a sweet taste. Glucose is readily absorbed from the stomach. Glucose is used to detect the disorders in carbohydrate metabolism because it is in the form of carbohydrate circulating in blood. A normal healthy person has 80-100 mgs of glucose/100 ml of blood. Glucose is present in fruits and honey.

Fructose known as fruit sugar is a ketosugar. It is sweeter than glucose. Fructose enters the cells without the aid of insulin and so it is recommended for diabetics. Honey is the richest source of fructose (30-40%). Fructose on reduction yields a mixture of sorbitol and mannitol.

Galactose is not present in nature. It is present only in milk sugar lactose; on hydrolysis lactose yields galactose and glucose. Galactose is present in cerebrosides in brain and nervous tissues.

Disaccharides

They are complex sugars with two saccharide groups and are formed by the condensation of two monosaccharides. On hydrolysis or by digestion they are split into monosaccharides. Disaccharides have a structure of $C_{12}H_{22}O_{11}$. They are water soluble, diffusible and crystallisable. They vary in their sweetness.

Commonly found disaccharides are sucrose, maltose and lactose.

Sucrose, otherwise known as invert sugar, is the commonest form of sugar in the diet. Either by hydrolysis or by enzyme action sucrose is simplified into glucose and fructose. It is present in sugarcane, beetroot and in many fruits and vegetables, and honey. Sucrose is formed by the condensation of one molecule of glucose and one molecule of fructose.

Maltose is a disaccharide which contains two molecules of glucose. It is otherwise known as malt sugar. Starch is converted to maltose before breaking down into glucose. It is present in sprouted grains. Cereal grains are rich in maltose.

Lactose is also known as milk sugar and contains glucose and galactose. Cow's milk contains about five per cent of lactose and human milk has about 6.8 per cent. It is easily digestible but it is not as sweet as cane sugar. Lactose is synthesised in the mammary gland. It is less in sweetness compared to other sugars.

Trisaccharides

They are with three saccharide groups but are not of any nutritional significance. The fibrous parts of certain beans and root vegetables which are not digestible contain trisaccharides, e.g., Raffinose is present in beetroots and cottonseed meal.

Tetrasaccharides

They contain four monosaccharides and like trisaccharides they are of no nutritional significance, e.g., stachyose and scorodose.

Polysaccharides

They are large complex molecules of monosaccharides linked together. Several hundreds of glucose units are linked together in polysaccharides. They are insoluble in water. Starch, dextrins, glycogen, pectin and cellulose are the common forms of polysaccharides.

Starch: Plants store carbohydrates in the form of starch and it is the main source of nourishment for human race. Cereal grains, seeds, roots like potato, tapioca, yam and plantain contain considerable amount of starch. On cooking, starch absorbs water and it swells and ruptures. This thickening quality of starch is used in cookery to produce a variety of dishes. Different sources of starch behave differently. Maize starch and cornflour are better 'thickening agents' than rice or wheat starch. All starches are broken down into glucose in the digestive system.

The characteristics of starch molecule depend upon the way in which 2,000 or more glucose units are linked. The number of glucose molecules in starch vary from 2,000 to 15,000. The glucose chain in starch are of two types. They are amylose and amylopectin.

(i) *Amylose:* Amylose is a long chain of glucose and starch has about 10-20 per cent of amylose molecule in it. One molecule of amylose has 500-5,000 glucose molecules. Amylose is easily soluble in water and it is mainly responsible for the stiffening of cooked rice on keeping.

Amylose chain - G-G-G-G-G-G-G-G-G

(ii) *Amylopection:* Starch contains about 80-90 per cent of amylopectin in them. Amylopectin molecule has more glucose units. Usually one amylopectin molecule has 50,000-5,00,000 glucose molecule. Glucose molecules are arranged in branches.

$$
\begin{array}{l}
\text{G} \\
\text{G} \\
\text{G-G-G-G-G-G-G} \\
\text{G} \\
\text{G-G-G} \\
\text{G-G-G} \\
\text{G-G-G-G-G-G} \\
\text{G}\qquad\text{G} \\
\text{G}\qquad\text{G} \\
\text{G} \\
\text{G}
\end{array}
$$

Fig. 2.1: Amylopectin

Small branches of amylopectin has 20-30 glucose units and it has a colloidal property and this is responsible for thickening of starch water on heating.

Dextrins: When starch is partially broken into fragments either by digestion or by acids they are called dextrins. They are like starch itself. Dextrin is broken down into maltose. Starch is broken down into amylodextrin, erythrodextrin, achrodextrin and maltose.

Pectin is a polysaccharide with no nutritional significance. But it is useful in the preparation of jam and jelly and thus it contributes to the palatability of foods.

Glycogen can be described as the animal starch as it is in this form animals store carbohydrate in the body. Glycogen is stored in the liver and muscles. This is the form of immediate energy for the body. About 350 gms carbohydrate is stored as glycogen in the body.

Cellulose is an insoluble, indigestible polysaccharide. More than 3,000 glucose units are there in cellulose but it is not of human utilisation. Cattle can digest cellulose. Even though it is not of much food value it provides bulk to the diet and thus helps movements in the large intestine. It prevents constipation and to an extent cancer of the bowel. It reduces the cholesterol level in blood as well as body weight. A high fibre diet can help in the treatment of obesity as it delays digestion and contributes satiety to obese people.

Sugar Alcohols

There are three sugar alcohols available commercially. They are sorbitol, mannitol and dulcitol. Sorbitol is used by diabetic patients. D-sorbitol or D-glucitol is an alcohol made from glucose by hydrogenation. By this process the aldehyde (CHO) group of glucose is reduced to alcoholic groups (CH_2OH). Mannitol is produced from mannose, a monosaccharide which does not occur free in nature.

Functions of Carbohydrates

1. Energy Supply

The most important function of carbohydrate is to supply energy or fuel for the body. Energy from carbohydrate is utilised by the body for immediate use. Nervous tissues and erythrocytes use glucose for their energy whereas other tissues can make use of fatty acids for energy.

2. Special Functions of Carbohydrates in the Liver

Carbohydrates have protective and detoxifying action in liver. Liver is protected against bacterial toxins by producing glycuronic acid or acetyle groups from carbohydrates. They are excreted throught kidneys. Since the defences of the liver against toxic agents are of great importance to the body, this function of the liver is very valuable. For this purpose glycogen is made use of and thus carbohydrates play a significant role in removing poisonous substances from the liver.

Carbohydrates, especially lactose, help the growth of desirable bacteria in the small intestine and help the synthesis of some B-complex vitamins in the intestinal tract. Lactose also helps in the absorption of calcium.

3. Carbohydrates and the Heart

Carbohydrate is used as the most efficient fuel for muscular exercise. Glycogen stored in the heart muscle is used for this purpose, especially in an emergency.

4. Carbohydrates and the Central Nervous System

Continuous supply of carbohydrate is essential for nervous tissues to function normally. Glucose as such has a specific influence in maintaining the functional integrity of nervous tissues.

5. Carbohydrates and Protein-sparing Effect

If carbohydrate supply is enough in the diet, protein is spared for important functions of it. This effect exerted by carbohydrate is called protein-sparing effect. Insufficient intake of carbohydrate forces amino acids to be de-aminated and converted to fatty acids for energy purpose.

6. Carbohydrates and Non-essential Amino Acids

Carbon skeleton of carbohydrate is used by the body for the synthesis of non-essential amino acids.

7. Carbohydrates and Fats

Carbohydrate is essential for the oxidation of fat. In extreme restriction of carbohydrate, fat may be metabolised rapidly.

8. Carbohydrates in Diet

Carbohydrate provides flavour and variety to the diet. Cellulose and other indigestible polysaccharides add bulk to the diet. Carbohydrate also retains water content of colon which helps intestinal motility

Sources of Carbohydrate

The best sources of carbohydrates are cereals like rice, wheat, millk like ragi, maize, roots and tubers like potato, tapioca, sweet potato, yan and colocasia, pulses, sugar and jaggery; honey, fruit and vegetables are the other sources of carbohydrates. Banana, apple, plantain and dried fruit are also good sources of carbohydrates.

In an average Indian diet carbohydrates are the cheap sources of calories. One gram of carbohydrate gives 4 kcals and an average Indian diet contains about 300 gms of carbohydrate.

Digestion and Absorption of Carbohydrates

In the mouth salivary digestion takes place. Carbohydrates are broken down by mastication and the saliva prepares the broken pieces of food for swallowing. Ptyalin, the enzyme present in saliva, acts on starch splitting it into dextrin and maltose. This action continues in the stomach till the acidity of the gastric glands interferes. There is not any digestive action on carbohydrates in the stomach as there is no enzyme in the stomach to act on carbohydrates.

The main digestive action on carbohydrate takes place in the small intestine. Amylase of the pancreatic juice hydrolyses the remaining starch into maltose. The intestinal mucosa cells contain sucrose or invertose, maltose and lactose. These enzymes convert sucrose into glucose and fructose, maltose into glucose and glucose and lactose into glucose and galactose, respectively.

The end products of carbohydrate digestion—glucose, fructose and galactose—are absorbed in the intestine. Bulk of these sugars are absorbed in the duodenum and jejunum and small amounts are absorbed in the ileum. Glucose and galactose are readily absorbed while fructose is absorbed slowly. These monosaccharides are absorbed by the capillaries in the walls of the intestines and they are carried by the bloodstream to the liver and the tissues.

The absorption of carbohydrate from the intestine is controlled by certain factors like condition of the intestinal tract and muscle tone, endocrine glands like anterior pituitary, thyroid and adrenal cortex and their functions and vitamin B-complex content in the diet.

Carbohydrate Metabolism

Through portal circulation the absorbed monosaccharides are carried to the liver. There galactose and fructose are converted into glucose. The liver cells release some glucose into the bloodstream and blood carries it to the tissues. In the tissues this glucose is metabolised to release energy. Excess of glucose is polymerised in the liver into glycogen and stored in the liver and muscles. This is again converted into glucose when energy is required. This process helps the bloodstream to maintain the normal blood sugar level.

Glycogen is formed from glucose, fructose and galactose and it is shown below:

Glycogen Galactose

Glucose-1 - Phosphate ——→ Galactose-1-Phosphate

Glucose ——→ Glucose-6-Phosphate

Fructose ——→ Fructose-6-Phosphate.

Fig 2.2: Formation of Glucose from other Monosaccharides

The carbohydrate metabolism in the body involves a series of chemical reactions. Glycogen formation, breakdown of glycogen and glucose to supply energy, formation of glucose from amino acid and glycerols of fat and formation of fat from carbohydrate are the main changes related to carbohydrate metabolism.

Breakdown of glycogen and glucose to yield energy involves a series of gradual reactions. Some of these chemical reactions take place in the absence of oxygen and it is known as the analrobic phase of carbohydrate metabolism. In the aerobic phase of metabolism oxygen is used. In total 38 ATP are yielded by each molecule of glucose: 8 ATP through glucolysis, 6 from pyruvic acid to Acetyl-CoA, 24 from TCA cycle.

Anaerobic Phase of Carbohydrate Metabolism (Glycolysis)

In glycolysis glycogen is degraded to glucose and it is converted to lactic acid.

The energy release in the process of glycolysis is calculated from the breakdown of ATP (Adenosine Triphosphate) and regeneration of ATP. Two molecules of ATP are used and four molecules of ATP are formed. Glycolysis takes place in muscular tissues.

Glycolysis is also known as Embden-Meyerhof-Parnas scheme of carbohydrate metabolism. The basic steps involved in glycolysis are given in Fig. 2.3.

Aerobic phase of carbohydrate metabolism involves oxidation of lactic acid into pyruvic acid and pyruvic acid to Acetyl-CoA. Acetyl-CoA undergoes a series of a chemical reactions whereby carbon dioxide, water and CoA are formed.

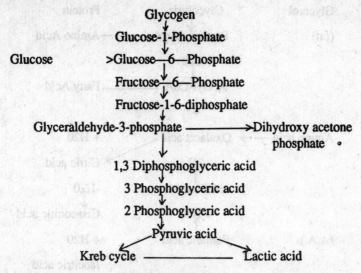

Fig. 2.3: Glycolysis

The conversion of Acetyl-CoA is otherwise known as Kreb's Tricarboxylic acid or T.C.A. cycle.

Oxalacetic acid reacts with Acetyl-CoA and this is repeated.

Most of the absorbed glucose is oxidized releasing energy. During this process carbon dioxide and water are also formed. Some portion of glucose is converted to fatty acids and some amount combines with free amino group to form amino acids.

B Vitamins like thiamine, niacin, riboflavin, pantothenic acid and B6 and minerals like magnesium and phosphorus are very essential for the proper metabolism of carbohydrates.

Certain hormones like epinephrine, thyroxine and gluoxine and glucagon and islands of Langerhans are essential to maintain normal blood sugar level in a person. A healthy person's blood shows the fasting sugar level as 80-100 mg./100 ml. of blood. After a meal it rises to 130-150 mg./100 ml. of blood. If the blood sugar level is above this the person is termed as a diabetic patient.

If the carbohydrate intake in the diet is inadequate, it leads to malnutrition and other metabolic disorders. Tissue proteins and fats will be utilised for energy purpose. If excess carbohydrate is taken, it will contribute towards obesity and diabetes.

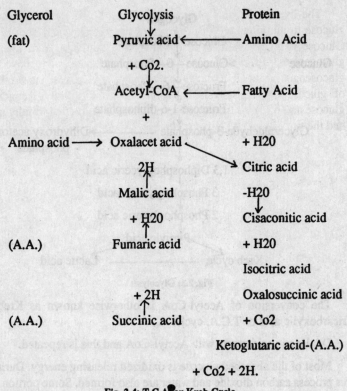

Fig. 2.4: T.C.A. or Kreb Cycle

Regulation of Blood Sugar

Blood circulates glucose continuously to each and every cell of the body as a source of energy and for the synthesis of a number of substances. From the blood if glucose is taken, the liver immediately replaces the blood glucose.

In the fasting state blood sugar level is 60-85 mgm per 100 ml of blood. Soon after a meal it rises to 140-150 mgm per 100 ml. If the body is in a good carbohydrate metabolic pathway this concentration will fall down to a normal level of 60-85 mgm. The liver very efficiently maintains the normal blood sugar level. If the blood sugar concentration is high this condition is known as Hyperglycaemia. Hypoglycaemia occurs when the blood sugar level is below normal level. This occurs in certain abnormalities of liver function or when insulin is produced in excessive amounts by the pancreas.

The liver is the only organ in our body which can either supply glucose to the circulation or to remove the excess sugar from blood. Glucose is made available to blood from absorption, from intestine glucogenesis, i.e., glycogen is produced from glucose and reconverts it; glucoseogenis, i.e., de-aminated amino acids are used for the synthesis of glucose, glycogenolysis is reconversion of stored glycogen to glucose and lipogenesis, i.e., excess glucose is converted to fatty acids and the use of glycerol to form glucose.

3

PROTEINS

In 1838, a Dutch scientist, Mulder, suggested the name 'Protein' to the complex nitrogen-bearing substance in tissues. The word 'protein' is derived fron the Greek work 'proteos' meaning 'to take the first place'. Proteins play a significant role in all activities of living organisms. Due to the multiplicity of their functions the name given to them is very apt. In our skin, muscles, skeleton and in body fluids protein is present. They are essential during growth because it is the main constituent in our tissues. In a person's life the first eighteen months are very important as eighty per cent of the brain development is over by this time. If protein is not sufficient during this time mental retardation takes place. Acute shortage of protein in early months of life brings intellectual dwarfism and it remains so for the rest of the life. That is why this nutrient is called 'protein'.

The Chemistry of Proteins

Proteins are complex organic compounds which contain carbon, hydrogen, oxygen, nitrogen, sulphur and phosphorus. Certain proteins contain iron, iodine, copper and other inorganic elements. The presence of nitrogen distinguishes protein from carbohydrate and fat. Protein contains an average of 16 per cent nitrogen.

On hydrolysis large molecules of protein give out smaller units called amino acids. Amino acids contain a carboxyl group (CooH) and an amino group (NH$_2$). They are otherwise known as the acidic and basic group, respectively. There are twenty-three amino acids in proteins. Amino acids are grouped into five groups based on the number of amino groups and carboxyl group in them. They are monoamino-monocarboxylic acids, monoamino-dicarboxylic acids, diamino-monocarboxylic acids, sulphur containing amino acids and aromatic and heterocyclic amino acids.

1. Monoamino-monocarboxylic acid.
   eg., Glycine, Alanine, Valine, Leucine, Isoleucin.
2. Monoamino-dicarboxylic acids
   eg., Aspartic acid, Glutamic acid.
3. Diamino-monocarboxylic acid
   eg., Arginine, Lysine
4. Sulphur containing amino acids
   eg., Cystine, Cysteine, Methionine
5. Aromatic and heterocyclic amino acids
   eg., Phenylalanine, Histidine, Tyrosine, Tryptophan, Proline, Hydroxyproline.

A protein contains a number of amino acids. Two amino acids are linked together through peptide linkage. In this, the basic group of one amino acids combines with the carboxyl or acidic group of another group of amino acids. Two amino acids are linked together to form a dipeptide and it combines with another amino acid. When a number of amino acids are linked together it is known as polypeptide.

CLASSIFICATION

Proteins are biochemically classified into three groups based on their chemical composition. They are simple proteins, conjugated proteins and derived proteins.

Simple Proteins

On hydrolysis simple proteins give nothing but only amino acids. Such proteins are called simple proteins. Examples of simple proteins are albumins, globulins and glutelins.

Prolamins, fibrousprotein, histamins and protamins.

Albumins and globulins are found within all body cells and in the blood serum. Potatoes and peanuts also have globulin in them. Globulin is in haemoglobin and myoglobin.

Glutelin is present in wheat glutens, zein in corn and gliadin in wheat has prolamine.

Collagen, keratin and elastin have fibrous proteins and histones are present in thymus and in globin. Protamins is present in salmine from salmonsperm.

Conjugated Proteins

On hydrolysis conjugated proteins give a protein fraction and a non-protein fraction. In our body conjugated proteins are present in various parts. Examples of conjugated proteins are haemoglobin, nucleoprotein, glycoprotein and lecithoprotein. Nucleoproteins are present in nucleus, glycoproteins in mucin and lecithoprotein in lecithin.

Derived Proteins

Derived proteins are derived from a mother protein either through hydrolysis or digestion. On digestion derived proteins are formed. Examples of derived proteins are metaproteins, coagulated proteins, peptides and peptones.

Metaproteins are products resulting from the action of acids or alkalies.

Coagulated Proteins

By the action of heat on protein or by the action of alcohol on proteins it coagulates. Cooked egg is an example.

Peptides, Proteoses and Peptones

Peptide linkage forms peptides from amino acids. Two amino acids linkage forms dipeptide and three amino acid tripeptides. Digested proteins form peptides.

Proteoses are derived from proteins by the action of digestive enzyme pepsin and precipitated by saturating their solution with ammonium sulphate.

Proteins are again classified based on their nutritive value. From the nutritional standpoint amino acids are of two types, essential and non-essential. Essential amino acids are termed essential because the body requires them through our daily food. Non-essential amino acids are also essential to the body but the body can manufacture them from the available chemicals. Thus, the nutritional quality of a protein is based on the presence of essential amino acids in them. There are eight essential amino acids in the case of adults and ten essential amino acids in the case of children and others are non-essential amino acids.

The essential amino acids are isoleucine, leucine, lysine, methionine, phenylalanine, threonine, tryptophan and valine. For infants and children arginine and histidine are also essential.

The non-essential acids are alanine, aspartic acid, cystine, cysteine, glutamic acid, glycere, hydroxyproline, proline, serine, tyrosine, citrulline and norleucine.

Proteins are classified into complete proteins, partially incomplete proteins and incomplete proteins based on the presence of essential amino acids in them. The presence of amino acids helps a protein to perform all the functions of proteins in our body. A complete protein food contains all essential amino acids in proper proportion. It helps the protein to promote growth, maintenance and repair. Examples of complete protein foods are milk, egg and fish.

Partially incomplete proteins lack some essential amino acids and so they will help to maintain our body but growth is not promoted. Vegetable proteins are examples of this group.

Incomplete proteins neither help maintenance nor growth. Gelatin is an example of this type of protein.

There are certain methods to evaluate the quality of a protein. Biological value of protein and growth gain or protein efficiency ratio (PER) are the important methods used for this.

Biological Value

Biological value of protein foods depends to a great extent on their amino acid composition and they are grouped as protein of low or high biological value. The biological value of protein also depends on the digestibility of a protein food. Cooking enables the digestibility whereas overheating and frying reduces the biological value of a protein because it destroys the essential amino acid, lysine. Egg, milk, fish, poultry and meat are of high biological value whereas proteins from cereals like wheat, rice, pulses and nuts are of low biological value. Vegetable proteins are low in essential amino acid pattern, especially of lysine, tryptophan, methionine and threonine. When a mixture of proteins from different sources is consumed mutual supplementation takes place. For example, rice or wheat protein is low in lysine whereas pulse is rich in lysine and low in methionine. Rice is rich in methionine and a mutual suplementation results when rice and pulse are consumed together.

Protein efficiency ration (Growth method): The ability of a protein to bring increase in weight or growth gain is considered on the efficiency of a protein or its nutritive quality. Nutritive value is expressed as growth per gram of protein consumed.

$$PER = \frac{\text{Gain in body weight (gm)}}{\text{Protein intake (gm)}}$$

Functions of Proteins

1. *Building Block*

The most important function of protein is to supply amino acids to cells for the continuous replacement of cells throughout life. It is the most abundant organic compound in our body. It is the building block of our body. From conception to growth at various levels, foetus, infant, child, and during pregnancy and lactation period protein is very essential.

In our body, tissues are not in a static position. Degradation and resynthesis of protein and other nitrogenous compounds always take place in our cells. Tissue proteins are broken down and new substances are continually synthesised in our body. Muscles and other tissues, bones, cartilage and trabecula contain fairly high percentage of proteins. Our hair, nails and skin also contain protein. All body fluids except bile and urine have protein in them.

2. *Regulatory Functions*

Different proteins perform highly specialised regulatory function in the body. Haemoglobin, which is the chief constituent of the red blood cells, carries oxygen to the tissues. Oxyhaemoglobin and their alkaline salts permit oxygen to enter into the tissues and receive carbonic acid from the cells. This process helps the removal of 92-97 per cent of all carbon dioxide from the tissues. Plasma proteins, especially albumin and globulin, play an important role in regulating osmotic pressure and water balance within the body. When plasma proteins are decreased the water balance is upset and accumulation of fluids in the body takes place. Proteins enable the blood to maintain their slight alkalinity. Proteins function as buffers, thus helping various sites of chemical reaction to maintain its pH. Nucleo proteins contain the blueprint for the synthesis, of all body proteins.

3. *Formation of Enzymes, Hormones and Other Secretions*

Proteins supply raw materials for the body to synthesise enzymes like trypsin and pepsin. Hormones like insulin and thyroxine are protein in nature. Digestive juices contain protein in them. Antibodies which give resistance power to the body are protein in nature. They are known as immune proteins.

4. Sources of Energy

Protein is generally considered as the building material of our body. But when the diet contains insufficient carbohydrate and fat for fuel, proteins are used as a fuel by the body. Each gramme of protein yields four calories. But it is not a wise contribution because the nitrogen excretion increases along with the cost of the food.

5. Proteins form Part of Vital Compounds in Body

Nitrogenous compounds are present in certain substances of immunological and antigenic reactions. Examples of these are globulin of blood serum and chromatin in nucleus. Methionine, an amino acid, provides methyl groups for the formation of creatinine and choline. Tryptophan, an amino acid, is converted to niacin, a B-complex vitamin, in emergencies. Glutathione, a tripeptide of crystine, is present in small amounts in all our active tissues and this helps oxidation-reduction reactions. Histidine, an amino acid, is decarboxylised to histamine and it is a stimulator of gastric glands to secrete gastric juice. It is also used as a dialator of capillaries. Threonine, another amino acid, acts as a lipotropic agent which prevents deposition of excess fat in the liver. Proteins also help the transport of drugs by binding them into protein molecules. Contractile proteins (myocin, actin) regulates muscle contration.

Acts as a Binding Factor

Retional binding protein, lipo proteins, transferin and serum proteins are very essential to our body for transporting many chemical substances.

Digestion of Proteins

There is no protein-splitting enzyme in saliva and so in salivary digestion protein is not affected. Hydrolysis of protein begins in the stomach. Pepsin, the enzyme secreted by gastric glands in the stomach, breaks down proteins into proteoses and peptones. Milk proteins are first converted to casein by a special enzyme called rennin. Casein combines with calcium to form calcium caseinate. Pepsin converts this into peptones. All the peptide linkages are not broken by gastric digestion. Stronger enzymes of pancreatic and intestinal juices complete the digestion of protein into peptones. Pancreatic juice contains trypsin and chymotrypsins. They hydrolyse peptones and proteoses into polypeptides. The final breakdown of all protein fractions to amino acids is brought about by erepsin secreted by intestinal mucosa.

Amino acids are absorbed by the small intestine and they are carried to the tissues or to the liver. A small amount, that is, about eleven per cent of the total protein is absorbed by the stomach, sixty per cent by the intestine and twenty-eight per cent by the colon. The absorbed amino acids reach the tissues where then metabolism takes place.

Metabolism of Proteins

In the tissues amino acids undergo breakdown and synthesis. They are also transaminised, deaminised or decarboxylated. The anabolic activities consist of a formation of new cells or the repair and maintenance of existing ones and secretion of various substances. If there is excess of amino acids after these anabolic activities, they will be either used for energy purpose or are converted to fat.

Deamination

One of the catabolic action is deamination. In deamination, the amino group is removed from an amino acid. This reduced amino group is used for the synthesis of new substances like simple amino acids or eliminated as urea. The carbon, hydrogen and oxygen may be used for carbohydrate or fat metabolism.

Transamination

The deaminated amino group may be utilised for transamination process. Transamination is a process whereby a new amino acid is formed using the deaminated amino group and another precursor. If all the amino group is not used for transamination, nitrogen freed from the amino group forms urea.

Formation of Urea

Amino acid is oxidised to ketoacids and ammonia. The ammonia, if it accumulates in the tissues, is toxic. So in the liver ammonia is converted into urea and excreted as urine. Therefore, the end product of protein metabolism is urea.

Ammonia is converted into carbamyl phosphate. This reacts with ornithine to form citrulline. Citrulline combines with aspartic acid and forms arginosuccinic acid which is converted to arginine. Arginine is hydrolysed into ornithine and urea. This ornithine again combines with carbamyl phosphate and this cycle is repeated.

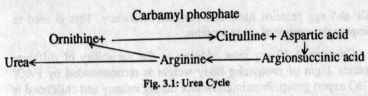

Fig. 3.1: Urea Cycle

Another catabolic change which takes place in an amino acid is decarboxylation. In this carbon dioxide splits off from carboxyl group and amines.

Nitrogen Balance

Tissue proteins are broken down at various times. When tissue proteins are utilised by the body for different functions nitrogen is excreted in urine and faeces. When protein food is taken new tissue proteins are formed. Nitrogen balance is the difference between the amount of nitrogen taken in through the diet and the sum of nitrogen and nitrogenous substances excreted from the body. When the nitrogen intake is more and the nitrogen loss is less the body is said to be in a positive nitrogen balance. When the nitrogen intake is less and nitrogen loss is more the body is said to be in a negative nitrogen balance. When the nitrogen intake equals the nitrogen lost from the body, the body is said to be in nitrogen equilibrium. During deficiency state the body shows a negative nitrogen balance.

Factors affecting Protein Utilisation

If sufficient calories are present in the diet, protein will be effectively used for its function. Certain minerals and vitamins are essential for the proper utilisation of protein. Potassium, phosphorus, vitamin A, riboflavin, niacin and vitamin B6 are the factors which enable the utilisation of proteins. Heat treatment or processing improves the utilisation. Heat destroys inhibitors of certain enzymes and that is how it helps digestion. But if direct heat is applied to meat it retards protein utilisation. Examples of this action is roasting meat in direct heat or frying.

Requirement of Proteins

Determination of protein requirement is based upon the nitrogen expenditure pattern and the estimation of nitrogen intake. Assessing nitorgen intake or protein quality of a mixed or complex diet is difficult. Efficiency of a protein source is based on its amino acid patterns and milk and egg proteins have 100 per cent efficiency. This is used to compare the quality of other proteins.

Covering a 30 per cent addition to the variability of different proteins 1 gm of protein/kg body weight is recommended by FAO/WHO expert group. Protein allowance during infancy and childhood is more as there is rapid growth. Studies have shown that well nourished pre-school children can attain heights and weights close to Western children. During pregnancy and lactation there is an increase in protein content. Protein requirement during various phases of life is given in table 3.1.

Table 3.1: Protein Allowance

Man	1 gm/kg/day...55 gm (55 kg)		
Woman	1 gm/kg/day...45 gm (45 kg)		
Pregnancy	2nd, 3rd trimester 14 gm/day		
Lactation	0-6 months + 25 gm/day		
	0-3 months - 2.3 gm/kg (for milk protein)		
	3-6 months - 1.8 gm/kg		
	6-9 months - 1.8 gm/kg		
	0-12 months - 1.5 gm/kg		
Children	1 - 3 years - 1.83 gm/kg day -	22 gm (12.03 kg)	
	4 - 6 years - 1.56 gm/kg	29 gm (18.87 kg)	
	7 - 9 years - 1.35 gm/kg	36 gm (26.37 kg)	
Boys	10 - 12 years - 1.24 gm/kg	43 gm (34.30 kg)	
	13 - 15 years - 1.10 gm/kg	52 gm (47.03 kg)	
	16 - 18 years - 0.94 gm/kg	53 gm (56.50 kg)	
Girls	10 - 12 years - 1.17 gm/kg	43 gm (36.47 kg)	
	13 - 15 years - 0.95 gm/kg	43 gm (45.53 kg)	
	16 - 18 years - 0.88 gm/kg	44 gm (50.00 kg)	

Protein Deficiency

Deficiency of protein-predominant foods during growth period is known as kwashiorkor and protein-calorie malnutrition is known as 'marasmus'. Protein calorie malnutrition is one of the largest nutritional problems in India.

Kwashiorkor

Kwashiorkor is a term used by Ga tribe in Ghana and the meaning of this word is 'the sickness the old child gets when the next baby is born'. Dr. Cicely Williams in 1933 reported the occurrence of kwashiorkor (red baby) in poorer sections of population in Africa. Internal and external changes occur in the structure and functional efficiency of various organs in the body. Starting from hair and skin to tissues, blood, water content in the cells, blood cells, organs like liver, alimentary canal and nervous tissues are affected by protein deficiency. The child will maintain an apathetic, anaemic, anorexic, oedematous and diarrhoeic condition.

The early symptoms of kwashiorkor include loss of weight, fatigue, reduced resistance to infection, delay in recovery from illness and retarded growth. As the protein deficiency prolongs, changes in the body take place. Discoloration of the skin, oedema with ascites, peeling of skin, cracks in the skin, angular stomatitis, cheilosis and atrophy of the tongue and anaemia occur. Degeneration of the epithelial tissues and reduced secretions of digestive juices result in diarrhoea. Absorption of nutrients is delayed and result in general weakness and mental retardation. Liver may be palpable and soft. Fatty liver, especially in the periphery, is seen. Functions of liver are affected adversely, especially the synthesis of lipoprotein is reduced, hence fat accumulates in the liver. Deficiency of all vitamins occurs. Deficiency symptoms of B-complex vitamins lead to stomatitis and ulcers in the mouth and stomach, vitamin A deficiency leads to night blindness and xerophthalmia, severe protein deficiency results in permanent retardation of mental development, psychomotor development and behaviour. (Refer chapter "Diet during Deficiency Diseases" for further reading.)

Marasmus

Marasmus is the result of starvation in children. Marasmus occurs when the diet is low in both calories and in protein. The term Marasmus is derived from the Greek word meaning 'to waste'. Tissues are wasted and unlike kwashiorkor the body looks shrunken. The child has an emaciated look. Irritation, apathy, loss of appetite, dehydration, wasting of muscles and weight loss and incessant diarrhoea are the other symptoms of marasmus. All these result in retardation of growth and severe wasting of subcutaneous fat. Deficiency of vitamins A and B complex is common in these patients.

Marasmic Kwashiorkor

This occurs when a combination of marasmus and kwashiorkor of varying degrees is present in a child. The child shows signs of both kwashiorkor and marasmus. Gastrointestinal and respiratory infection may accompany the other symptoms.

Protein Sources

The best sources of protein are animal sources like meat, fish, poultry, eggs, milk and milk products. They are otherwise known as first class proteins because they are rich in essential amino acids.

Cereal grains and legumes are the important sources of plant proteins. They are also known as second class proteins. Pulses are commonly knows as "poorman's meat" because they are comparatively cheap and fair in the nutritive content. The biological value of vegetable proteins can be improved when cereals and pulses are taken together.

Mutual Supplementation of Amino Acids

Amino acid content of the diet can be improved by supplementing one protein source with the other. In Indian diet this method has a significant role to play. For example, cereals and pulses. Lysine, the limiting amino acid in cereals, is supplemented by pulses, which is rich in it. Methionine, the limiting amino acid in pulse, is supplemented by cereals. Soyabeans is also rich in lysine but deficient in methionine. A small quantity of animal foods can also do the same to vegetable proteins.

4

LIPIDS (Fats)

Lipids are heterogeneous groups of compounds with same properties. Fat is the common household name given to lipids.

Like carbohydrates, fats are organic compounds composed of carbon, hydrogen and oxygen. But they differ from carbohydrates in that they contain much less oxygen and much greater proportions of carbon and hydrogen. Seventy-six per cent carbon, twelve per cent oxygen and twelve per cent hydrogen are present in fats. True fat has one molecule of organic ester of glycerol and three molecules of fatty acids. Fats vary in their structure due to the presence of different fatty acids with glycerol molecules. If the glycerol in a fatty acid is combined with three fatty acid units such fats are called triglycerides. Fats are insoluble in water and soluble in organic solvents like ether, benzene or chloroform. Their cooking properties depend upon the type of fatty acids present in them.

Classification

Lipids are classified into (a) simple lipids, (b) compound lipids, (c) waxes, and (d) derived lipids.

Simple Lipids

These are esters of fatty acids with various alcohols. Fats are esters of fatty acids with glycerol. Oils are liquid at 20°C while fats are solid at 20°C. Combination of fatty acids and sterol alcohol form cholesterol. Food fats contain neutral fats. Fat is stored in the body as adipose tissue. This is also neutral fat.

Compound Lipids

When fatty acids and glycerol combine with other organic compounds they are known as compound lipids. Examples of compound lipids are phospholipids and glycolipids.

(i) *Phospholipids* (phosphatides) are substituted fats in which phosphoric acid and a nitrogenous base take the place of one fatty acid radical. These are present in vegetable oils and in the fats of animal tissues in the blood and in egg yolk. Phospholipids help the absorption of fat in the body, and also help the transfer of fat from one place to another. They have prominent role in the functions of the nervous tissue. Lecithin and cephalin are the two important forms of phospholipids in our body.

Lecithin is composed of glycerol, two fatty acids in ester linkage, phosphoric acid and choline. This is the most common form of phospholipid.

Cephalin contains nitrogen compounds other than choline, phosphoric acid, glycerol and /fatty acid esters. Phosphatidyl ethanolamine and phosphatidylserine are the common forms of cephalin.

(ii) *Glycolipids* are compounds which contain a carbohydrate molecule with fatty acids and a nitrogenous base. Cerebrosides are the best example of glycolipids. Cerebrosides occur largely in the brain. Galactolipids, glycolipids, and sulfolipids are examples of cerebrosides.

Waxes

These are esters of higher fatty acids and alcohol other than glycerol. Cholesterol esters, sterol esters, esters of fat-soluble vitamins are the common waxes.

Derived Lipids

Substances derived from one fat on hydrolysis or by enzyme activities are called derived fats. Examples of derived lipids are fatty acids like stearic acid, linoleic acid, butyric acid, alcohols like glycerol, cetanol and lanol. Sterol alcohols like cholesterol, ergosterol and sistosterol are also derived fats.

Sterols are nutritionally important. They are classified as animal sterols, plant sterols and mycosterols.

Cholesterol is the precursor of steriod hormones and bile salts. Hormones like progesterone, oestrogen and adrenal corticoids contain cholesterol. Sodium glycocholate and sodium taurocholate and the bile salts have cholesterol in them. Cholesterol esters produced by the liver regulate the cholesterol content in the blood. It is present in all animal and human tissues. The white matter of the brain has 1-14 per cent cholesterol while the grey matter has 60 per cent on dry basis. Sebum secreted by sebaceous gland also has large amounts of cholesterol.

Properties of Fat

The properties of fat are based on its composition and structure. Melting point of fat is the most important physical quality. Fats which have a high proportion of saturated fatty acids are solid at room temperature and unsaturated fatty acids are liquid at room temperature. If the melting point of a fat is above 50°C or 122° F it is poorly utilised by the body.

The most important chemical properties of fats are hydrogenation, saponification, emulsification and rancidity. All these reactions are related to their chemical structure. The double bond linkages in the unsaturated fats make them readily available for all chemical reactions.

Iodine value (number)

Iodine value gives the number of grammes of iodine which combine with 100 grammes of fat. Iodine value depends on the number of bonds it makes at the site of double bonds. This gives the degree of unsaturation of fats.

Saturated and Unsaturated Fatty Acids

Saturated fatty acids have all the carbon atoms in the chain saturated with hydrogen atoms. When a double bond is present between two carbon atoms the fatty acid is termed as unsaturated fatty acid. The degree of unsaturation varies according to the presence of double bonds. If one or more double bonds are present in a fat it is called unsaturated fatty acid. If there are more double bonds in a fat it is called polyunsaturated fatty acid.

Palmitic, stearic and butyric acids are saturated fatty acids. Oleic, linoleic, linolenic and arachidonic acids are unsaturated oils. They have one, two, three and four double bonds, respectively. The unsaturated fatty acids are often described as essential fatty acids. Vegetable oils are rich in linoleic acid and fish oils and animal fats are rich in arachidonic acid.

Table 4.1: Saturated and Unsaturated Fatty Acids

Common name (saturated fatty acids)	Molecular formula	Unsaturated fatty acids	Molecular formula	Double bonds (Nos)
N-Butyric	C4 H8 O2	Palmitoleic	C16 H30 O2	1
Caproic	C6 H12 O2	Oleic	C18 H34 O2	1
Caprylic	C8 H16 O2	Elaidic	C18 H34 O2	1
Capric	C10 H20 O2	Vaccenic	C18 H34 O2	1
Lauric	C12 H24 O2	Linoleic	C18 H32 O2	2
Myristic	C14 H28 O2	Linolenic	C18 H30 O2	3
Palmitic	C16 H32 O2	Ylinolenic	C18 H30 O2	3
Stearic	C18 H36 O2	Eleostearic	C18 H30 O2	3
Arachidic	C20 H40 O2	Arachidonic	C20 H32 O2	4

Table 4.2: Percentage Composition of Some Fatty Acids in Common Oil and Fats

Fat	Oleic acid (C18.1)	Linoleic acid (C18.2)	Polyunsaturated fatty acids
Butter fat	3.3	4	2
Coconut oil	8	1.6	-
Cottonseed oil	30	56	2
Egg fact	52	9	3
Groundnut oil	65	17	Trace
Olive oil	65	15	Trace
Pig fat	47	4	3
Rapeseed oil	28	15	59
Red palmoil	52	5	Trace
Safflower seed oil	31	51	-
Sesame oil	45	41	Trace
Soyabean oil	29	51	6
Sunflower seed oil	14	73	1
Sardine oil	17.3	2.5	30.1

Some of the chemical reactions of fats are related to its unsaturated status.

Hydrogenation

Unsaturated fats have a tendency to combine with hydrogen at the site of its double bonds. Hydrogenation is such a process. Vegetable fats are exposed to hydrogen at high temperature in the presence of an alkali. Nickel or cobalt is used as a catalyst. For example, groundunt, coconut, cottonseed and other oils are usually used for hydrogenation. On hydrogenation liquid fats turn into solids. Vanaspati is an example of hydrogenated fat from groundnut oil.

Rancidity

On keeping, fats develop an unpleasant odour and this is known as rancidity.

There are two types of rancidity: hydrolytic and oxidative rancidity. One of the common reactions which cause the spoilage of fat is hydrolytic rancidity.In hydrolytic rancidity lipase hydrolyses fats into free fatty acids. Fatty acids with low molecular weight give an unpleasant odour to fats which is easily spoiled.

In oxidative variety unsaturated fatty acids are oxidised. The addition of oxygen may give rise to peroxides which on decomposition yield aldehydes and ketones. They have a foul odour. These peroxides are oxidising agents. They destroy important vitamins present in fats. This oxidation is prevented by the presence of antioxidants in the fat. Vegetables oils have tocopherols or vitamin E as a natural antioxidant in them. There are α β γ (alpha, beta, gama) tocopherols. Among these alpha tocopherol is the most powerful antioxidant.

There are some other substances which can be used as antioxidants which give a prolonged shelf life to fats. Ascorbic acid or vitamin C, gum guaiac acid and propylgilate are some of them.

Saponification of Fats

The ester linkage of fatty acids with glycerol brings this process of saponification. Neutral fats are rich in ester linkage. When neutral fats are heated with sodium or potassium hydroxide the fat molecules may readily rupture at the ester linkage. It is thus hydrolysed into glycerol and sodium or potassium salts of fatty acids and this is known as soap. Thus, the formation of soap from the hydrolysis of fat with heat and alkali is termed as saponification. Saponification of fats, when performed under standard conditions, is used as an index to find out the molecular weight of fatty acids in a fat.

Emulsification

Fats and oils are insoluble in water because they are lighter than water.

When fat forms a homogeneous mixture with water it is called emulsification. This property is made use of in cookery.

Essential Fatty Acids

Nutritionally important fatty acids are known as essential fatty acids (EFA). Since the body cannot synthesise them the EFA must be supplied to the body through foods. Linoleic acids, linolenic acids and arachidonic acids are the essential fatty acids.

Functions of Fat in the Diet

The most important function of fat is due to its highest calorie density in foodstuffs. One gramme of fat supplies 9.3 kcal while 1 gramme of carbohydrate and protein supply 4.3 and 5.6 kcal respectively. Fats are the carriers of fat-soluble vitamins A, D, E and K. Fats also exert a thiamine-sparing action. Fats have a protein-sparing action also. Essential fatty acids help to maintain tissues, their normal structure and efficiency. Fats, especially phosphatides, form an essential part of nervous tissues. Adipose tissue, where fat is stored, serves as an insulation material in injury. Vital organs of the body are thus protected. In growth period it promotes growth. It also enables proper sexual maturity, especially in female experimental animals. Fat provides flavour and palatability to food.

Digestion and Metabolism of Fats

There is no digestive change for fat in the mouth. In the stomach a little fat is mechanically separated from other foodstuffs. Since carbohydrate and proteins are partially digested in the stomach fat is set free. In the stomach fat forms a coarse emulsion and is eventually released into the duodenum as small portions. Even though there is not much digestive action in the stomach for fat, digestion is delayed in the stomach by fat. The emulsified fat, known as chyme, takes three to four hours to transfer it from the stomach into the intestine. Pancreatic lipase is the most powerful enzyme in fat digestion. This lipase breaks the alpha position of triglycerides and makes them free fatty acids and 1, 2, diglycerides. 1, 2 diglycerides are hydrolysed to 2, diglycerides and fatty acids. They combine with bile salts and emulsify fats. They reduce the surface tension of fat and make it available for enzyme activity. Bile salts promote emulsification and help the fat into partial solution of fats and fatty acids. The water-soluble glycerol is quickly absorbed. Short chain fatty acids which are also soluble in water are trasported into the portal blood. The products of fat digestion which reach the intestinal wall are resynthesised into new triglycerides by the intestine. In the jejunum triglycerides are absorbed. These triglycerides pass into the lymphatics in the form of small scattering particles called chylomicrons. Thorasic duct carries them into the systemic circulation.

Fats which are quickly absorbed are readily available for the tissues. If the fats remain in the gastrointestinal tract for a longer period for utilisation they add satiety value to the meal.

Absorption of fat is based on its digestibility, melting point, the size of the fat molecules and its quantity. The age of a person is another factor which affects the absorption. Old people utilise fat slowly.

Lipids in Blood

In the post-absorptive state plasma contains about 500 mgs of total lipids/100 ml of blood. In this 180 mg/100 ml is cholesterol. Neutral fat occurs in blood plasma largely in the form of chylomicrons. In the liver triglycerides are resynthesised and they combine mainly with cholesterol and form beta lipoproteins and are passed into the circulation. Cholesterol esters are converted to bile acids in the liver, re-excreted into the small intestine and reabsorbed. The concentration of bile may affect cholesterol synthesis in the intestine. Only forty per cent of cholesterol in the circulating blood is from food. The remaining portion is synthesised in the liver and intestine. Cholesterol synthesis in the body is controlled by various factors like calorie intake, cholesterol intake, fat intake and essential fatty acid content of the fat. Liver, skin, intestine, adrenal cortex, kidney and lungs are the organs which synthesise cholesterol. Acetate is the precursor of cholesterol and so all substances which yield acetate become precursor of cholesterol. Apart from fatty acids, carbohydrates, ethyl alcohol, alanine, and certain amino acids yield acetate or pyruvic acid or glycogen or glucose which can in turn form acetate. Thus every foodstuff forms acetate and cholesterol while calorie restriction and essential fatty acid deficiency inhibit hepatic cholesterol synthesis.

The adult human body synthesises about 2,000 mgs of cholesterol daily. The dietary intake of cholesterol ranges from 500 mg to 1,200 mg depending upon the consumption of milk, butter, eggs, meat and fish. Apart from these foods coconut oil and hydrogenated fat increase the blood cholesterol level. Unsaturated fats or essential fatty acids reduce the blood cholesterol level. Safflower oil, sesame oil, sunflower oil and soyabean oil are the unsaturated fats.

Metabolism

The metabolism of fatty acids and glycerol are separate. Glycerol enters the glycolytic pathway through the formation of 2 glycerophosphate. Fatty acids are oxidised to acetyl-CoA and it is again oxidized to CO_2 and water through Kreb's cycle of carbohydrate metabolism. Energy is the end product in the metabolism of fat also. In the stepwise reactions two carbon atoms are added or subtracted using co-enzyme A. For this reaction ATP or Adenosine triphosphate is required. The enzyme which catalyzes the reaction is thiokinase. In the next step dehydrogenation of fatty acids takes place. Fatty acids are dehydrogenated into alpha beta unsaturated fatty acid. Alpha beta unsaturated fatty acids are converted or hydrated to hydroxyacyl-CoA. Hydroxy acid is oxidised to keto acid. The last step in the fatty acid oxidation is the thiolytic cleavage of Keteacyl-CoA ester to yield a fatty acid-CoA derivative. This is repeated and Acetyl-CoA molecules are released. Different fatty acids yield varying numbers of acetyl-CoA. For example, one molecule of steraic acid gives 9 molecules of acetyl-CoA and 1 molecule of palmitic acid gives 8 molecules of acetyl-CoA and 1 molecule of lauric acid gives 6 molecules of acetyl-CoA.

Acetyl-CoA thus formed is oxidised through Kreb's cycle and glycerol is converted into glyceraldehyde - 3 - phosphate and it enters into the glycolysis pathway.

Summary of Fat Metabolism

(1) Fatty acid - α β unsaturated fatty acid

$+ H2O$

(Beta) hydroxy fatty acid

Keto acid

Acetyl CoA

(2) Glycerol ⟶ Glycerophosphate

Glyceraldehyde - 3- phosphate.

Ketone Bodies

Normally acetyl-CoA combines with oxaloacetic acid which is oxidised in the TCA cycle. When large amounts of fat are metabolised in the absence of carbohydrate more acetyl-CoA is formed. When there is not enough oxaloacetic acid from carbohydrate, two molecules of acetyl-CoA condense to form acetoacetyl-CoA. This is hydrolysed into acetic acid and later converted into β-hydroxybutric acid and acetone. These metabolic end products of fats are known as ketone bodies. When the concentration of ketone bodies in the blood increases the condition is known as ketosis. When it is excreted through urine it is called ketonuria. In normal condition acetoacetate is either oxidised directly to carbon dioxide and water or converted to two molecules of acetate which are later oxidised. In diabetes and during fasting ketone bodies are formed in excessive amounts. Apart from fats, amino acids like leuine also produce ketone bodies.

Lipo Proteins and Lipotropic Factors

Lipo proteins are lipids containing protein in blood and other parts of the body. The insoluble lipids when attached to proteins form soluble lipo proteins. Cholesterol, neutral fats and phospholipids bind them with protein to form lipo proteins.

Lipo protein in the liver along with choline enhances the oxidation of fatty acids. On diets which are high in fats with saturated fatty acids and which are low in protein or in choline there is an increased deposition of fat in liver. A high cholesterol diet also leads to the production of fatty liver. An increased choline intake will bring down the fat in the liver. This effect of choline on fat release is known as lipotropic action. Methionine likewise exerts a marked lipotropic action owing to its ability to promote the synthesis of choline by the transfer of methyl groups to suitable precursors. Inositol (B-complex vitamin), tryptophan and glutamic acid exert this lipotropic action. Essential fatty acid deficiency can also produce fatty liver, pantothenic acid or riboflavin deficiency may also lead to it.

Requirements

The requirement of fats is about 50 to 60 gms for a normal person. The dietary fat is used for energy and it is also a source of essential fatty acids. At least fifty per cent of the fat must be from vegetable oils which are rich in essential fatty acids.

An average Indian adult derives about 20 per cent of energy from dietary fat.

Sources

Vegetable oils, like groundnut oil, coconut oil, mustard oil or gingelly oil, hydrogenated oils, butter and ghee and lard are the common sources of fats.

Deficiency of Fats

During infancy a deficiency of essential fatty acids results in perianal irritation and skin changes like dry skin and itching. In adults phrynoderma is easily cured by essential fatty acids with vitamins B2 and A.

5

ENERGY METABOLISM

Energy is defined as the capacity for doing work. From sunlight plants store energy as carbohydrate with the help of chlorophyll. Animals and men avail their energy through foods. When food is metabolised in the body, energy is released. Body requires this energy for all its activities. For all muscular activities and for the function of vital organs like heart, lungs, alimentary canal, nervous tissues and glandular tissues energy is required.

The energy requirement of a person depends on various factors. The most important factor in assessing the energy requirement is the basal metabolic rate of the person.

Basal Metabolic Rate (BMR)

This is defined as the amount of heat or energy required by the body to do the involuntary work of the body. Functions of brain, heart, liver, kidneys, lungs, secretery activities of the glands and intestinal movements are the basal activities in our body.

Factors Affecting the BMR

Basal metabolic rate of a person depends on the size, shape, composition, body weight, age and physiological condition of the person. Nutritional status and endocrine system of the body also exert their influence on basal metabolic rate of a person. Climatic condition of the surroundings also affects the basal metabolic rate.

1. *Size*: Since the heat loss in body is proportional to the skin surface, a tall and thin person has greater surface and thus higher basal metabolic rate compared to the short person. The body composition shows varitations in energy use. With little fat deposition in the body the basal metabolic rate increases and thus a tall, thin person has higher rates of basal metabolism compared to a short, fat man. Constant muscular activities of an athlete demand about 5 per cent more basal metabolic rate.

2. *Sex:* Sex also makes a variation in energy requirement. The metabolic rate of women is 6-10 per cent lower than that of men.

3. *Growth period:* During the growth period the basal metabolic rate and thus the energy requirement are increased. The highest BMR is during the first two years. After the growth period, especially after 25 years of age, there is a decline in energy requirement.

4. *Endocrine glands:* The thyroid gland exerts influence over energy requirements. Thyroid hyper-activity will speed up basal metabolism. The pituitary gland also increases the metabolic rate if it has disturbance. Adrenaline increases the BMR.

5. *Nutritional status:* During undernourishment the basal metabolic rate also declines to an extent of thirty per cent.

6. *Pregnancy condition:* During pregnancy and lactation the basal metabolic rate is increased by about 5 per cent during the first and second trimester and 12 per cent during the third trimester.

7. *Sleep:* During sleep the BMR is less than in the waking state.

8. *Climate:* Climatic conditions of the environment also affect the energy requirement. If the temperature falls below 14°C the energy requirement increases.

9. *Body temperature:* Fever increases the BMR.

10. *Disease conditions:* Diseases like typhoid fever, medullary diseases and lymphatic leukaemia show an increase in the BMR.

11. *Physical activities*: Physical activities half an hour before BMR measurement show high rates of BMR.

Total energy requirement of a person varies according to the basal metabolic rate, effect of food, activity involved, age, sex, physiological conditions and climatic conditions of the surroundings.

Energy requirements of an adult in India was reviewed by 'The Expert Group' of the FAO/WHO in terms of a reference man and reference woman. The reference man is in the age group of 20-39 years, with a weight of 55 kgs, without any disease and with a capacity to perform 8 hours of moderate activity. When not engaged in work a reference man spends 8 hours in bed and 4-6 hours in moving around or in a sitting position and 2 hours either walking or doing household activities.

In the case of a reference woman, the difference is only in her body weight, that is, as against 55 kg of a man she weighs 45 kg. Instead of the physical activity of the occupation, the woman does household duties. Other conditions are the same in the case of a reference woman.

The energy expenditure for man and woman is calculated considering their internal and external activities. The FAO/WHO expert group (1983) suggested some recommendations as given in Table 5.1.

Table 5.1: Energy Allowance for Various Groups

Category	Reference body weight	Activity	Energy allowance kcals.
Man	55 kg	light	2400
		moderate	2800
		heavy	3900
Woman	45 kg	light	1900
		moderate	2200
		heavy	3000
	Pregnancy	2nd and 3rd trimester	+300
	Lactation	first six months	+550
		6-12 months	+400

Additional requirement of energy is needed for the growth of the foetus, placenta and maternal tissues during pregnancy. The BMR is also increased due to increased internal activities. Daily 150 kcals during the first trimester and 300 kcals during the rest of pregnancy is recommended. The energy cost during the term of pregnancy is 62,500 kcals. Additional energy requirement during lactation is for the secretion of milk. For a normal output of 850 ml of milk during the first 6 months 550 kcals/day is recommended.

During infancy the energy requirement is high. For 0-3 months 120 kcals/kg, 3-5 months 115 kcals/kg, 6-8 months 110 kcal/kg, 9-11 months 105 kcal/kg and at one year 112 kcals are recommended.

For children, the energy requirement varies according to their body weight. The ideal weight of the children according to their age must be considered for assessing energy requirements. Thus in the latest recommendations, some suggestions were made as shown in Table 5.2.

Table 5.2: Energy Allowance for Children

Age group	Body weight kg.	Energy allowance kcal.
Children		
1-3 years	12.03 kg	1220 kcal
4-6 years	18.87 kg	1720 kcal
7-9 years	26.37 kg	2050 kcal
Boys		
10-12 years	34.30 kg	2420 kcal
13-15 years	47.03 kg	2660 kcal
16-18 yrars	56.50 kg	2820 kcal
Girls		
10-12 years	36.47 kg	2260 kcal
13-15 years	45.53 kg	2300 kcal
16-18 years	50.00 kg	2200 kcal

Specific Dynamic Action

Energy requirement is affected by the type of food ingested. The extra heat which is produced after taking food is known as the specific dynamic action (SDA). The stimulating effect of carbohydrates, fats and protein on energy metabolism is different. Protein foods produce the highest per cent increase in energy metabolism. The SDA of protein is about 30 per cent while carbohydrates and fats exert 6 per cent and 4 per cent, respectively. The average SDA of a mixed diet is about 8-10 per cent.

The activities which demand maximum energy are in the following order.

Walking very fast, severe exercises, running, swimming, sawing wood, labourer's work, carpentry, metal and industrial work, walking slowly, laundry work, typing and ironing.

Units for Measuring Energy

Energy is measured in terms of Kcalorie. A Kcalorie is defined as the amount of heat requied to raise the temperature of 1 kilogramme (1 litre) of water by 1°C. But joule is the new term used to measure energy. A joule is defined as the amount of work done or heat generated by an electric current of 1 ampere acting for 1 second against a resistance of 1 ohm. This unit is very small for measuring energy in nutrition and so 1 kilojoule (KJ) or megajoule (MJ) is used for practical use.

1 Kilojoule	=	1000 joules
1 Megajoule	=	10,00,000 joules
1 Calorie	=	4.184 joules (J)
1 Kcalorie	=	4.184 Kjoules
1,000 Calories	=	4.184 Mj (Megajoules)

Energy Value of Foods

Energy value of foods is otherwise known as the caloric value of foods. To measure the caloric value of food, an apparatus known as Bomb Calorimeter is used. In this apparatus a known amount of food is burnt and the rise in temperature of water in a container is recorded. The heat liberated by 1 gramme of carbohydrate is recorded as 4.1 kcals, protein 5.6 kcals and fat 9.4 kcals.

The energy value of food is otherwise known as the fuel value of foods. This is determined by means of an instrument known as Bomb calorimeter (Fig. 5.1).

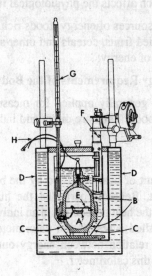

Fig. 5.1: Bomb Calorimeter

A weighed sample of dried food in pellet form is placed in a heavy steel container called a bomb. The bomb is held in place in a well insulated vessel. This is surrounded by a known volume of water.

The bomb is charged with oxygen to a pressure of about 300 pounds to the square inch. After the temperature of the water has been determined the sample is ignited by means of an electric fuse. The heat from the sample is dissipated into the water. By noting the change in the temperature of the water the energy value of the food can be calculated.

Physiological Fuel Value of Foods

Small losses occur in digestion when carbohydrates, fats and proteins are utilised by the body. Digestability coefficiency of western diets are available and based on these data:

the physiological fuel value of carbohydrate	- 4 kcals
the physiological proteins	- 4 kcals
the physiological fats	- 9 kcals

Among these nutrients the body loses maximum energy from protein. This is due to the loss during digestion. The digestibility of various foods varies which affects the physiological fuel value.

Among the various sources of energy, foods rich in fats and dairy produce are the best. Dried fruits, cereals and other starchy foods and legumes are fair sources of energy.

Determination of Energy Requirements of the Body

There are two methods generally applied for measuring the energy requirements of human body. They are direct and indirect calorimetry methods.

Direct Calorimetry

In this method the amount of heat produced by the body is measured directly. At Water-Rosa, Benedict perfected the human respiration calorimeter. To measure the heat production in an individual a specially constructed chamber, called a respiration calorimeter, is used. It is determined through the relation between energy output and oxygen consumed in a person in this calorimeter.

Respiration calorimeter consists of an airtight copper chamber insulated by wooden wall with air spaces in between. Enough provision for sitting or to lie down is made through a folding bed, chair and table. Food is provided through the opening at one end and the excreta is removed through another opening at the other end. The chamber is very well arranged for the individual to relax, read or write. It is insulated to prevent the entry and exit of heat through the walls. The chamber is ventilated by a current of air, the CO_2 and water given off are removed by soda lime and sulphuric acid respectively. For oxygen supply, a known amount of oxygen is introduced to the chamber through a gas metre with an air current. The oxygen consumption and CO_2 production are calculated using a formula. The heat produced is also measured by circulating a current of water through copper pipes and measuring the quantity of water that has been circulated through the chamber and also the difference between the temperature of the water entering and leaving the chamber.

Respiratory Quotient: Respiratory Quotient is the ratio between the volume of CO_2 given out and the volume of O_2 consumed by the human subjects.

$$\text{Respiratory Quotient (RQ)} = \frac{\text{Volume of } CO_2 \text{ produced}}{\text{Volume of } O_2 \text{ consumed}}$$

The RQ varies with the type of food being oxidised. When glucose is oxidised RQ is 1, for a fatty acid it is 0.7 and for protein it is 0.8. Under resting condition with no food for 12-14 hours the RQ is 0.82. In this condition carbohydrate, fats and protein present in the body are utilised.

Indirect Calorimetry

In this method oxygen consumed and carbon dioxide excreted in a given time under basal condition is measured. Many experiments on people of different ages have shown that 1 litre of oxygen is equal to 4.825 kcals when the person is in Basal Metabolic condition. The basal metabolic rate is measured by indirect calorimetry. The person has to observe certain conditions before measuring the basal metabolic rate. They are:

1. In a post-absorptive state, i.e., 12-16 hours after the last meal— preferably in the morning.
2. In a reclining state but awake.
3. Before the test the person must take one hour rest if he is engaged in any work.
4. Relaxed and free from emotional upset, excitement or fear.
5. Body temperature must be normal.
6. Room temperature must be comfortable.

In these favourable conditions the BMR is measured. For an adult man the BMR rate is 34.2-36.7 kcals/sqm/hr. and for an adult woman 30.9-35.1/kcals/sqm/hr.; for children it is more. For 7-8 year boys it is 49.1/kcals/sqm/hr. and for girls it is 45.2/kcals/sqm/hr.

6
VITAMINS

Vitamins are the discovery of 20th century scientists. Carbohydrates, proteins and fats were considered as the nutrients essential for health. In the history of nutrition, the findings of a Polish chemist, Casimir Funk; in 1911 was a turning point. He found out for the first time that a disease syndrome could be produced in an experimental animal if inadequate supply of certain factors in food other than carbohydrates, proteins and fats takes place. He gave the name for the water soluble substance as "vitalamine" which was later known as vitamin. Scientists from various parts of the world were engaged simultaneously in finding out these specific factors which promote growth and maintenance of various organs in our body. Takaki, a physician in the Japanese Navy, first demonstrated that fatal diseases like beriberi could be treated with rice bran, vegetables, fish and meat. Thus the study of vitamins brought to light about 17 different vitamins. Each one of them has its own history, chemistry, structure, function, sources, requirements and disorder symptoms.

Vitamins are defined as organic compounds which are necessary for good health and vitality. Vitamins are required in minute quantities and their deficiency results in structural and functional disorders of various organs in the body. Thus vitamins are essential for life.

Classification of Vitamins

Vitamins are classified broadly into two groups: (a) fat-soluble vitamins, and (b) water-soluble vitamins.

Fat-soluble Vitamins

Fat-soluble vitamins are soluble in fats and fat solvents. They are insoluble in water. So these vitamins are utilised only if there is enough fat in the body.

Vitamin A and carotene, vitamin D, vitamin D2, vitamin D3, vitamin E and vitamin K are fat-soluble vitamins.

Water-soluble vitamins are soluble in water and so they cannot be stored in the body. Therefore, a day-to-day supply of these vitamins is essential.

Water-soluble Vitamins

B-complex vitamins: 1. Vitamin B (Thiamine), 2. Riboflavin, 3. Nicotinic acid and Nicotinamide (NIacin), 4. Pyridoxin (B6), 5. Pantothenic acid, 6. Folic acid, 7. Biotin, 8. Choline, 9. P-amino benzoic acid, 10. Inositol, and 11. Vitamin B12.

 II. Vitamin C or Ascorbic acid, and

 III. Vitamin P. (Bioflavonids)

FAT-SOLUBLE VITAMINS

Vitamin A

Vitamin A was the first fat soluble vitamin to be discovered. In 1913 Osborne and Mendel found that certain natural fats and oils stimulated growth in rats. Again McCollum and Simmonds (1917) demonstrated that Xerophthalmia was due to the lack of a fat-soluble vitamin. Steenbock (1919) discovered the vitamin A activity of carotenoids. In 1920 Roseheim and Drummond demonstrated that the carotene of plants had similar biological action to that of vitamin A. In 1930 Moore discovered that when carotene was fed to vitamin A-deficient experimental animals vitamin A was found in their liver. In 1931 Karser obtained the structure of vitamin A. In 1937, Kuhn and Morris synthesised vitamin A. In the same year Holmer and Corbet obtained vitamin A in a crystalline form.

Chemistry

Vitamin A in its pure form is a pale yellow substance soluble in fat. It is unsaturated alcohol which is stored in the body as esters. Vitamin A as such occurs only in animal foods. Retinol is the generally accepted chemical name for vitamin A. It is stable to heat. Vitamin A is present in the form of retinol (vitamin A), Retinal (retinene) or vitamin A aldehyde, retonic acid or vitamin A acid, dehydro retinol (vitamin A2) and carotene (provitamin A). Carotene has alpha, beta and gamma isomers. Vitamin A_2 is poor in its biological activity. Upon hydrolysis each molecule of beta-carotene yields 2 molecules of vitamin A. But the biological value of beta carotene is only half of vitamin A.

Functions of Vitamin A

Vitamin A is essential for the building and growth of all cells, especially skeletal cells. Vitamin A is also needed for proper tooth structure. It also helps in the integrity of the epithelium, especially the mucous membranes, which line the eyes, mouth, alimentary canal, salivary glands, respiratory and genito-urinary tracts. In the deficiency of vitamin A the epithelial tissues of these parts are keratonised.

Vitamin A maintains normal reproductive function in males. Vitamin A is again essential for the maintenance of normal vision in dim light. This vitamin combines with protein to form rhodopsin or visual purple which is present in the retina. Visual purple absorbs light and is decomposed to retinene and protein. The protein and retinene are partially recombined to form rhodopsin in the dark. Vitamin A is essential for this reaction and so continuous supply of this vitamin is required.

Rhodopsin Cycle
(Rods of the retina)

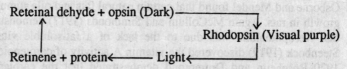

Reteinal dehyde + opsin (Dark) ⟶ Rhodopsin (Visual purple)

Retinene + protein ⟵ Light ⟵

Vitamin A plays an important role in maintaining the structure of myelin sheath. Vitamin A also helps the synthesis of mucopolysaccharides.

High serum retinol levels reduce the risk of cancer. This is a new finding in vitamin A studies and further research is going on.

Vitamin A is also known as anti-infective vitamin as it provides resistance power to the body by maintaining normal structure of the organs.

Deficiency of Vitamin A

Vitamin A deficiency in man may be due to low intake of vitamin A sources or due to interference with absorption or storage of vitamin A in the body. In certain diseases proper assimilation of vitamin A is affected. Loss of vitamin A occurs in the blood during some infectious diseases.

Clinical manifestations of vitamin A deficiency are retardation of growth and lowered resistance to infection. Deficiency of vitamin A shows in delayed adaptation to darkness on coming from the lighted area because it produces changes in the eyes. In a healthy person the eyes adapt quickly to dim light and bright light. In vitamin A deficiency state rhodopsin is not formed effectively, therefore vision in dim light is not easy. This symptom is known as night blindness. As the deficiency advances a condition known as xerophthalmia develops. The conjunctiva becomes dry and lustreless. The transparent appearance of the eye and its elasticity is lost. The eye becomes grey and opaque. If this condition persists the eye becomes infected and ulcerated. This is a serious conditon of the eye which results in blindness. Softening of the cornea brings blindness. Advanced neglected xerophthalmia leads to degeneration of cornea and blindness. This condition is known as keratomalacia.

Bitot's spots: Grey coloured triangular spots are located in the conjunctiva in severe cases.

Phrynoderma: In vitamin A deficiency, the skin becomes rough because the epithelial tissues are affected. This condition is known as follicular keratosis or toad skin or phrynoderma.

Mucous membraneous structures of respiratory tract, alimentary tract and genito-urinary tract are affected and infectious diseases of these areas result due to a deficiency of vitamin A. Thickening and dryness of the alimentary canal reduce the secretion of digestive juices which leads to diarrhoea.

Experimental animals showed that vitamin A exerts a protective effect against artificially induced cancer and urinary calculus.

Hypervitaminosis: If excess amount of vitamin A is consumed it shows ill-effect in the body. The symptoms are drowsiness, headache, vomiting, itching, skin lesions and loss of appetite.

Sources of Vitamin A

Vitamin A activity is in the form of retinol and carotenoids. The best sources of retinol are co/shark and halibut liver oils, and liver of animals like sheep, goat and cow. Butter, ghee, egg, especially egg yolk, and all milk powders are good sources of vitamin A.

Carotenoids are present in green leafy vegetables, yellow vegetables like carrot, pumpkin and yellow fruits like papaya and mangoes. Vegetable oils are available in processed forms (vanaspati) and they must contain specific amounts of retinol as per government rules.

Loss of Vitamin A during Cooking and Storage

Under Indian conditions 50 per cent of available vitamin A in food is lost during cooking. However, cooking loss of carotene is negligible. Since most of our dietary vitamin A is from the conversion of carotene, cooking loss is not considerable.

Requirements of Vitamin A

In our diet vitamin A is present as preformed vitamin A or retinol or as carotene which is converted into vitamin A. Retinol or preformed vitamin A is present only in animal foods. In an average Indian diet vitamin A is present in the form of beta carotene. It is converted into retinol. Due to various physiological reasons only one-third of beta carotene is absorbed. But from leafy vegetables and from carrots and papaya the conversion rate is about 50 to 99 per cent. Considering these factors the ICMR Expert Group recommended a daily intake of 750 mg of retinol/day for an adult. If beta carotene is consumed the recommendation is 3000 mg of beta carotene for an adult/day.

Prophylatic Treatment

In India a majority of the people consume vitamin 'A' deficient diet. As per 1978 studies half of the world's 15 million blind persons are in developing countries. Out of this two out of every three cases are preventable nutritional or infective conditions. The age group most affected in our country is 1-5 years and males are affected more than females.

Low availability of vitamin A in the diet and its poor utilisation due to protein deficiency are the main causes for deficiency. Now the Government of India has introduced prophylatic measures to combat vitamin A deficiency. Intake of one teaspoonful of codliver oil daily provide 3000 I.U. Four ml of red palm oil, supplying oral dose of 1,00,000 microgrammes of vitamin A palmitate through 5 ml of arachis oil are some of the measures.

In severe cases of deficiency large doses of 50,000 mg are administered for a few weeks.

Vitamin D

Vitamin D is otherwise known as 'sunshine vitamin' as it can be synthesised from sunlight by our body. Palm (1890) first demonstrated that a bone deformity, ricket, can be prevented by exposure to sunlight. Mellanby (1919) discovered that codliver oil can cure rickets produced in experimental animals. McCollum (1922) showed that codliver oil contained two vitamins, vitamin A and vitamin D. Recrink and Van Wijk (1931) isolated crystalline vitamin D from activated ergosterol. Schenck (1937) obtained a crystalline vitamin D from activated 7 dehydrocholesterol.

Chemistry

Vitamin D is fat soluble. It is a group of different sterol compounds with antiarchitic properties. They are vitamin D, vitamin D2 and vitamin D3. Among these vitamin D2 or calciferol and vitamin D3 or cholecalciferol are biologically important. Ergosterol and 7 dehydrocholesterol act as provitamin of vitamin D. When ergosterol of vegetable origin is exposed to ultraviolet light caliciferol is formed. Vitamin D3 is produced by the action of ultraviolet rays of sunlight on 7 dehydrocholesterol which is present in our skin. If the body is kept in 'purdah' cholecalciferol is not produced by the body.

Functions

Vitamin D itself is in an inactive form. Vitamin D is concentrated in the liver and in minute quantities in skin, lungs, brain, spleen and kidneys. In the liver vitamin D is hydroxylated to 25-hydroxy vitamin D_3 (25-OH-D_3). It is also known as 25-hydroxyl-cholecalciferol. From the circulating blood vitamin D_3 reaches the kidney and here it is further hydroxylated to form 1, 25-Dihydroxy cholecalciferol (1, 25, (OH)D_3). This is the active form of vitamin D.

Vitamin D promotes the absorption of calcium and phosphorus from the small intestine. In the DNA vitamin D helps to form active calcium binding protein. It also maintains the concentration of calcium and phosphorus in the blood. Vitamin D helps the deposition of calcium phosphate in the bone. In rachitic children there may be delay in dentition and malformation of the teeth occurs.

Sources

Fish liver oils, egg yolk, milk, butter and ghee are the best sources of vitamin D.

Some brands of butter are fortified with vitamin D. Sunlight is the best natural source of vitamin D.

Vitamin D is absorbed from the intestine with dietary fat from where it is taken to the liver.

Deficiency of Vitamin D

Deficiency of vitamin D results in poor absorption of calcium and phosphorous from the intestine and excessive loss of them in the urine and faeces. Concentration of calcium in the plasma is diminished and it produces tetany which is charaterised by hyperexcitability of the nervous system. This stimulates the parathyroid glands to decalcify bone calcium to raise the plasma calcium level. Deficiency of vitamin D leads to rickets in children and osteomalacia in adults.

Rickets: The name ricket is given to vitamin D deficiency after a famous English bone-setter by Ell. In mild deficiency of vitamin D, the symptoms shown are restlessness and irritability. Ricket is a disease of infancy and childhood. Calcium and phosphorus are not deposited enough to form strong bones and as a result the leg bones become bent and deformed. Small round unossified areas are developed near skull bones and projections are formed on the osteochondal junction of the ribs. It resembles a rosary and it is known as 'rickety rosary'. The abdomen is distended and chest deformities like depression of ribs attached to diaphragm take place. This is known as Harrison's sukus. This gives an appearance of 'pigeon breast'. In a later stage pelvic deformities, bow legs and knock knees develop. Nutritional rickets occur in infants and children of poor families. Premature infants are more susceptible to rickets.

Osteomalacia occurs among adults. It is often known as 'adult rickets'. Osteomalacia is most common among women who live on a poor diet lacking in calcium and vitamin D. Pregnant women are more prone to this. It is mainly because of the increase in weight during pregnancy accompanied by the deficiency of vitamin D. It is again common among women who observe 'purdah'. Repeated pregnancies and prolonged lactation further deplete calcium stores which results in osteomalacia. Pain, softening and tenderness in the bones and fractures are the common complaints of the patients of osteomalacia.

Prophylatic treatment: For the treatment of rickets and osteomalacia 1,000 to 5,000 I.U. of vitamin D should be administered orally for about a month. If there is marked improvement the dose can be reduced to 800 I.U./day for at least six months. A massive dosage of 1,000,000 I.U. can also be administered but small dosage is safer.

Storage

Cholecalciferol is converted to 25-hydroxy cholecalciferol in the liver. This is the active form of vitamin D. Vitamin D is stored in body tissues in the inactive form. Adipose tissues and skeletal muscles are the major storage sites. Brain, lungs, skin and spleen are other places where it is stored.

Vitamin E

Evans and Bishop (1923) discovered that for normal reproduction of experimental animals a fat soluble vitamin is needed. It was later named vitamin E or tocopherol. Female rats with vitamin E deficiency are unable to carry the young ones throughout the gestation period. The word tocopherol is derived from the Greek word tocos (childbirth or offspring).

Chemistry

There are eight naturally occurring tocopherols with vitamin E activity. Among these Alpha tocopherol is the most active. Tocopherols inhibit oxidation; therefore it is known as antioxidant vitamin. Vitamin E is soluble in fats and stable to ⌐ ¹ls and heat.

Sources

Cereal gem oils are the richest source. Vegetable oils except coconut oil and nuts are fair sources.

Functions

Vitamin E has a prominent role in maintaining the stability and integrity of cell membranes. One latest discovery about its function is its role in erythrocytes survival among premature infants. Experimental animals showed that deficiency of vitamin E results in anaemia in monkeys. Vitamin E deficiency produced muscular dystrophy in rabbits and reproductive failures in rats. One important function of vitamin E is its antioxidant properties. Through this activity it reduces the oxidation of vitamins A and C and sulphur containing amino acids. Through this activity it stabilizes the lipid parts of cell membrane. The presence of vitamin E as a natural component of vegetable fats protects against rancidity. Recent studies on rats have shown that vitamin E may protect lung tissues from damage by air pollution through nitrogen dioxide and osazone. In experimental animals vitamin E has been shown to promote the effectiveness of linoleic acid in preventing essential fatty acid deficiency. Studies have suggested the possibility of polyunsaturated fatty acids having a role in brain development during infancy. The antioxidant property of vitamin E helps fatty acids from oxidation and thus it indirectly helps the brain development.

Vitamin E Deficiency

Vitamin E deficiency is not common among human beings as it is widely distributed in foods. Experimental deficiency in female rats results in foetal death and in males testicular changes in sterility. Muscular dystrophy and paralysis are the other symptoms of vitamin E deficiency. Premature babies with vitamin E deficiency showed impaired fat absorption. If vitamin E deficiency is present in the pregnant mother transfer of placental blood to foetus is poor and so haemolytic anaemia may occur in the baby after delivery. Vitamin E deficiency in adults results in poor absorption of fat and increased haemolysis and increased excretion of urinary creatinine. Brown muscle pigment deposition called ceroid occurs with tocopherol deficiency. Liver necrosis, erythrocyte haemolysis and anaemia are the other symptoms.

Requirements

For males 30 I.U. and for females 25 I.U. are recommended. Human milk supplies enough tocopherol for the infants.

Vitamin K

In the 1930's a Dutch scientist Dam and his associates found that "Koagulation vitamin" is necessary for clotting or coagulation of blood. It was named vitamin K. Karrer and coworkers (1939) isolated pure vitamin.

Chemistry

There are two naturally occurring forms of vitamin K, vitamin K1 and vitamin K2. Vitamin K1 is vegetable origin and vitamin K2 is produced by bacterial sythesis.

Sources

Plant oils are the best sources. Rice bran oil and wheat germ oil, soyabean and cottonseed oils are the best sources. Wholegrain cereals, fleshy foods and organ meats are fair sources. Vegetables and fruits are poor sources. It is a fat soluble vitamin and is easily oxidised by acids, alkalies and light.

Functions of Vitamin K

Vitamin K is essential for the formation of prothrombin which helps normal clotting of blood. Vitamin K is not directly involved in the coagulation but it is essential for the coagulation of blood. It takes part in the carboxylation of glutamic residue.

Requirements

The exact requirement is not known. If lowered prothrombin level is there 1-2 mg of vitamin K/day is recommended.

Deficiency

Dietary deficiency is not common. Deficiency of vitamin K is indicated by a tendency to bleed from skin and mucous membranes. Deficiency occurs due to deficient production of it by the gut, with prolonged antibiotic therapy, due to poor absorption of vitamin K, in malabsorption of fats and due to low prothrombin synthesis in liver disease. Pyloric obstruction and diarrhoea or dysentery can result in poor absorption.

Deficiency of vitamin K among newborns, especially among premature babies, delays clotting of blood. If the mother's intake during pregnancy is poor it can lead to this condition.

Excess of vitamin K due to excessive administration produces hypoprothrombinaemia and disorders in liver.

Vitamin K is not stored in large quantities in the body. Only in the liver vitamin K is stored.

WATER-SOLUBLE VITAMINS

There are 13 vitamins in this group. Vitamins C and B complex family, comprising twelve vitamins, are soluble in water.

In 1882 Takaki, the Director General of the Naval Medical Service in Japan, demonstrated that 'beriberi', a fatal disease in the navy, could be cured by including a mixed diet of whole cereals, vegetables and milk. In 1897 Eijkman found that fowls on a poor diet manifested symptoms like beriberi. He suggested that instead of rice, rice polishings must be included in the dietary pattern to avoid beriberi. In

1911 Casimer Funk described a group of water-soluble substances present in food which can act as ar.'i-scorbutic, anti-beriberi and anti-pellagra factor. In 1926 McCollum and Kennedy suggested different substances in food with different properties which were later identified as anti-beriberi and anti-pellagra factors.

Thiamine (B1)

The occurrence of beriberi led to the discovery of thiamine. Followed by the findings of Takaki, Eijkman established that rice polishings prevented a disease similar to beriberi in fowls. Dr. Grijins, an associate of Eijkman, suggested beriberi was a deficiency disease and rice polishings contain the factor. Funk, Suzuki and Edic attempted to isolate the 'anti-beriberi' factor. In 1926 Jausen and Donalth isolated crystals of thiamine. In 1936 Dr. R.R. William synthesised thiamine.

Chemistry

It is a white powder which is readily soluble in water. Alkali destroys thiamine. Thiamine is commercially produced as thiamine hydrochloride. It has a yeast-like odour and it is stable in its dry form.

Physiological Functions

Thiamine combines with pyrophosphate and forms thiamine pyrophosphate. (TPP) Thiamine pyrophosphate participates in intermediary metabolism of carbohydrates. Transketolase and enzyme has thiamine pyrophosphate as a co-factor. It acts as a co-enzyme in the metabolic pathway of carbohydrates at different places. Animal experiments showed that thiamine pyrophosphate is essential for protein metabolism. Thiamine is also required for the synthesis of glycine in the body. Thiamine pyrophosphate is present in the peripheral nerve cells. It has a specific effect on nerve tissues. In thiamine deficiency the peripheral nerves degenerate. Thiamine is also required for the maintenance of normal gastro-intestinal tone and motility. Thiamine seems to help the heart in its normal action. Thiamine is otherwise known as "morale vitamin" because it helps the transmission of nervous impulses and maintains the stability of nerves.

Deficiency of Thiamine

It is difficult to identify the deficiency earlier. In mild deficiency loss of appetite, fatigue, irritability, depression and constipation occur. Gastrointestinal and cardiovascular disorders with peripheral nervous problems initiate the deficiency state of thiamine.

In mild deficiency loss of appetite, loss of weight and strength fatigue, emotional upsets, irritability, depression, anger and fear are manifested. Constipation is common among such people. Headaches, insomnia, and techycarida with slight exertion occurs during thiamine deficiency. Severe deficiency of thiamine causes beriberi. Two forms of beriberi occur in human beings. They are dry beriberi and wet beriberi.

Dry beriberi: In dry beriberi, the peripheral nerves of the legs and arms are affected first. Degeneration of the myelin sheath of the nerves is followed by the degeneration of the axis cylinder. Calf muscles become tender. Numbness in the toes and ankles takes place. The knee and ankle jerk and later on the sensation is lost. Tingling and numbness of the legs and hands are followed by wasting of muscles and difficulty in walking.

Wet beriberi: All the symptoms of dry beriberi are seen in wet beriberi also. In addition to these oedoma in legs and in between cardiac muscle fibres is observed. These changes in the heart muscles lead to enlargement of the heart. Later palpitation, oliguria, and dyspnoea may develop. Oedema on the legs will be prominent. The patient may be bed-ridden and cardiac failure may take place. If untreated it leads to death within hours.

Infantile beriberi: It affects infants within six months. The early symptoms are restlessness, sleeplessness and loss of appetite. The affected child is pale, oedematous and ill-tempered. Vomiting and green-coloured diarrhoea are common. If treatment is delayed it leads to death.

Requirements

Thiamine requirement is related with energy intake. The Nutrition Expert Group of ICMR and FAO/WHO recommended 0.4-0.5 mgs of thiamine per 1000 kcals. For infants 5.9 mgs/kg and from 1 year onwards proportionate kcals requirements are recommended.

During deficiency state 5 mgs of thiamine orally three times a day is recommended. It is readily absorbed from the small and large intestines. It is not stored in the body.

Sources

Rice polishings, dried yeast and wheat germ are rich sources of B1. Whole cereals like wheat, oats, legumes, oil seeds and nuts are good sources. Milled cereals, vegetables, fruits, milk, meat and fish are fair sources. On milling, thiamine is lost from cereals. Commercial preparation of B1 is extracted from natural sources or it is synthesised. Nowadays cereals are enriched with thiamine. Flours are enriched and labelled to show the amount of enrichment.

Riboflavin

Scientists from various parts of the world reported that a growth promoting factor substance remained even after the beriberi preventive factor is destroyed from yeast. A yellow green fluorescent compound was known to be in the whey from milk. In 1932 the German scientists Warburg and Christian discovered the first flavoproteins from yeast. It was first known as 'Yellow enzyme'. In 1933 Kuhn and Gyorgy isolated riboflavin and Booker recognised the growth promoting property of it. It was synthesised by Kuhn and Karrer in 1935.

Chemistry

Riboflavin is dimethyl-iso-alloxazine 'attached to ribose.' It is slightly soluble in water and stable in acid medium. In alkaline medium it is easily destroyed. Bright light also destroys riboflavin.

Functions

Riboflavin is part of food co-enzymes as riboflavin monophosphate or flavin mononucleotide (FMN) and flavin adenine dinucleotide. Riboflavin is closely related to biological oxidations in cells. Flavoprotein enzyme system is present in different parts of our body. It takes part in cell respiration. Cellular growth cannot evolve in the absence of riboflavin. Riboflavin through the enzyme system possesses the ability of transferring hydrogen in chemical reactions. Thus, it takes part in carbohydrate and protein metabolism. Riboflavin is essential for the health of skin, mucous membraneous structures of alimentary canal and eyes. For normal vision riboflavin is essential. The retina has free riboflavin which is converted by light to a compound that stimulates optic nerves.

Deficiency

In mild deficiency of riboflavin weakness, anorexia, apathy, burning at the angles of mouth, in the eyes and over the skin occur. Normal metabolism of carbohydrate and protein is affected. Riboflavin deficiency symptoms are generally known as ariboflavinosis. Ariboflavinosis consists of angular stomatitis, with cheilosis, glossitis, skin changes, seborrheic dermatitis and vascularisation of the cornea.

The angles of the mouth become pale and crust is formed in the corners. Fissures occur at the corners of the mouth and it is known as cheilosis. Crust is formed on the surface of lips and removal of it makes it red in colour. Papilae of the tongue are peeled off and the tongue shows a 'magenta' or red tint on the surface. This is referred to as glossitis. On the nasolabial folds, ears, vulva in the female reproductive organs and on the scrotum in the male, scaly desquamation of the skin takes place. These are known as nasolabial seborrhoea and scrotal lesions. The lesions are cured by the administration of riboflavin.

Even in a mild deficiency state burning and watering of the eyes, sensitivity to light and dimness of vision take place. Vascularisation of the cornea and abnormal pigmentation of the iris are the other symptoms manifested. Vision is blurred and conjunctivitis and itching may occur in riboflavin deficiency.

Requirements

Various studies on the requirement of riboflavin showed that 1.4 mg per day for a sedentary man, 1.7 mg for a moderate worker and 2.3 mg for a heavy worker are essential. For females the requirement is 1 mg, 1.1 mg and 1.5 mg, respectively. During pregnancy and lactation additional 0.2 mg and 0.3 mg riboflavin are required. During infancy (0-6 months) 0.71 mg/kg and 6-12 months, 0.65 mg./kg. For 1-3 years 0.7 mg, 4-6 years 0.9 mg, and 7-9 years, 1.00 mg. of riboflavin are required. During adolescence 1.5 mg in the earlier stages, that is, 10-12 years and 1.6 mg during later adolescence for boys and 1.4 mg in early adolescence and 1.4 during later adolescence for girls are recommended.

Sources

Fleshy foods like liver, egg, skimmed milk powder and other milk products are rich sources of riboflavin. Milk, meat, fish, whole cereals, legumes, dals, oil seeds, nuts and leafy vegetables are good sources of riboflavin. Milled cereals and flours, roots and tubers and other vegetables are fair sources of riboflavin.

Riboflavin is readily absorbed from the intestine and the excess is excreted through urine.

Niacin (Nicotinic Acid)

Niacin is also known as nicotinic acid or nicotinamide. In 1725 a Spanish physician Casal described the occurrence of red sickness. In the eighteenth century, the Italian physician Frapoli named the disease as pellagra, meaning rough skin. In 1911 Funk isolated niacin from rice polishings. In 1937 Elvegem and co-workers showed that the deficiency disease (black tongue in dogs) was cured by an isolated substance from liver. Goldberger cured and prevented pellagra by adding meat, vegetables, fruits and eggs in the diet. Thus, pellagra preventing factor (P-P-factor) was identified from foods. Further investigations showed that nicotinamide was equally effective as nicotinic acid in curing pellagra.

Chemistry

Niacin is a white crystalline compound soluble in water, stable to heat, light, acids and alkalies. In the body niacin is converted into niacinamide.

Physiological Functions

Like thiamine and riboflavin niacin takes part in the metabolism of carbohydrates, proteins, and fats through the enzymatic action. It is part of co-enzyme I and co-enzyme II which are essential for the conversion of lactic acid to pyruvic acid. They are otherwise known as NAD and NADH. More than 40 biochemical reactions depend on these enzymes. Dehydrogenation reaction in Kreb's cycle, oxidation of alcohol to aldehyde, of glucose to gluconic acid, of malic acid to oxaloacetic acid, of lactic acid to pyruvic acid, glucose -1-6-phosphate to phosphohexouric acid and reactions in the synthesis of fatty acids, cholesterol and for the conversion of phenylalanine to tyrosine are some of them. It takes part in tissue oxidations. Nicotinic acid is essential for the normal functioning of the skin, intestinal and nervous systems.

Effects of Deficiency

In a mild deficiency state weakness, loss of weight, loss of appetite, lassitude, irritability, burning tongue, and constipation occur. Pellagra is the characteristic disease resulting from niacin deficiency. It is otherwise known as three 'D's disease—dermatitis, diarrhoea and dementia. The dermatitis of pellagra is different from other skin diseases. It occurs mainly on the exposed portions of the body. Lesions are seen on the face, neck, surfaces of the hands, elbows, feet and other parts of the body which are exposed to sunlight. Another peculiarity of dermatitis is that the skin lesions are symmetrical in shape, and they always occur on both sides of the body simultaneously. The skin is cracked and scaly. Burning sensation and itching are common. The lesions leave a reddish, dark brown colour. The mucous membrane of the alimentary canal is affected and glossitis, abdominal pain, and loss of appetite are some of the symptoms. Nausea, vomiting and diarhoea are the other symptoms of niacin deficiency. Delirium is the common mental disturbance in pellagra. Earlier symptoms of nervous disturbances are depression, dizziness and insomnia. It leads to death.

Pellagra is common among jowar eaters. Jowar has a very high leucine content and this excessive leucine interferes with the utilisation of nicotinic acid. Leucine precipitates mental changes but isoleucine promptly reverses them to normal.

Dr. Gopalan and his co-workers in India have done extensive studies for a decade (1960-69) in this connection. Among maize eaters pellagra is common because of the high leucine content in them. Leucine interferes in the conversion of tryptophan to niacin and also the conversion of niacin to NAD and NADP in the tissues.

Sources

Cereals, especially whole cereals, dried yeast, liver, groundnut, legumes, fleshy foods and fish are good sources. Milk, eggs, and vegetables are fair sources.

Tryptophan-niacin relation: Tryptophan is an essential amino acid and it is a precursor of niacin. Vitamin B1 or thiamine, B2 or riboflavin and pyridoxine are essential for this conversion of tryptophan to niacin. Another essential amino acid leucine interferes with the conversion of tryptophan to niacin and niacin to co-enzymes. Milk is a rich source of tryptophan. Animal foods rich in protein are good sources of niacin.

In a healthy person's body 60 mg of tryptophan is equivalent to 1 mg of niacin. Thus the dietary allowances are usually made in terms of niacin equivalents.

Niacin equivalents (mg) = Niacin content (mg.) + tryptophan content (mg)/60

Requirements

The FAO/WHO expert group has recommended an allowance of 6.6 mg niacin equivalents per 1,000 kcals. For all age groups this requirement pattern is suggested.

Pyridoxin (B6)

Three naturally occurring compounds with similar activities are together known as Vitamin B6. They are pyridoxine, pyridoxal and pyridoxamine. It is also known as adermin. In 1934 Gyorgy found a factor leading to a type of dermatitis in rats. In 1938 it was isolated and named pyridoxine.

Chemistry

It is a white crystalline substance soluble in water, quite stable to heat and acid. In an alkaline medium it is easily destroyable.

Physiological Function

Vitamin B6 acts as a co-factor for several enzymatic reactions in all the three metabolisms. In protein metabolism, transamination takes place with the help of this enzyme system. In carbohydrate and fat metabolisms, there are intermediary reactions where vitamin B6 acts as a co-factor.

It is part of the transaminase system which has a number of enzymes, e.g.,

1. Glutamic acid + oxalo acelate - alphakete-glutarate + aspartate.
   Alanine + alpha ketoglutarate = glutamic acid + pyruvic acid.
2. Amino acid decarboxylase- Amino acids to amines
   e.g., Histidine = Histamine + CO_2
          Tyrosine - Tyramine + CO_2

Tryptophan conversion to niacin has a series of biochemical reactions. In pyridoxine deficiency this conversion step will not materialise and niacine is not formed.

Removal and transfer of sulphur groups from sulphur-containing amino acids like cysteine requires pyridoxine.

In carbohydrate metabolism pyridoxal phosphate is essential for the action of phosphorylase enzyme which converts glycogen to glucose.

Vitamin B6 helps in energy transformation in brain and in nervous tissues. In its deficiency, convulsive seizures occur in animals and in human beings. Especially infants fed on evaporated milk develop nervous irritability and convulsive seizures.

Deficiency

Separate deficiency of B6 is not common. But as a part of general deficiency of B complex, vitamin B6 deficiency also occurs. In experimental cases anorexia, nausea, restlessness, lethargy, seborrhoea, hyperpigmentation, pellagra like dermatitis, cheilossis, glossitis and angular stomatitis were observed. Changes in the periphery of nerves with sensory impairment and motor abnormalities were also observed. In infants convulsions are seen. Immune response is impaired in B6 deficiency.

Sources

Dried yeast, rice polishing and liver are rich sources. Millets like cholam, cambu, pulses, beetroot, cabbage and fleshy foods are rich to fair sources, respectively.

Pantothenic Acid

In 1933, R.J. Williams reported that a factor present in food is essential for growth in yeast. It is named pantothenic which is derived from a Greek word 'Panthos' meaning everywhere. In 1939, it was isolated and synthesised in 1940.

Chemistry

It is soluble in water and it contains the amino acid alanine. It is stable to heat but prolonged exposure to dry heat destroys it. It is also destroyed by acid and alkali.

Functions

Pantothenic acid forms a complex compound co-enzyme A (CoA) and acyl carrier protein and thus it takes part in the metabolism of carbohydrates and fats. It is also necessary for the formation of acetyle choline, which is a precursor of heme which in turn is essential for haemoglobin synthesis. CoA is also essential for the synthesis of cholesterol and sterols.

In our body pantothenic acid is present in the liver, adrenal glands, kidneys, brain and heart.

Deficiency

Deficiency of pantothenic acid is rare. Experimental production of its deficiency showed loss of appetite, fatigue, weakness, headache, insomnia, nausea, emotional instability, dizziness, imparied motor coordination, muscle cramps, burning sensations in the feet and changes in the heart beat rate and in blood pressure.

Burning feet syndrome is associated with neurological and mental disturbances and it is cured only by pantothenic acid. Gopalan (1946) suggested the treatment for burning feet as administration of capantothenate. He also found that other B-complex vitamins like thiamine, riboflavin and niacin were not effective in its cure.

Sources

Dried yeast, liver, rice polishings and wheat germs are the rich sources. Whole cereals, legumes, nuts, fleshy foods, eggs and fish are fair sources.

Requirements

For adults 10 mg/day, for adolescents 8-10 mg/day, children 5-8 mg/day and for infants 1.5-2.5 mg/day was recommended by the FAO/WHO expert committee. During pregnancy and lactation 10-15 mg/day was recommended.

Vitamin B12

Minot and Murphy in 1926 reported that pernicious anaemia could be controlled by feeding liver in large quantities to patients. Castle found that beef muscle is also effective in controlling pernicious anaemia. He established that two factors were involved in curing pernicious anaemia, the intrinsic factor of normal gastric secretion and the extrinsic factor vitamin B12. In 1948, two British scientists, Smith and Parker, and Dickes from the USA isolated B12. Its structure was determined in 1955.

Chemistry

Vitamin B12 contains the mineral cobalt which gives its characteristic dark red colour. Cyanocobalamin and Hydroxy cobal are the two forms of B12.

Functions

B12 is essential for the maturation of red blood corpuscles and it combines with globulin. B12 takes part in the enzymatic reaction. Especially co-enzyme B12 is very prominent in the body. Niacin, riboflavin and magnesium are essential for this conversion of B12 to co-enzyme B12 . B12 co-enzyme is required for the action of dehydrase reaction.

Vitamin B12 acts as a necessary substance for the lipo protein action in the nervous tissues. It is also necessary for the synthesis of myelin. Within the bone marrow B12 co-enzyme participates in the synthesis of DNA.

Co-enzyme B12 is essential for carbohydrate, protein and fat metabolism. In experimental animals vitamin B12 has been found to stimulate growth. B12 co-enzyme is also essential for the synthesis and transfer of single carbon units such as the methyl group, eg., methionine and choline synthesis.

Deficiency

Due to the deficiency of vitamin B12, pernicious anaemia occurs. To prevent anaemia two factors are required: an intrinsic factor produced by the gastric parietal cells and the extrinsic factor of vitamin B12. If due to any cause enough intrinsic factor is not secreted, B12 is not absorbed and utilised properly. B12 is otherwise known as extrinsic factor. Congenital intrinsic factor deficiency and low absorption of B12 or its deficiency leads to pernicious anaemia. In pernicious anaemia the life span of red blood cells is reduced to 60 days instead of the normal 120 days and their size and shape also is changed. Skin changes show a yellowish pallor. Soreness and shine on the tongue are other manifestations of skin lesions. Gastric secretion is reduced. Stomach mucosa shows atrophic changes. Nervous tissues are degenerated, especially the posterior column of the spinal cord is affected. Peripheral neuropathy and later on mental changes are common. Tingling, numbness, loss of sensation in the limbs, exaggerated knee jerks and ankle jerks are the other symptoms. Depression and other psychosis symptoms are common in later stages.

Sources

Organ meats like kidney, liver, brain, meat, poultry, egg, fish and milk are good sources of B12. Vegetable foods lack B12.

Requirements

B12 requirements for a normal person is 1 mgm (microgram) per day. During pregnancy and lactation it is increased to 1.5 mgm (microgram). Infants and children up to 10 years require 0.2 microgram and adolescents need 1 microgram.

Choline

In 1934, Best and Huntsman discovered fatty liver in choline deficiency among rats. Choline is a component of phospholipid lecithin and it forms acetyl choline with alcohol and takes part in biochemical reactions. It is involved in the transmission of parasympathetic and other nerve impulses to effective organs. It promotes growth in animals.

In its absence neutral fats and cholesterol esters accumulate in the liver which produce fatty liver. Choline is otherwise known as a lipotropic factor as it prevents fatty liver. Choline enhances the oxidation of fatty acids and promotes the formation of lipo proteins in the liver. Phospholipids take part in the transport of fatty acids and cholesterol in the blood and from the liver and their deposition and removal in adipose tissues. It is essential for the transfer of nerve impulses. It takes part in the formation of methionine from homocystine. In its deficiency production is reduced.

Sources

Egg yolk, wheat germ, organ meats like kidney, brain, heart, meat, yeast, soyabean and peanut and skimmed milk are good sources of choline. The amino acid methoinine acts as a donor of methyl group to convert eltanolamine to choline.

Requirements

Choline requirements of human beings is not known and its deficiency is also uncommon.

Biotin

The importance of biotin was first observed by Boas in 1927. He found that raw egg white produces dermatitis, loss of hair, and muscular incoordination in experimental animals. Therefore, it was first called anti-egg white injury factor. In 1931, Gyorgy gave the name vitamin H or Haunt, which means skin. It is sparingly soluble in cold water and alcohol. Biotin is present in human tissues and is necessary for bacterial growth. It is also necessary for normal gestation and lactation in experimental animals. Biotin plays an important role in maintaining the skin structure and for the health of nervous system. Biotin also acts as a co-enzyme for carboxylation of acetyl-CoA to form malonyl-CoA in fatty acid metabolism.

Egg White Injury Factor (Avidin)

Rats kept on a diet of uncooked egg white developed dermatitis, muscular incoordination and spasticity of legs and loss of hair. This is produced by a protein present in egg white called avidin. Avidin combines with biotin which is unavailable to the body. This avidinbiotin compound is excreted in the stool. Since avidin is present in egg white it is also known as egg white injury factor. Since heat destroys avidin, cooking of egg destroys it.

Deficiency of biotin among human beings is not common. Sydenstricker and co-workers in 1942 produced biotin deficiency in man by giving 30 per cent of the total calorie intake from fresh egg white. Dermatitis of varying types on the necks, hands, arms and legs were seen. It was followed by lassitude, muscle pain, anorexia, nausea and anaemia. Injection of biotin brought rapid cure.

Sources

Dried yeast, rice polishings, liver, groundnut, soyabean, whole cereals, legumes and fleshy foods are good sources of biotin.

Requirements

A normal balanced diet supplies the requirement of biotin. Its deficiency is not common. The exact requirement of biotin is not known.

Inositol

Wolley and co-workers in 1940 reported that deficiency of inositol produced alopaecia in the mouse. Inositol is a component of phospholipids.

Inositol is essential for the growth of fibroblasts. It is present in phospholipids and it exerts a lipotropic effect. It is present in different tissues, especially in heart and skeletal muscles. It also enables peristalisis of the intestine.

Effects of Deficiency

In experimental animals deficiency of inositol produced retarded growth, loss of hair or alopaecia. It also produces spectacled eye or loss of hair around the eye.

Sources

It is widely distributed in nature. Fruits, milk, vegetables, nuts, meat, wholegrains, yeast and bacteria are good sources of inositol.

Para-amino-benzoic Acid

In 1941, Ansbacher found out that para-amino-benzoic (PABA) is essential for normal growth of rats. For normal lactation and for the prevention of greying of hair para-amino-benzoic acid is necessary. It is present in folic acid.

Para-amino-benzoic acid inhibits the bacteriostatic effect of sulphonamides. It also inhibits the production of thyroid hormones.

Requirement of PABA for human beings is not known. Average diets provide adequate amounts of PABA.

Vitamin C (Ascorbic Acid)

In the eighteenth century James Lind, a British naval surgeon, demonstrated that citrus juices cured scurvy among sailors. Holst and Frolich produced scurvy in guinea-pigs. The study of ascorbic acid was thus actually initiated in 1907 by these scientists. Later in 1928, Szent-Gyorgy isolated a factor from orange and cabbage juice. It was hexuronic acid which prevented scurvy. Wangh and King in 1932 showed that hexuronic acid was identical with vitamin C and they isolated it from lemon juice.

Chemistry

Ascorbic acid is a white crystalline substance readily soluble in water. It is present in two forms: L-ascorbic acid and D-ascorbic acid. L-ascorbic acid has anti-ascorbutic property while D-ascorbic acid has no such property. It is easily destroyed by oxidation, heat and alkalies. Even when it is exposed to air it is oxidized to dehydroascorbic acid. During cooking much of it is destroyed. Iron and copper act as catalysts and cooking in these vessels increases the loss of vitamin C. Ascorbic acid is also lost by the action of an enzyme, ascorbic oxidase, present in vegetable oils. When vegetables are cut into fine pieces more enzyme is released and it causes more loss. This can be minimised by immersing vegetables in boiling water as heat destroys the enzyme. Adding sodium bicarbonate to preserve the colour of vegetables destroys vitamin C. As it is readily soluble in water washing vegetables after cutting, cooking in too much water and cooking in cold water enhances the loss of vitamin C.

Ascorbic acid is readily absorbed from the intestine.

Physiological Functions

Due to its great affinity for oxidation it takes part in oxidation and reduction reactions in the tissues. Ascorbic acid is essential for the formation of collagen present between cells. It is otherwise known as the cementing material or intercellular cement of the body. If collagen is defective tissues in the capillaries, teeth and bone matrix are not formed properly. Ascorbic acid is also necessary for the formation of osteoblasts. Vitamin C is essential for cholesterol metabolism. It is also necessary for the conversion of phenylalanine to tyrosine and for the oxidation of tyrosine. It takes part in the conversion of tryptophan to 5-hydroxy-tryptophan. Ascorbic acid reduces the ferric iron to ferrous iron and iron is absorbed only in this form. It is also essential for rapid healing of wounds as it helps in the formation of connective tissues. Vitamin C is also essential for the utilisation of folacin.

Deficiency of Vitamin C

Prolonged deficiency of Vitamin C produces scurvy. In mild deficiency fatigue, weakness, irritability and frequent infection occur. Pain in bones is common.

Scurvy among infants is known as infantile scurvy. The infant cries on moving its legs and arms. Early symptoms include listlessness, fatigue, fleeting pains in the joints and muscles, bleeding gums, internal haemorrhages and shortness of breath. In severe deficiency of vitamin C scurvy occurs. Swollen gums, loose teeth, soft or malformed weak bones, anaemia, degeneration of muscle fibres including heart muscles are some of the symptoms of vitamin C deficiency. Separation of ribs through beading is also observed. This can be distinguished from rickets from its shape. The skin becomes rough and dry. Pyrexia, rapid pulse and susceptibility to infection are common in scurvy.

In adults, weakness, spongy bleeding gums, loose teeth, swollen joints and haemorrhages in various tissues are the symptoms.

Propylaxis for infantile scurvy include 50 mgs of vitamin C with orange juice three or four times a day. In the case of adults 100 mgs of ascorbic acid twice daily is recommended. Citrus fruits, sprouted pulses and soaked cereals must be liberally used for vitamin C.

Dietary Sources

Citrus fruits like lime, orange, pineapple, ripe mango, papaya, cashew fruit and tomato are good sources. Amla or Indian gooseberry is the richest source of vitamin C. One hundred grammes of amla contain 700 mg of vitamin C. Guava is also rich in this vitamin C. Leafy vegetables are good sources of vitamin C. But this vitamin is readily destroyed by oxidation during cooking and storing. About half of the vitamin C in raw food is lost during cooking.

Requirements

The ICMR (1984) recommended 40 mgs of vitamin C as sufficient for an adult considering its cooking loss. During pregnancy and lactation the requirement was reviewed and the committee recommended that no additional allowances were needed during pregnancy but 80 mgs of vitamin C is required during lactation. For infants 20 mg per day and for children 40 mg per day is enough.

Folic Acid (Folacin)

Folic acid has been called folacin, pteroylglutamic or vitamin Bc. In the early 1930s a search for anaemia-preventing factor was done by many scientists. Dr. Lucy Wills (1934) showed that there was a factor in yeast and crude liver extracts which cured tropical macrocytic anaemia. This factor was known as "Wills factor". In 1946 Keresztesy and Silverman isolated folic acid from liver. The word folic acid is derived from the Latin word folium (leaf) as it is found in green vegetables. Many bacteria synthesize folic acid but lactobacillas grows well only if folic acid is supplied. So folic acid is otherwise known as Lactobacillas.

Chemistry

Folic acid is a yellow crystalline compound widely distributed in nature. Both folic acid and folinic acids occur in foods as conjugates of glutamic acid. It is slightly soluble in water, relatively unstable to heat and easily destroyed by exposure to light. Folacin occurs in different forms. Most of it occurs as pterolypolyglutamates. It is sensitive to light and cooking loss is reduced by anti-oxidant agents like vitamin C.

Physiological Functions

Folic acid is converted to active folinic acid. Folic acid acts as a co-enzyme. Co-enzyme takes part in metabolic process when it transfers single carbon units from one compound to another. Folacin co-enzymes are involved in many methylation reaction. Folic acid is essential for nucleoprotein synthesis and it is required for cells division and also for maturation of erythrocytes. The role of folacin in protein synthesis is made in cancer therapy. Folacin inhibitor like methortrexale are used in chemotherapy to inhibit tumor growth. It is essential for reproduction in animals. Folic acid also helps the hair growth and health of skin.

Deficiency

Lack of folacin results in megaloblastic anaemia. It is otherwise known as macrocytic anaemia. This mainly affects pregnant women. A study in Madras showed that 20 per cent of maternal deaths occurred due to anaemia. Poor vegetarian diet supplies very little folacin. This type of anaemia is due to inadequate formation of nucleoproteins. This prevents the megaloblasts in the bone marrow from maturing into erythrocytes. In megaloblastic anaemia the number of red blood cells produced in the bone marrow is reduced. The haemoglobin level is also reduced to 6-9 per cent and R.B.C. count to two to three million per mm. Along with inadequate diet it also results from malabsorption syndromes like tropical sprue. Often B12 deficiency after a surgical removal of some part of the stomach also produces megaloblastic anaemia.

Requirements

100 mgm for adults and 300 mg during pregnancy are recommended by the expert committee. Breast-fed infants will receive about 25 to 30 mg of folate daily. Requirement for children is not known.

Sources

Organ meats like kidney, liver and dark green leafy vegetables, soyabean and groundnuts are rich sources of folic acid. Other vegetables, legumes, eggs, wholegrain cereals and fruits are good sources.

7

MINERALS

In an adult 4 per cent of the body weight is from minerals. There are 24 minerals in the body. Mineral substances are important in maintaining good health because they are part of our tissues, skeletal structure and the body fluids. Hormones, enzymes and vitamins contain minerals. Vital organs like heart and nervous tissues cannot function normally in its absence. Water balance, regulation of fluids, and the acid base balance in the body depend to a great extent on certain mineral balance in the body. Neuromuscular activities, coagulation of blood and fluid movement in the tissues are under the control of certain inorganic substances in the body.

Minerals are inorganic substance that are present in the body tissues like phosphomin, iron, sulphur, zinc or copper or soluble minerals in the body fluids like sodium chloride or mineral components in the bones and teeth and hormonal secretions. Water balance in the body is regulated by minerals like sodium and potassium. Our body has calcium, phosphorus, sodium, potassium, chlorine, iron, magnesium, copper, iodine, cobalt, zinc, aluminium, arsenic, bromine, fluorine, nickel, chromium, cadmium, selenium, silicon, vanadium, and molybdenum as minerals. Each one of this has some role in maintaining the structure and function of vital organs of our body. Few milligrams of a mineral element decide the skeletal growth or the mental ability of a person.

Optimum intake of minerals and favourable environment for its utilisation are equally important to maintain mineral balance. During the growth period and also during pregnancy, lactation and old age, certain minerals are very essential to maintain health and growth.

Calcium

The most abundant mineral element in the body is calcium. Nearly 99 per cent of the calcium in the body is present in the skeleton. The remaining part of calcium performs a variety of functions in the body. About 850-950 gms of calcium is present in a healthy man.

Functions

The most important function of calcium is the ossification of bones. If calcium content in the blood is below normal, bone calcium is depleted and serum level is brought to normal. Parathyroid hormone regulates calcium level in blood and its metabolism in the bone. The bones constitute a mineral reserve which may be drawn upon in need. Calcium is also essential for the formation of teeth and for the contraction of the heart and muscle. The regulation of muscle irritability is dependent upon the serum calcium level. Calcium is also required for normal nerve impulse transmission and excitability of nerve fibres and nerve centres. Calcium forms part of acelytcholine which is necessary for the transmission of nerve impulses. Calcium helps in the coagulation of blood and is needed for permeability of capillary walls. Calcium exerts its influence in the absorption of vitamin B12 from the intestine. The mineral has been shown to activate certain enzymes, especially lipase and certain proteolytic enzymes, adenosine triphosphate and rennin.

Factors Affecting Calcium Absorption

The most important factor promoting calcium absorption is vitamin D content in the body. Utilisation of calcium is more when it is needed by the body. For example, during growth the absorption of calcium is more than in adults. Calcium content in the diet increases the absorption of calcium. Phosphates and calcium ratio in the diet also influences the absorption. If the ratio is 1:1, absorption rate is high. If phosphate ratio is high, calcium absorption is low. Phytic acid which is present in cereals combines with phosphorus and forms insoluble calcium salts and calcium phytate and inhibits calcium absorption. Abnormal intake of fats and fatty acids reduces the calcium level in blood and its metabolism in the bone. The bones constitute a mineral reserve which may be drawn upon in need. Minerals like iron which forms insoluble phosphates interfere with phosphorus absorption which indirectly affects calcium absorption. Absorption of calcium is facilitated by low intestinal pH. Normal acidity of stomach due to the presence of hydrochloric acid is essential to stimulate the absorption of calcium. Parathyroid hormone also aids in the absorption of calcium from the stomach. If cereals with husk are used in the diet, calcium absorption is reduced. Whole flours, oatmeal, and preparation with these, if not fermented, increases the inhibition of calcium utilisation. On fermentation of the enzyme phytase splits up calcium phytate and then increases its absorption.

Like phytic acid, oxalic acid is present abundantly in leafy vegetables and certain fruits. This forms an insoluble compound calcium oxalate and thus diminishes the absorption of calcium. Magnesium, if taken in abundant quantities, often interferes with calcium absorption and results in poor calcium absorption. During sprue, steatorrhea or in biliary fistula fat is absorbed poorly and thus accumulated fats help the formation of calcium soaps. Good quality protein content in the diet helps calcium absorption. During rickets citric acid increases calcium absorption.

There are many factors which hinder the absorption of calcium. Phytic acid, oxalic acid, magnesium and fat reduce the absorption of calcium. Cereals contain phytic acid which combines with calcium to form insoluble calcium phytates. Phytic acid is present in the outer parts of certain proteolytic enzymes.

Deficiency

Calcium deficiency symptoms are usually accompanied by a lack of phosphorus and vitamin D. Any of the factors which affect calcium absorption can lead to its ineffective utilisation. Vitamin D deficiency alone can produce calcium deficiency symptoms. Pure calcium deficiency is osteoperosis. In osteoperosis serum calcium level is normal but body store is reduced. During old age the capacity of the body to absorb and utilise calcium is diminished. In women hormonal imbalance during menopause or removal of ovaries at earlier stages results in osteoperosis. Corticosteroid injection for any purpose may result in osteoperosis. In osteoperosis pores are seen in the bones due to decalcification. Back pain, loss of weight, fracture of bones for no reason and loss of teeth are some of the clinical symptoms. Calcium and vitamin D deficiency results in rickets and osteomalacia among children and adults, respectively.

Tetany is another symptom of calcium deficiency. In tetany there is hyperexcitability of the nervous system. A series of spasmodic movements take place in the muscles. Depending upon the level of serum calcium symptoms of tetany vary. Irritation, confusion, pain, involuntary muscle spasm, bronchial spasm, spasm in the gastro-intestinal tract, pain and convulsions are again symptoms of tetany. If parathyroid gland is in hypoactivity, calcium is not properly assimilated and results in chronic tetany. In this condition nervous changes occur and impairment of memory takes place. Depression, irritation, loss of hair and nails, roughness of the skin, pitting of teeth and epileptic fits are other symptoms of this condition. Cataract is common in such patients.

Hypercalcemia

Hyper-vitaminosis-D or Hyperparathyroidism produces hypercalcemia. Normally infants of 5-8 months get this problem. Loss of appetite, vomiting, constipation and flabby muscles are the symptoms.

Sources of Calcium

Milk and milk products are the best sources of calcium. Calcium is absorbed maximum from milk and milk products because of the presence of lysine and lactose in it. Ragi is the cheapest source of calcium; therefore it is known as 'poor man's milk'. Sesame seeds and leafy vegetables are also good sources of calcium. But the availability from these sources is not insured as in sesame seeds calcium is present in its husk and on dehusking it is removed. In leafy vegetables the presence of oxalates inhibits its absorption. Molasses and vegetables like peas, beans, potatoes, pulses, and small fish and dried fruits are rich in calcium. Unabsorbed calcium is excreted through faecal matters.

Requirements

The FAO/WHO expert group (1984) has recommended 400-500 mg of calcium per day for an adult man and woman. During pregnancy and lactation the requirement increases to 1,000 mg/day. For infants 500-600 mg and for children of between 1 and 9 years 400 to 500 mgs and for age group 10 to 15 years 600-700 mg are recommended.

Phosphorus

No other mineral takes part in a number of functions as phosphorus in different parts of our body. An adult human body contains about 400-700 mgs of phosphorus. About eighty per cent of the body's phosphorus is deposited in the bones and teeth as calcium phosphate. The remaining portion is located as sodium phosphate and potassium phosphate in the body fluids and in cells. Phosphorus is also present in many enzymes and co-enzymes and co-carboxylase. Thus it takes part in metabolism.

Functions

Phosphorus takes an important role in the calcification of bones. It also plays an essential part in carbohydrate metabolism in phosphorylation of glycogen. Phosphorus is an essential constituent of co-enzyme I and co-carboxylase enzyme system in the oxidation of carbohydrate, proteins and fat metabolism. Phosphorus compounds control the storage and release of energy through ATP, ADP system. Phosphorus is present in the nucleoproteins which are an integral part of the cells. Phospholipids, which are present in various cells of our body, contain phosphorus. Inorganic phosphates in the body fluids act as a buffer system in the body.

About seventy per cent of ingested phosphorus is absorbed. If iron, aluminium and magnesium are present in excess amount in the diet they interfere with the absorption of phosphorus. The proportion of calcium and phosphorus is an important factor which regulates its absorption.

Requirements

The daily requirement is about 1 gm. Phosphorus requirement is similar to calcium for various groups.

Sources

Animal foods like meat, fish, poultry and eggs are excellent sources of phosphorus. Milk and milk products are good source of phosphorus. Though cereals and legumes are good sources, phosphorus is less available from them as it is present in the form of phytic acid which is not utilised well.

Iron

Iron is a component of the complex protein haemoglobin, a haemoprotein component of the red blood cells. It is the pigment of red blood cells. Of the 3 to 5 gms of iron present in our body more than half of it is present in haemoglobin. The rest of it is stored in the liver, spleen, bone marrow and muscles. In the muscle it is present in the form of myoglobin. Iron is also present in some enzymes like cytochromes, catalase and peroxidase.

Functions

The most important function of iron is to form a constituent of haemoglobin which takes part in the transportation of oxygen from the lungs to the tissues. This oxygen is used by the body for the processes of metabolism. In its deficiency the oxygen-carrying capacity of the blood is reduced. In red muscles myoglobin, a pigment substance, is formed with the participation of iron. This also has the same oxygen-transporting function like the haemoglobin. During strenuous activity this muscle is involved. In our body there are certain cytochrome protein pigments with iron as an essential component. They act as respiratory enzymes. Certain flavin enzymes also contain iron in them.

Absorption of Iron

Dietary iron is absorbed primarily from the duodenum by the mucosa. Depending upon the need of iron in the body its absorption varies. If the haemoglobin concentration of the blood is satisfactory, little or no iron is absorbed and it is excreted in the faeces. Ferrous iron is absorbed more efficiently than ferric iron. In the intestine most of the iron is reduced to ferrous state. Absorption of iron is enhanced in an acid medium. Vitamin C also enhances the absorption of iron, in the intestinal tract, because of its strong reducing capacity. Protein content in the diet helps the absorption of iron to some extent. Sulphur containing amino acids reduce iron which helps its absorption. Excess of calcium phosphate, phytates and oxalic acid interfere with iron absorption by forming insoluble iron salts or oxalates. Minute traces of copper help the formation of haemoglobin. The rate of absorption of iron is affected by the magnitude of iron store in the body and the rate of erythropoiesis. Malabsorption syndromes also reduce iron absorption.

Deficiency of Iron

Anaemia is a conditon where the haemoglobin level is lowered in the blood. Shortage of iron in the diet is the most common cause of anaemia. Iron, folic acid, proteins, B12, copper, cobalt, vitamin C and pyridoxine are the nutrients required for erythropoiesis. Folic acid deficiency produces megaloblastic anaemia.

Symptoms of Anaemia

When the haemoglobin level falls below 12.5 gm/100 ml of blood, it results in the diminished oxygen-carrying power of the blood. Iron deficiency anaemia is otherwise known as hypochromic anaemia. In this condition the number of RBC is not much reduced but the quantity of haemoglobin is less. The pallor of skin and tissues, fatigue, weakness, giddiness, blurred vision, anorexia, heartburn, palpitation, dysproea, oedema over feet, headache and a feeling of tiredness are some of the symptoms. The nails show koilonychia and tongue and papillary atrophy are seen. Among women menstrual disturbances like menorrhagia or phases of amenorrhoea take place.

Nutritional megaloblastic anaemia occurs due to dietary deficiency during old age, increased requirement during pregnancy, lactation, prematurity, rapid growth and in endocrine disturbances. Haemolytic anaemias occur during malignancy, rheumatoid arthritis, pulmonary tuberculosis and in skin diseases. Alcoholism and side effects of drugs also result in anaemia. In diseases like idiopathic steatorrhoea, tropical sprue and in partial gastractomy anaemia takes place. During pregnancy this type of anaemia usually occurs in the second trimester. Weakness, palpitation and fatigue are followed by fainting bouts.

Anaemia must be treated with ferrous sulphate tablets and iron-rich diet.

Hemosiderosis

It is a disorder of iron metabolism. In this condition large deposits of iron are made in the liver and in the recticulo endothelial system. Iron with carrier protein which is known as transferrin of circulation becomes saturated with iron. When transferrin is unable to bind all the absorbed iron this metabolic disorder of iron takes place. If iron vessels are used for almost all cooking much more iron is ingested in the body, which may result in hemosiderosis. The Bantu population of Africa is an example of this condition.

In hemolytic anaemia a large number of red blood cells are destroyed and this can lead to hemosiderosis. Prolonged prophylaxis with massive doses of iron can often produce hemosiderosis.

Sources of Iron

Liver, kidney, heart, lean meat, egg yolk and shellfish are the best sources of iron. Dried beans, legumes, dried fruits, nuts, green leafy vegetables, whole cereals, enriched grains and molasses are good sources. Milk is a poor source of iron.

Requirement of Iron

Recommended intake of iron is calculated, based on its loss and absorption. For an adult man weighing 55 kg the iron requirement is 24 mg/day and for a woman of 45 kg weight 32 mg is the requirement. During pregnancy 40 mg and during lactation 32 mg of iron is required.

For infants till one year 1 mg/kg body weight and for children of 1 to 9 years of age 20 to 25 mg of iron are required. For boys and girls between 10 and 12 years of age 30 to 25 mg and for boys 13 to 15 years of age 25 mg and for girls from 13 to 15 years 35 mg of iron are required. During later adolescents for boys (16-18 years) 25 mg and for girls 35 mg is the recommended allowance.

Magnesium

The human body contains minute quantities of magnesium in the bones along with calcium and phosphorus and the rest in soft tissue. An adult human body has about 25 gm of magnesium.

Functions

Magnesium plays an important role in normal calcium and phosphorus metabolism in man. It is also present in certain enzymes like co-carboxylase which decarboxylase pyruvic acid. Magnesium also takes part in the phosphorylation in metabolic pathways.

Magnesium is easily absorbed from the intestine. Excess magnesium is excreted in the faeces. Normal human serum contains about 2 to 3 mg/100 ml.

Deficiency

Prolonged starvation brings magnesium deficiency, vomiting and intestinal fistula. Diabetic acidosis is associated with raised serum level of magnesium. Neuromuscular irritability, tremors, cramps, twitching and convulsions occur in its deficiency. Confusion, disorientation and visual hallucinations are some other complaints with magnesium deficiency.

Sodium

Sodium is essential for the normal functioning of the body. Sodium plays an important role in the regulation of acid-base balance and water metabolism in the body. Sodium in the form of sodium chloride is ingested directly through food and many food materials contain this mineral. Almost all the body sodium is found in the extracellular fluids of our body. Through sodium the osmotic pressure is also regulated by the body. A healthy kidney regulates the excretion of sodium according to the requirement. During kidney diseases sodium is retained in the body and oedema takes place. Under normal conditions 90 per cent of ingested sodium is excreted in the urine in the form of sodium chloride and sodium phosphate. Sweat contains some amount of sodium. Sodium helps to contribute alkalibility of the gastrointestinal tract.

Sodium plays a special role in controlling the heartbeat by helping in its origin and maintenance. Contraction of muscles and regulating the permeability of cell membranes are the other functions of sodium.

The adult human body contains about 100 gm of sodium. On an average diet about 3 to 5 gms of sodium is excreted in the urine. In profuse perspiration sodium chloride is depleted from the body. In sodium depletion muscular cramps, weakness, headache and vascular collapse take place. In decreased water intake the serum level of sodium is increased and this condition is known as hypernatraemia. Blood urea is increased and cellular water is depleted during dehydration and in hyponatraemia. In infants shrinkage of brain causes rupture of cerebral veins and further cerebral thrombosis. Retention of sodium produces oedema and ascites. In renal diseases, cardiac failure, hepatic cirrhosis with ascites, toxaemia of pregnancy, prolonged administration of corticosteroids sodium must be restricted through diet. Normally 4-5 gm sodium is injested through food and it is restricted to 250 mg, 500 mg, or 750 mg depending upon the condition.

Requirements

For an adult 1-2 gms of sodium and for children 350 mg-1 gm is recommended. For infants 150-400 mg is enough.

Sources

Animal foods like meat, meat extractives, fish, poultry, milk, milk products, nuts, bakery items, salted biscuits, egg-white, dried fruits, roots like beetroot, carrot, radish and leafy vegetables like spinach are excellent sources of sodium.

Abnormalities of Sodium Level in Blood

Hyponatraemia and hypernatremia are two conditions which manifest the sodium level in the blood.

Hyponatraemia

When serum sodium level falls below normal the condition is known as hyponatraemia; various conditions lead to this symptom. Severe dehydration, decrease in blood volume, decrease in blood pressure, circulatory failure are some of them, prolonged vomiting, diarrhoea, chronic renal diseases with acidosis, Addison's disease due to adrenocestical deficiency are the common causes for hyponatraemia.

Hypernatraemia

In this condition the plasma sodium iron content is higher than normal. Hyperactivity of adrenal cortex as in cushing's syndrome, prolonged treatment with cortisone, ACTH and sex hormones are some of the causes of hypernatraemia. Deficient water intake due to vomiting, nausea, difficulty in swallowing with sore throat, oesophegal disease, cerebral impairment, increased water loss through respiration diarrhoea, excessive urination in diabetes mellitus, chronic renal diseases, increased sodium intake and deficient sodium excretion brings hypernatraemia.

Potassium

In contrast to sodium, potassium is present in the intracellular fluids of the body. It is an important constituent of cells. In adult body 250 gm of potassium is present. Most of it, that is, 97 per cent is found in the intracellular fluids and the remaining 3 per cent in extracellular fluids. The other important function of potassium is that it influences the cellular excitability of smooth, skeletal, cardiac and nervous tissues. If potassium content is high muscular irritability is increased. Diminished calcium and magnesium also result in such a condition. Involuntary muscular function is controlled by potassium content in the body. When the potassium level in the myocardium is changed it is reflected in the electrocardiogram. Potassium is also necessary for the acid base balance in the body.

Potassium deficiency shows weakness in muscular functions, mental disorientation and cardiac irregularities. Hyperpotassemia results from kidney diseases when renal excretion is less. In dehydration these symptoms occur. Deficiency of potassium is not common unless as a complication of diseases. Deficiency condition shows hypokalaemia during operation when food cannot be ingested. In diabetic acidosis this condition occurs. Deficient intake due to starvation and excessive loss from gastro-intestinal tract leads to deficiency.

Hypokalaemia occurs due to deficient intake of it while a surgical patient is exposed to prolonged parent therapy, excessive loss from gastro-intestional tract through persistent vomiting, fistulae or diarrhoea before and after surgery, the patient may be on a poor diet which may enhance the excretion of potassium. Surgical cases due to low intake produces hypokalaemia.

In diabetic acidosis potassium is lost through dehydration on insulin therapy, sugar is converted to glycogen and starch. This glycogen formation depletes some potassium from extracellular fluids and serum potassium level falls and it is dangerous.

While diuretics are administered considerable loss of potassium through urine leads to hypokalaemia. Nephritis and other kidney diseases, tumours of large intestine, treatment with steroids, deficiency disease like kwashiorkor, megaloblastic anaemia, heatstroke and violent exercise are some of the other causes which produce hypokalaemia. Prolonged hypokalaemia causes injury to myocardium and kidney.

Hyperkalaemia

When the potassium level in the serum is high the condition is known as hyperkalaemia. This occurs due to diminished urine volume, intake of potassium salts of penicillin, iodide, acidosis, endogenous tissue breakdown, Addison's disease, kidney failure due to kidney disease or chronic renal failure and rapid intravenous administration of potassium are some of the reasons for hyperkalaemia. Cardiac and the central nervous system are affected by this condition. Anorexia, weakness of the muscles, diminished tendon jerks, low heart sounds followed by peripheral vascular collapse and general apathy are some of the symptoms.

Trace Elements

Elements which occur in our body in small quantities are known as trace elements. Copper, iodine, zinc, manganese, molybdenum, fluorine, selenium, nickel, chromium, cadmium, silicon, vanadium, strontium, cobalt and chlorine are some of the trace elements. Though these trace elements are present in traces they are very essential to maintain the structure of various organs in good condition. RBC formation, thyroxine production, formation of healthy bones, haemoglobin formation and proper enzymatic actions are some of the important functions of trace elements in our body.

Iodine

The significance of iodine as an essential trace element lies in its role in thyroxine production. Thyroxine is the hormone produced by the thyroid gland. Iodine is the main component of thyroxine and a normal adult has only about 10 mg of iodine in the thyroid. The absorbed iodine combines with a thyroxine bindi.ng protein. Thyroxine plays an important role in carbohydrate metabolism. Deficiency of thyroxine interferes with the normal physical and skeletal development of the child during the growing period. Iodine also helps the tissues in its oxygen consumption. Conversion of glycogen to glucose occurs only in its presence. Thyroxine increases the heart rate and depletes bone calcium.

Deficiency

If the iodine intake is deficient the thyroid gland enlarges and this condition is known as simple or endemic goitre. The normal thyroid gland weighs about 25 gm. In goitre it enlarges from 200 to 500 gm. Iodine deficiency goitre results in hypofunctioning of the gland. If diagnosis is done early and iodine supplements are given the thyroid may become normal. If timely treatment is not given the enlargement will become permanent. During the growing period if severe deficiency occurs it results in retarded growth and the condition is known as cretinism. People living mainly in submountain zones are affected. In India residents of sub-Himalayan regions and Kashmir and parts of adjoining plains are the victims. The most affected are among girls between the ages of 12 and 18 years and boys from 9 to 13 years. The areas where goitre is common is known as the goitre belt. According to the latest data available, about 40 million people are affected with goitre. In these areas air, water, soil and foods grown are poor in iodine which results in its high incidence. Goitre can be prevented by the regular use of iodized salt.

Goitrogenic Substances in Foods

Certain foods of brassica genus like cabbage, cauliflower, turnip, soyaflour and oil contain substances which react with iodine present in the food and make it unavailable. These substances are known as goitrogenic substances. Consumption of these foods in large quantities makes the iodine non-available to the body.

Requirement of Iodine

An adult requires about 0.15 to 0.2 mg of iodine and for infants and children 0.05 to 0.1 mg daily is enough.

Sources

Iodine is present in minute quantities in all foods. The iodine content of foods depends on the iodine content of the soil. In certain parts the soil contains less iodine and the foods grown in such places are iodine poor. The soil of mountainous regions is usually iodine-poor soil. The best sources of iodine are seafoods, common salt and vegetables; cereals and legumes are poor sources of iodine. Most of the iodine in the vegetables is in their leaves and flowers.

Copper

Copper is found in all tissues of our body. It is an essential element in the formation of haemoglobin. About 100 to 150 mg of copper is present in the human body. The brain, liver, heart and kidney contain the highest amounts. In the blood, copper is present in the plasma and RBC. Copper is absorbed rapidly into the blood.

Copper is a component to certain enzymes in our body. It is part of the enzyme cytochrome oxidase which is essential for glucose metabolism. It is also part of tyrosinase, an enzyme necessary for converting the amino acid tyrosine to melanin, the dark pigment of the skin. Copper stimulates the absorption of iron. Copper is a constituent of the elastic connective tissue protein elastin.

Deficiency

Copper deficiency is not common in human beings. In malnourished persons iron is not absorbed properly and anaemia occurs. Premature babies fed on cow's milk develop anaemia due to copper and iron deficiency.

Requirement

An adult person requires about 2 mg/day. During pregnancy and lactation the copper requirement is increased to 3 mg/day. Infants from 0 to 12 months require 0.5 mg to 1 gm and children 2 gm and adolescents 3 mg of copper.

Sources

Millets like cholam, bajra, raw rice, whole grams, cow gram, dried peas, red gram dal, vegetables like drumstick are good sources of copper. Liver is the richest source of copper. Organ meat like kidney is also a good source of copper.

Zinc

In an adult 2 to 3 gms of zinc is present. It is present in certain parts of the eye, certain glands and in their secretion. Liver, muscles, bone and hair contain some of the remaining zinc. Blood, especially the RBC, has some zinc. In small amounts it is present in tissues and bone cells.

The important function of zinc is its role in enzymatic action. At least in 25 enzymes of digestive and metabolic action zinc takes part. It is also present in an enzyme carbonic anhydrase which is essential for the transport and elimination of carbon dioxide. Co-carboxypeptidase and alkaline phosphatase contain zinc in them. Zinc plays an essential role in the formation of DNA and RNA. It is a constituent of insulin and it is necessary for the formation of connective tissues. Zinc also aids in the healing of burns and wounds.

Deficiency

Zinc deficiency in animals results in growth failure, loss of appetite, degeneration of the male sex glands, testes, skin lesions, alopaecia or loss of hair, changes in the epithelial and cutaneous tissues, dermatitis and scaling and cracking of the paws. Abnormal bone formation, thickening and metabolism also occur during zinc deficiency. In human beings zinc deficiency produces anaemia, growth retardation and delayed genital maturation.

Requirement

Infants require 3 to 5 mg. For children 10 to 15 mg and during pregnancy and lactation 20 to 25 mg of zinc are required.

Sources

Seafoods, meat, poultry and eggs are good sources of zinc. Cereals, legumes, and nuts contain considerable amounts. Fruits and vegetables are poor sources. On milling eighty per cent of zinc is lost.

Cobalt

In an adult body about 1.1 mg of cobalt is present. It is found in the blood, liver, kidney, spleen and pancreas. It is also present in minute quantities in all tissues.

The most important function of cobalt is that it forms an integral part of vitamin B12. In animals, if the feed is deficient in cobalt, severe anaemia occurs. Addition of cobalt to feed or injection of vitmin B12 cures this condition. In human beings vitamin B12 synthesis occurs in the colon. At that phase absorption is not taking place. So preformed B12 must be ingested for the cobalt requirement. But deficiency of cobalt is not common among human beings. Cobalt also takes part in the enzymatic action and also in thyroid function.

Requirement

Since deficiency is not known, the requirement is not studied. In pernicious anaemia B12 deficiency is present and on administration of B12 it disappears.

Sources

Cereals, beans, peas and organ meats like kidney and liver are good sources.

Manganese

About 20 mg of manganese is present in an adult. Bones, liver, pancreas, kidney and pituitary gland contain manganese.

The manganese functions in many enzyme systems. It activates certain enzymes which take part in the digestion and metabolism of carbohydrates, proteins and lipids. In the synthesis of ATP cholesterol, fatty acids and RNA, the manganese plays an important role.

Manganese deficiency in human beings is not known. Experimental deficiency symptoms are slowing of growth, abnormalities in bone, depressed reproductive functions, neurological weakness of the limbs, ataxia and lack of balance. Among birds a condition known as perosis occurs on manganese deficiency. It is characterised by bone deformities and dislocation of bones.

Sources

Cereals, bran, dried beans, peas, green vegetables and nuts are good sources. Tea and coffee are high in manganese content. But animal foods are relatively poor in it.

Chromium

An adult body contains about 6 mg of chromium. Chromium is present in skin, hair, muscles, brain, tissues, adrenal glands and in body fats.

An important function of chromium is its role in glucose tolerance factor formation in the body. Chromium niacin complex factor helps the action of insulin on glucose. Chromium is also essential for the activating enzymes involved in carbohydrate, protein and fat digestion and metabolism. The serum cholesterol level was raised on experimental animals in chromium deficiency.

Requirement

The exact requirements is not known. A normal balanced diet supplies enough chromium.

Sources

Organ meats like liver, meats, wholegrain cereals and brewer's yeast are good sources of chromium.

Fluorine

Fluorine is present in the body as fluoride. It is present in teeth, bones, thyroid gland, skin and liver.

Fluoride is necessary for the formation of caries-resistant teeth. Small amounts of fluorine prevent dental caries in children. It promotes calcification.

Fluoride and Tooth Structure

For healthy tooth formation some amount of fluorine is essential. Though the exact mechanism by which it prevents dental caries is not fully understood, it is assumed that fluorine is incorporated into the tooth enamel. This reduces the solubility of enamel in the acids produced by bacteria. In its absence the enamel is soluble in the acid and tooth decays. In experimental animals fluoride seems to help normal growth during the growing period, but in human beings its role is not yet proved.

Toxicity or Fluorosis

If water contains more fluorine, dental fluorosis occurs. The enamel of the teeth loses its natural lustre and becomes rough. Opaque white patches with yellow or brown stains are found irregularly on the teeth. Ridges or diffused spots and pitting occur over the teeth. The surface of the teeth gives a corroded appearance.

Skeletal Fluorosis

The bones of vertebral column, especially the cervical part of the spine, pelvis and bones of the lower extremities, are affected in this condition. Hypercalcification of the bones and the collagen take place due to excessive fluorine deposition. Stiffness and pain are the earlier symptoms. Weakness and spasticity of lower limbs, wasting of the distal muscles of hands, deep jerks on lower extremities and numbness or girdle pain are the other symptoms of skeletal fluorosis. Gradually the person becomes crippled as he cannot bend or squat for the joints become stiff.

Requirements

Water containing 1 to 2 ppm prevents caries and so it is considered as the requirement.

Molybdenum

The adult human body contains only 9 mg of molybdenum. It is present in the liver, kidney, adrenal glands, bones, skin and tissues. Molybdenum is essential for the normal enzymatic system and its function. Enzymes like xanthine oxidase and aldehyde oxidase make use of molybdenum. These enzymes are essential for the proper nucleic acid and iron metabolism. Molybdenum seems to aid in preventing teeth decay. The requirement of molybdenum is not known. Whole-grain cereals, dried beans, peas and dark green leafy vegetables are good sources. Meat is also an excellent source.

8
WATER

About sixty to seventy per cent of the total body weight of a person is water. Water is present inside the cells of tissues (the intracellular water) and outside the tissue cells (the extracellular water). The extracellular water is present in the blood plasma, water in the space between the tissues is known as interstitial water and in lymph. Water and electrolytes are essential constituents of cellular metabolism. It is not only a component of our body but also acts as a vehicle for chemical transport. Water and electrolytes must be supplied to the body regularly to maintain the cellular function and to regulate the excretion through kidneys, lungs and skin.

Water intake and loss must be balanced. Water is injested through food and also as drinking water. Apart from this, a considerable amount of water is formed in the tissues through the oxidation of carbohydrates, fats and protein in their metabolism.

Water Intake and Loss from the Body

Water intake	(Ml)	Daily excretion	(Ml)
As fluids	1,500-1,750	Urine	1,200-1,500
Water in solid food	600-900	Perspiration	700-900
Water from oxidation of carbohydrate, protein, fat metabolism	300-350	Faeces	100-200
Total	2,400-3,000		2,400-3,000

Water is lost through urine, skin, lungs and faecal matter. In a normal healthy person the water intake and water loss is more or less equal. The excretion through the kidneys and skin changes according to the climatic conditions. In a dry climate more perspiration and in the cold weather more urination takes place. If the fluid intake is less thirst occurs. When two per cent of the body weight is lost dehydration starts.

Water is absorbed quickly and it is circulated to the tissues. From the tissues water is passed on to the capillaries. The capillary walls and cell membranes separate the water compartments. Water can move in and out of all cells by osmosis. The osmotic pressure in the plasma proteins regulates the exchange of water from tissues to capillaries. Antidiuretic hormone of posterior pituitary, hypothalamus, electrolytes like Na and K and adrenal cortex hormone aldosterone regulate the water metabolism in the body.

Antidiuretic hormone of the posterior pituitary increases the reabsorption of water in kidney tubules by increasing the permeability of distal tubules and collecting tubules. This mechanism enables them to retain more water in the body.

Hypothalamus is having the thirst centre. In dehydration plasma is concentrated and osmoconcentration stiumulates the thirst centre of hypothalamus. This induces the person to be very thirsty. By taking water the water balance in the body is regulated.

Various solutes present in the body fluids also help to regulate water metabolism. Plasma proteins exert low osmotic pressure and this helps to maintain the water in the blood vessels. Aldosterone increases reabsorption of Na^+ by the kidney.

About 170 litres of fluid pass through the glomeruli of the kidneys daily. A healthy person's kidneys excrete about 1.5 litres of urine from the above fluids. The urine formation is reduced if the intake of fluids is less. Then the urine becomes more concentrated with urea which forms the main bulk in urine. The normal output of urea is 30 mg for which 750 ml of urine must be formed. If urine formation is less urea is retained in the body which is harmful to the body; when less urine is formed in summer season more sweat is formed. Excessive sweating occurs with increased external temperature and humidity, fever and exercise. Water is also lost through insensible perspiration.

Apart from maintaining the intracellular and extra cellular water metabolism, water also takes part in a number of activities. All the vital functions of the body depend on the presence of proper water content. Digestion depends on its juices and all digestive juices are watery in nature. Urine, the excretory medium of our body, contains 97 per cent water. Water also helps in regulating body temperature. By evaporation of water, by respiration and through sweating the body temperature is regulated.

Requirement of Water

Water requirement of a person varies with climate, age, activity, dietetic habits and body build. Activity is an important factor which affects the water requirements. When activity is more intense more heat is produced and more water is needed to dissipate the heat produced. The type of diet also influences the water requirement. A high mineral content increases the water requirement. Consumption of sweets demands extra water for their dilution in the stomach. Beverages like tea, coffee and cocoa are diuretics and they stimulate excretion of water. If excess water is injested the kidney responds to it after 13-50 minutes and the extra water is excreted within three hours. The water balance will be maintained by the excess urine output. The sensation of thirst is one means of meeting the body's need for water.

Dehydration

Water depletion occurs when water loss is not met by water intake. On water depletion changes occur in the body fluids. Thirst, weakness, loss of weight, dryness of the skin, mucous membranes, tachycardia, disorientation and delerium are the symptoms manifested by dehydration. If not corrected coma and death occur. The urine changes in its specific gravity and concentration. The salt level is diminished in the urine and serum levels of sodium, urea and chlorides are elevated. Intercellular water is depleted to compensate the water content of the secretions. This results in cellular dehydration and vital organs fail to function. Plasma volume and blood volume are reduced which leads to reduced output and further cardiac failure.

Acid-base Balance

Acid-base balance refers to the regulation of the hydrogen ion concentration of body fluids. From metabolic processes acids are continuously produced and have to be eliminated. Lungs and kidneys are the major agents in carrying out this function in our body. Normally the body is maintained in neutrality. In some pathological conditions like diabetes mellitus or fasting for weight reduction and in renal failure the acid-base balance is affected. Acidosis occurs in this conditon.

Carbonic acid is the main form of acid formed in the body from metabolism. Carbohydrates, protein and fats yields Co_2 and water during their metabolism. The hydrated form of carbon dioxide is carbonic acid. Intermediary products like lactic acid, pyruvic acid, keto acids, uric acid, sulphuric acid, phosphoric acid from phosphoprotein are acidic in nature.

Certain foods in the body produce alkaline ash as the cations (Na^+, K^+) will allow the body to retain more bicarbonate ions thus producing alkaline effect. The neutrality of the body is maintained through the body fluids and their circulation, the acid buffer system like bicarbonate carbonic acid through haemoglobin and its capacity to form carbamate, regulation in respiration and the final effort from kidney on emergencies.

Acidosis

It is a condition in which the hydrogen ion concentration is increased or there is an excessive loss of base. The ratio of bicarbonate to carbonic acid is less than 20:1 and the pH is below 7.35.

Alkalosis

This is a condition in which the hydrogen ion concentration is decreased or the base is increased. The ratio of bicarbonate to carbonic acid is greater than 20:1 and the pH is 7.45.

Part II
FOODS

9

CEREALS

Cereals and millets form the staple food of human race. Wheat, rice, maize (corn), barley, oats, jowar, ragi and bajra are the common cereals and millets used. Cereals as a whole are rich sources of starch or carbohydrate, and good sources of protein in an Indian diet. Millets like ragi are a rich source of mineral calcium. Cereals are also good sources of B group vitamins.

WHEAT

Wheat is one of our important food crops. Next to rice wheat is the most extensively grown foodgrain.

Wheat varies in its nutritive value, especially its protein content depending upon the seeds, variety in soil and water supply. The protein content varies from 7 to 20 per cent. In the 'green revolution' new vaieties of superior quality wheat were produced. Sonalika, safed lerma, kalyan sona, sharbati sonora are some of these new varieties of wheat.

The wheat grain consists of three main parts. The germ or embryo is rich in protein and oil, the endosperm is rich in starch and fair sources of proteins and the outer coverings such as pericarp.

Various wheat products available are broken wheat, semolina, wholewheat flour (atta) and white flour. These flours are made from different kinds of wheat. Hard wheat, durum wheat and soft wheat are the different types of wheat from which flours are made. Flours' of different percentages of extraction are obtained. Depending on the extent of milling, flour made from hard wheat has an extraction of 85 per cent and it is used for chapati making. With 75 per cent extraction white flour or soft wheat products are obtained. Biscuits, cakes, crackers and breakfast items are prepared from this flour. Semolina is prepared from hard wheat and durum wheat. It is granular wheat and it is used for the manufacture of macaroni products like noodles.

Composition of Wheat Flour

Wheat is a very good source of carbohydrates and proteins; 100 gms of wheat provides 350 calories. Wheat contains carbohydrate in the form of starch; 66 to 68 per cent of flour is carbohydrate. Wheat flour has cellulose and hemicellulose and its quantity enhances the quality of dough prepared from it.

Protein

Wheat flour contains glutenin and glidin as proteins which are commonly known as gluten. Wheat flour contains about 12 to 12.5 gms of protein per 100 gm. The strength of wheat flour is based on the quality of gluten in it. Gluten is comparatively poor in amino acid lysine. Pulses, soya bean and groundnut are good in lysine content and they can be supplemented with wheat.

Lipids

Wheat flour contains 1.88 per cent fat; its kernel has about 3 per cent and bran contains about 4.8 per cent fat. Fat is present in the gluten of the flour.

Minerals

Wheat flour is poor in calcium content. The iron content of whole wheat flour is high but refined flour has less iron. Phosphorus content in whole flour is high compared to refined flour. But this high phosphorus content interferes with the absorption of calcium and iron.

Vitamins

Wheat is comparatively a good source of thiamine, riboflavin and nicotinic acid. But cooking results in loss of these B complex vitamins. During chapati making about 33 per cent of thiamine is destroyed and during fermentation much more thiamine is lost. In the preparation of puri 40 to 90 per cent of thiamine is lost. During bread making about 10 to 30 per cent lysine is destroyed. If the bread is toasted again this vitamin is lost. Bulgar wheat is much more nutritious. Wheat is parboiled in the preparation of bulgar wheat. During this process vitamins and other nutrients in the outer layers of the seeds move to the centre. Thus bulgar wheat is better in its nutritive value.

Processed Wheat Products

Bread, biscuits, toast and breakfast cereals like wheatflakes and shredded wheat are processed wheat products. The nutrivtive value of bread, especially fresh bread, is similar to two-thirds of wheat flour in its quantity. In the preparation of biscuits thiamine and protein is lost. On baking, a part of thiamine is lost and lysine is also lost. The average protein content in biscuit is 5 to 8 per cent as against 12 per cent in wheat flour. In the preparation of toast heat is applied on bread slices and part of thiamine is again destroyed. Lysine is also lost considerably. Readymade breakfast items are also inferior in nutritive value.

RICE

Rice is the staple food not only in India but also in many of the South-East Asian countries like Ceylon, Burma, China and Japan. Rice with its husk is called paddy. Husk is the loose covering of rice. It has no nutritive value. About 20 per cent by weight of paddy is husk. Removing the husk is called milling. Bran, aleurone layer, embryo or the germ and endosperm are the other layers. Bran is the outermost layer which contains nutrients and cellulose. Aleurone layer which lies beneath the bran is rich in vitamins, minerals, proteins and fats. Embryo or the germ is at the base of the grain which is rich in all nutrients and vitamin E. Endosperm forms 75 per cent of the grain and it comprises mainly starch. On milling vitamin B lost considerably. Parboiling improves the vitamin content of rice.

Parboiling of Paddy

In the conventional method of parboiling paddy is steeped in cold water for two to three days. Then it is steamed for about 5 to 10 minutes and then dried under the sun. During soaking paddy is fermented and at times gives out a foul smell. B complex vitamins in the pericarp and germ penetrate into the endosperm and get fixed into the grain. If parboiling is not done with care certain moulds present in the grain grow and produce toxins like aflatoxin. This can be rectified by using modern techniques in food processing. Through hot soaking process developed by CFTRI (Central Food Technological Research Institute) in Mysore this can be rectified. In this method paddy is soaked in water at 65° to 70°C for about 3 to 4 hours. Then water is drained and the soaked paddy is steamed in the same vessel for 5 to 10 minutes. This paddy is dried in the sun or in mechanical driers.

The nutritive value, especially of thiamine and niacin, is improved by parboiling.

Nutritive Value of Rice

Rice contains carbohydrate in the form of starch. Though it is a fair source of protein, it is a poor source of fat, iron and calcium. Rice provides about 335 calories per 100 gm of dry weight. The protein content is about 7 per cent which is not an appreciable amount. But since it is consumed in large quantities, rice supplies a good amount of proteins. In poor Indian diets cereals or millets are the main source of proteins. Though the protein content is low in rice compared to wheat the quality of rice proteins is superior to wheat proteins. Rice protein is deficient in lysine which can be improved by supplementing the diet with pulses. High yielding varieties of rice are cultivated in our country. The protein count of hybrid variety rice like IR-20 is 9 per cent as against 7 per cent of ordinary rice.

Rice is poor in its mineral content especially calcium. Iron content is also negligible, therefore rice-eaters must depend on other sources for minerals. Green leafy vegetables can be used for mineral supplementation.

Rice is a poor source of carotene or vitamin A, and vitamin B is present in good amount. Since it is present mainly in the outer layers polishing reduces the vitamin content. As polishing is increased the content of B vitamins decreases. In 20 per cent polishing thiamine (B.1) content is only 40 mg/gms whereas in parboiled rice at 20 per cent polishing thiamine is 200 mg/100 gm. Niacin content is 0.6 mg/100 gm in 20 per cent polished rice whereas in parboiled rice it is 2.8 mg/100 gm. Among people who depend entirely on polished rice, a burning sensation in the feet, tingling and numbness occur. This is due to the deficiency of thiamine in the diet. Even though rice is a good source of B complex vitamins its high solubility in water makes it non-available after various processes of cooking. About 60 per cent of it is lost through washing, if rice is washed twice or thrice. In the cooking water the remaining B complex gets dissolved. If the "conjee" water is thrown out this amount is also lost. Cooking rice in just enough water and utilising the excess water, if any, are the useful tips to make use of this vitamin.

Gelatinisation

Starch is present in cereals. This is insoluble in water, but in hot water it dissolves and forms colloidal dispersions. It swells and forms a sticky substance. In cereals about 65 to 80 per cent starch is present. Next to cereals roots like tapioca, potato and sweet potato are with starch granules. These roots and tubers contain about 22 to 39 per cent of starch. In starch there are two components—amylose and amylopectin. Amylose is about 15 to 30 per cent and amylopectin about 70 to 85 per cent. In different sources of starch it is present in different proportions. Amylose is soluble in water and amylopectin is insoluble in water. On 5 per cent concentration starch forms gels. Among the various sources of starch corn starch is the finest. This property of starch to gel is exploited in cookery. In many preparations starch is used as a thickening agent. To get a good gel, gelatinisation temperature of different starches must be known. Usually it starts to gel at 65° to 72°C. The enzymes in the starch are the other factors which affect the gelatinisation. Commercial products like sago, custard powder, corn syrup, glucose or dextrose and dextrimaltose are prepared from tapicao starch or from corn starch.

MILLETS

The common millets used in our country are jowar, ragi and bajra. Though millets are comparatively cheap they are superior in nutritive value. Usually people prefer rice or wheat as their cereals. If these millets are used more many deficiency symptoms among various groups can be minimised as they are excellent sources of vitamins and minerals.

Ragi

In India ragi is used mainly in Karnataka and Tamil Nadu as a staple food. In Kerala, ragi is used as a weaning food. Actually ragi is considered as a 'poor man's milk' by nutritionists because of its high calcium content. It can be easily substituted as a breakfast item. If we consider its cost it is cheap and at the same time rich in minerals that are lacking in rice or wheat. Like wheat or rice, ragi also contains 7 to 10 per cent protein and is equivalent to the above cereals in its carbohydrate content. It is considered superior because of high calcium content. Ragi is also a good source of iodine. No other cereal contains iodine. Another special feature of ragi is that the carbohydrate in ragi is digested slowly and so it can be given to diabetic patients because the sudden rise of blood sugar can be avoided by this. In certain hybrid varieties of ragi protein and iron contents are more and thus it is superior in its qualities. Ragi can be incorporated with pulse instead of rice in all breakfast items.

Bajra

Bajra is used in certain parts of the country as a staple food. It contains about 12 per cent of protein and calcium and iron content is more compared to rice. Bajra is a better source of vitamin B, especially thiamine and riboflavin.

Jowar

Jowar is used in Maharashtra, Andhra Pradesh, Karnataka, Tamil Nadu and Madhya Pradesh. The protein content in jowar is 10 per cent and the amino acid proportion is better. It has more B complex vitamins compared to rice. But certain varieties of jowar inhibit the availability of niacin and cause the deficiency symptoms of pellagra.

Effect of varying concentration of sugar syrup and crystallisation

Boiling temperature^0 C	Sugar percentage (Syrup)	Cold water test
110-112^0 C	78-80	Does not form a ball
113-115^0 C	83	Soft ball, eg., fondant.
118-120^0 C	86	Firmer ball, eg., caramels.
128-130^0 C	90	Hard ball, but still plastic, eg., candy
138-140^0 C	94	Very hard ball, eg, toffees
149-154^0 C	98	Very hard and brittle, eg., brittles.

To prepare the syrup add a small amount of sugar in water and heat. When the whole sugar is dissolved examine the consistency.

10
PULSES

Dried edible seeds of certain plants are called pulses. Split pulses are known as dals. Pulses are good sources of proteins and B vitamins. Even though vitamin C is not present in pulses, sprouting of pulses makes it a very good source of vitamin C. Pulses are the best supplements for cereals. Generally pulses contain about 20 to 28 per cent of protein but they are inferior in quality compared to animal foods. Methionine, the limiting amino acid in cereal proteins, is present in good amount in pulses. Thus cereal pulse combination improves the nutritional quality of the diet. This combination is the most economic way to provide protein. Pulses contain fair amounts of minerals like calcium and iron. About 8 to 10 mg of iron and about 100-200 mg of calcium are present in 100 gms of pulses. Pulses contain fair amounts of thiamine, riboflavin and niacin. Sprouting of pulses improves the carotene content and vitamin C.

Sprouted Pulses

Green gram, red gram, bengal gram, black gram, cow gram, horse gram, lentils, peas and soyabeans are the common pulses used in our cookery. All these pulses are good in protein, carbohydrate and vitamin B and fair in mineral content. But vitamin C is not present in them. On sprouting this deficiency can be rectified. To sprout, cleaned pulse is soaked for 24 hours and then it is spread on a muslin cloth, sprinkling water occasionally on it. After 24 hours tiny sprouts appear on the surface. These sprouts are very rich in vitamin C and carotene. Sprouted pulses are very tender and cooking is not necessary. They can be used as raw salad by sprinkling lime juice and salt or as raitas by adding curd and salt to it. As cooking destroys vitamin C it is better to use them as a raw item.

Vitamin 'C' Content of Sprouted Legumes

Period of Germination	Vitamin 'C'
Dry legumes	Trace
After 24 hrs germination	7-12 mgms/100 gm
After 48 hrs germination	11-18 mgm/100 gm
After 72 hrs germination	13-20 mg

If pulses are not cooked properly they contain much undigestible materials. But if pulses are used as flours they are completely digested and absorbed. In raw pulses trypsin inhibiter is present and it is anti-digestive in nature. Among the various pulses green gram is digested best. If more than 100 gms of pulse is consumed in a day it is not properly digested and gas is produced. If diarrhoea or other stomach complaints are present gas is produced by consuming small quantities of pulses. Bengal gram has the efficiency to reduce serum cholesterol level by increasing faecal excretion of total bile acids.

Lathyrism

Lathyrism is a paralytic disease seen in India and Spain where a type of pulse called kesari dal — Lathyrus sativus — is used liberally in food. In India Kesari is extensively cultivated in Madhya Pradesh, Bihar and Orissa. In Uttar Pradesh, West Bengal, Maharashtra, Gujarat, Karnataka and Andhra Pradesh it is cultivated in limited extent. Kesari dal is very cheap and highly nutritious. The flour prepared from this dal is used as a staple food in these areas. In these areas most of the agricultural labourers get kesari dal as their wage and about 250-500 gm of it is consumed by a person in a day. As a result about 4 per cent of population in these areas are crippled. Surveys in two districts of Madhya Pradesh (Rewa and Satna) showed 32,000 paralytic victims with lathyrism. The cause of lathyrism is the production of a toxin known as BOAA-B oxalyl amino L alamine which affects the nervous system. The toxin is produced more by the husk and its consumption causes high incidence of disease. The Indian Council of Medical Research has developed certain methods to destroy the toxin.

The disease occurs in different stages. The onset is sudden. But in the first stage itself it can be detected. On exposure to cold the calf muscles contract and backache occurs. An awkward manner of walking with short jerky steps and crossed gait are common. Muscular stiffness necessitates the use of a stick to maintain balance. Later spastic paralysis of the lower limbs, and exaggerated knee and ankle jerks occur. And at this stage the patient needs crutches for support. Finally the erect posture becomes impossible as the knee joints cannot support the weight of the body. The patient crawls by throwing his weight on his hands. The serum globulin and urinary glutamic acid are increased in this condition.

The National Institute of Nutrition identified the toxic factor and a simple feasible solution was suggested by them to destroy the toxin. The household procedure is to steep the dehusked grain is boiling water. The seeds are drained of water and sundried and thus the toxin is eliminated. About 90-95 per cent of the toxin is leached out by this method.

Soyabean

Soyabean is otherwise known as the miracle bean because it is a storehouse of proteins, fat, vitamin A, thiamine, riboflavin and nicotinic acid. The protein content in soyabean is about 43 per cent and fat content is 19.5 per cent. The proteins of soyabean consists of all the essential amino acids in proper proportion except methinine and cystine. It has a good amount of lysine and it can be used for supplementing rice which is deficient in lysine. Apart from the nutritive importance it is also made use of in the production of penicillin and other antibiotics for industrial purposes. Enamel paints, varnishes and printing inks are made out of soyabean.

Even though it is rich in nutrients, unless it is processed properly, proteins and carbohydrates of soyabeans are poorly digested. Soyabean contains a factor which inhibits the protein digesting enzyme, trypsin. Heat destroys it and after cooking if it is used, the protein is properly digested. Soaking, steaming, germinating and fermenting are other processes which improve the nutritive value. Soyamilk is very nutritious, but soyabean seems to produce goitre at times because it interferes with iodine metabolism. Soyamilk has about 4.2 gm of proteins, 3.4 gm of fat and 0.75 gm of salts. Soyabean can be parched and used like parched bengal gram. It can be used as a substitute for bengal gram flour in recipes.

Cooking of Dals

Soaking, use of sodium bicarbonate, acids, alkali or calcium salts affects the quantity of cooked pulses. Dals absorb water before they can be cooked. If dal is soaked in cold water overnight or in warm water for 4 to 5 hours it can be cooked within 30 to 40 minutes. But if hard water is used for cooking it takes more time. If sodium bicarbonate is added to cook pulses cooking time is reduced. B vitamin like thiamine is destroyed. Addition of acid helps the cooking of pulses whereas salts retard the cooking. Addition of formic acid of the pulse also influences the cooking quality. The exact causes for these variations are not yet found out.

11

VEGETABLES

Edible parts of plants like bulbs, tubes, roots, seeds, fruits, stems, leaves or flowers are considered as vegetables. Vegetables as a whole are important sources of minerals and vitamins and certain vegetables have starch, cellulose and water. In meal planning and for dietary calculation vegetables occupy a prominent place. To check their sufficiency and also for convenience, vegetables are grouped into green leafy vegetables, and roots and tubers and other vegetables. Legumes like double beans, french beans, cluster beans and peas are also included into other vegetables. Vegetables are the best sources for calcium, iron, sodium, chlorine, cobalt, copper, magnesium, manganese, phosphorus and potassium. Carotenes, the precursors of vitamin A and ascorbic acid are present in abundant quantities in leafy and yellow vegetables. Vegetables are poor sources of calories except in the case of roots and tubers. Raw legumes and beans are good sources of proteins. Vegetables as a group supply a high amount of water and the mineral elements present in them contribute the alkaline substances in the body. This enables to maintain the acid-base balance of the body.

Green Leafy Vegetables

Cabbage, cauliflower, coriander leaves, lettuce, spinach, amaranth and drumstick leaves are the common leafy vegetables. Of all the vegetables green leafy vegetables are the richest in carotene and the carotene content depends upon the green colour. If the colour is deep the carotene is more in it. Green leafy vegetables are fair sources of proteins and good sources of folic acid, ascorbic acid and calcium. Some leafy vegetables contain oxalic acid which interferes with the absorption of calcium in the diet. Leafy vegetables act as a buffer and maintain the proper alkalinity of the blood by balancing the acidity of acid-producing foods like meat.

Roots and Tubers

Roots and tubers are good sources of starch and fair sources of protein, vitamin B and vitamin C. Roots and tubers include tapioca, potato, sweet potato, carrots and beetroots. Carrots are rich sources of vitamin A. The starch in roots is easily digestible. Potato, a root vegetable, is a fair source of proteins, ascorbic acid, and B vitamins. Sweet potato is a poor source of proteins but it is a fair source of B vitamins and ascorbic acid. The yellow variety of sweet potato is a rich source of pro-vitamin A or carotene.

Other Vegetables

Other vegetables are good sources of minerals, cellulose and water. They are also good sources of vitamins. Common vegetables like ladiesfingers, gourds, brinjals, pumpkins, green peas and all other vegetables fall in this group. Tomato is also considered as another vegetable. Green peas and yellow pumpkin are fair sources of carotene.

Cooking of Vegetables

Cooking affects the colour, texture and nutritive value of vegetables. Cooking methods can destroy the good qualities if not handled properly. Common methods of cooking are boling, steaming, baking, frying and pressure cooking. Before applying these methods the chemical structure of vegetables must be considered. Vegetables contain different chemical compounds like pigments, tannin, enzymes and flavouring substances. Common pigments in vegetables are chlorophyll, carotinoid, flavones and anthocyanins. On heating these pigments undergo certain chemical changes which affect the colour of the finished product. Vegetables also lose organic acids and nutrients in cooking water. Acid or alkali content, and the cooking media also affect the appearance and quality of the product.

Chlorophyll

Chlorophyll is the green pigment in leaves which is not readily soluble in water. In an acid medium chlorophyll turns an olive green and in alkali it becomes bright green. But the use of alkali to retain the green colour in salad vegetables destroys vitamin C and thiamine. Cooking in copper vessels turns chlorophyll into deep bluish green colour. Addition of sodium carbonate affects the texture and the cellulose becomes mushy. Cooking with a lid and in minimum time retains the colour. The green vegetables must be added to boiling water to reduce the cooking time.

Carotenoid

Carotenoid is yellow orange in colour and insoluble in water. It is soluble in ether and acetone. Carotenoids are present in different forms like carotenes, Ly copence, xanthophylls, cryptoxanthin and citroxanthin. Carotenoids are present in yellow vegetables like carrots, sweet potatoes, tomatoes, and xanthophyll in all vegetables. Cryptoxanthin is present in papaya, orange peel and yellow maize. Carotenoids are unchanged in acid or alkali and so vegetables with carotenoid pigments may be cooked with a cover. Such vegetables can be cooked by any method as the carotenoids remain unaffected.

Flavanoids

Flavones and flavonols are together known as flavanoids. Anthocyanins, anthoxanthins, leucoanthoxanthins and catechins are together known as flavonoids.

Anthocyanins are reddish water soluble pigments occurring in fruits and vegetables. They are destroyed by heat and oxidation. Passion fruit, apple, cherry, plum, grapes, blackberries are some of the fruits with anthocyanin in them. Beetroot has anthocyanin as its pigment. Anthocyanin is water soluble and in acid medium it turns blue. In some vegetables flavones and anthocyanin are combined together which gives a green colour on cooking in alkaline medium.

Another chemical substance present in plants is tannin. Tannin and ferric salts form a greenish purple compound. On oxidation this turns brown which imparts a brown colour. Certain vegetables show discoloration if an iron knife is used to cut it. If vegetables rich in tannin are cooked in milk, the milk curdles.

Effect of Cooking on Vegetables

At a high temperature the cellulose is disintegrated and protopectin, a non-dispensible substance in water, undergoes hydrolysis and makes it dispersible. This changes the structural framework of the vegetables and makes it soft. If it is overcooked the vegetable becomes mushy and unpalatable. Some vegetables lose their natural flavour on cooking. Strong flavoured vegetables like onion, cabbage and cauliflower must be cooked by suitable method either to retain or to lose the flavour. If a mild flavour is desired the vegetables can be cut into small pieces and cooked in a small amount of boiling water in a covered pan. If vegetables are in large pieces, large quantity of water can be used in an open pan. The plant acids are dissolved in water and the open lid allows the acids to escape.

Green vegetables turn brown because the plant acids and cholorophyll are disintegrated on cooking. Cooking time must be reduced so as to prevent their contact. Use of pressure cooker, large quantity of boiling water to cook the vegetables and use of an uncovered pan are some of the measures that can be used to reduce the colour change.

Retention of Nutrients on Cooking

Vegetables are rich in mineral salts and vitamins and most of them are water soluble. Some of them which are not soluble in water are destroyed by heat or by oxidation. If cooking water is thrown away considerable loss of mineral salts, especially of sodium, potassium and chlorine due to leaching occurs. To avoid this either use minimum amount of water or the excess water after cooking can be used for other preparations. Cut the vegetables as big as possible to reduce the cooking loss. Bring the cooking water to boiling before inserting vegetables. Cook just enough. Washing vegetables after cutting enables considerable loss of minerals in the water. About 40 per cent minerals and thiamine are lost if the rice is washed twice or thrice before cooking. Washing once and utilising the rice water are better methods for retaining nutrients. Absorption method of cooking can be adopted for rice cooking.

Vitamin A or carotene is not affected when food is cooked in water. But shallow frying or roasting brings considerable loss of these vitamins. If sodium bicarbonate is added especially for dals or pulses most of the thiamine is destroyed. Roots like potato, sweet potato and other roots which can be cooked with their skin must be cooked so as to prevent leaching out of nutrients. They can be boiled first and later cut into pieces. Vitamin C is the most unstable vitamin among water soluble vitamins. Washing, cutting with an iron knife, cutting into smaller pieces and prolonged cooking lead to oxidation of vitamin C content of food items. If tamarind or lime, which is high in acidity, is added to cooking water it has a preservative effect on this vitamin. Since vitamin C is leached the least possible amount of water must be used and the cooking done in a covered vessel.

Cooking just before consumption is another method to preserve vitamin C content in the foods. Use of pressure cooker minimises the loss of nutrients. Consumption of raw vegetables provides all nutrients without any loss. If boiling is the method used to cook vegetables put them only into boiling water and bring the cooking water again to boiling temperature. For strong flavoured vegetables use little boiling water and let them remain uncovered. For other vegetables smaller amounts of water and tightly covered untensils are recommended. Avoid the use of baking soda.

The Losses of Vitamins in Some Vegetables during Cooking

Name of vegetable	Method of cooking	Loss of		Vitmin C
		Tiamicne	Ribeflavin	
Beans	Boiling	29%	20%	42%
Cabbage	"	32%	18%	45%
Carrots	"	20%	10%	30%
Potato	"	25%	9%	23%
Peas	"	28%	17%	40%
Spinach	"	15%	10%	28%
Sweet potato	"	20%	13%	24%
Beans	Steaming	22%	14%	32%
Cabbage	"	18%	9%	38%
Carrots	"	15%	10%	25%
Peas	"	24%	11%	30%
Potato	"	20%	12%	25%
Spinach	"	16%	12%	25%

A fruit is the edible fleshy seed-bearing part of a plant or tree. Fruits are favoured by all due to their attractive appearance, appealing flavour and pleasing odour. Apart from their nutritive value they are also appreciated for their appetising effect. Fruits contain starch. On ripening the starch is converted into fructose and glucose and these sugars contribute to the sweetness of fruits. Water is the chief constituent of fruits. About 75 to 95 per cent of the total weight is from water. Fruits as a whole are rich sources of vitamin C and vitamin A and minerals like sodium, potassium, magnesium, fibre and cellulose. Characteristic flavours of fruits are due to the presence of organic acids in them. Citric acid and malic acid are the acids present in fruits. Grapes contain tartaric acid. Acid content of vaious fruits varies. Citrus fruits are the best sources of vitamin C. Dried fruits like raisins, dates and figs are rich in iron. Calcium is present in citrus fruits. Banana contributes a very high amount of carbohydrates and about 23 per cent of it is sugar. Jackfruits, figs and cherries are also very good sources of carbohydrates. For vitamin C guava is a cheap source. About 300 mg vitamin C is present in 100 gms of guava. Cashew fruit is also an excellent source of vitamin C. Lime, mango, papaya and orange are other sources of vitamin C. Fruits have alkaline reaction in the body.

Fruits with different colours have carotenoids, anthocyanins and flavanols in them. Fruits also contain enzymes like ascorbic oxidase and phenol oxidase. The vitamin A value of fruits is in the carotene in yellow fruits. Organic acids and salts are present in fruits. Dried fruits like dates and raisins are sources of iron. Potassium is the most important salt in fruits. Potassium is present in citrus fruits as citrates and in grapes as tartarate.

Pleasing colours of the fruits are due to their pigment content. In ripe fruits carotenoid pigments are present in different forms. Red, purple and blue shades of fruits are due to the presence of anthocyanine pigments in them.

Tannins and Browning Reaction

Tannins are present in almost all fruits. They contribute bitter taste and astringent quality and discoloration of cut surfaces of fruits on exposure to air. When certain fruits are pared a brown colour appears on their surface which becomes darker as the fruit is allowed to stand. Apple, banana, plum, guava and peach show this change. Tannins and flavone pigments give brown coloured pigments on oxidation. Oxidising agents present in fruit cells catalyse the reaction. If the fruits are cut with an iron knife, tannins and flavones react with iron salts forming a greenish purple compound which discolours the fruits. Acidic juices of fruits like lime, grape or pineapple are sprinkled on the fruits to prevent browning action.

Enzymatic browning occurs only when the fruits or vegetables are cut into pieces. The natural phenolic compounds present in tissues of plants do not come into contact with the phenoloxidase which is also present in some tissues. Practical methods for preventing enzymatic browning are to change the pH and the use of anti-oxidants which retard oxidation. By using the acidic juices of fruits the pH can be brought down.

Non-enzymatic browning occurs due to the formation of brown condensation products from reducing sugars and amino acids on heating. To prevent non-enzymatic browning storing the food materials at a low temperature, between $0°$ and $5°C$, and addition of sulphur dioxide in the case of dehydrated vegetables are recommended.

Browning reaction affects the nutritive value of food, especially the lysine content of it. Loss of nutrients of fruits on cooking is negligible.

Prevention of Browning

Thermal inactivation of oxidase enzymes, elimination of O_2 from the systems, change of pH to prevent enzyme action, and use of antioxidants are the measures to prevent enzymatic browning.

For non-enzymatic browning low temperature ($0°$-$5°C$), addition of SO_2 and keeping the moisture content low are some measures.

MILK AND MILK PRODUCTS

Milk is commonly considered as a complete food as it contains all six of the essential foodstuffs. Milk protein is of excellent quality and it promotes growth and maintenance of body tissues. Therefore, milk is an ideal food for infants and children. But milk is very low in iron and ascorbic acid content. Calcium and phosphorus levels in milk are very high. The ratio of calcium and phosphorus and the presence of vitamin A help its maximum utilisation. Milk is an excellent source of vitamin A. In it the cream is rich in vitamin A and if the same is removed as in skimmed milk, its vitamin A content becomes low. Riboflavin, a B vitamin, is present in significant quantities in milk. If the milk is exposed to light riboflavin is lost. Fats present in milk are readily digested. The carbohydrate of milk is lactose and it is hydrolysed into glucose and galactose. Whole milk contains 4.7 per cent carbohydrate, 4 per cent fat, 3.3 per cent protein and 88 per cent water. Fats in the form of oleic, palmitic and stearic acids is present in milk. Milk protein is casein and whey protein has lactalbumin and lactoglobulin.

The Average Composition of Milk and Milk Products (gm\100 ml)

Milk product	Protein (gm)	Fat (gm)	Calcium (mg)	Vit.A. (I.U.)	Vit.C. (mg.)	Calories (kcal.)
Buffalo's milk	4.3	8.8	210	160	3	118
Cow's milk	3.2	4.1	149	150	2	67
Buttermilk	0.8	1.1	30	...	...	15
Skimmed milk	2.5	0.1	120	...	...	29
Condensed milk	9.1	8.4	280	430	...	328
Cheese	24.1	25.1	790	273	...	348
Goat's milk	3.7	5.6	170	60	2	84
Human milk	1.0	3.9	20	70	3	67
Curd	2.9	2.9	120	40	4	51

In developing countries, the per capita availability of milk is poor whereas in developed countries it is more.

Among these buffalo's milk has a higher proportion of total solids and fats than cow's milk. Casein coagulation is also high.

Goat's milk is rich in cream and poor in protein compared to buffalo's milk. Human milk is easily digestible because it becomes solid on reaching the stomach. Casein is the chief protein of milk. It is a phosphoprotein which contains protein and phosphoric acid. An enzyme rennin aggregates and precipitates casein and it is coagulated or curdled. Bacterial action also curdles milk. Casein is present in milk in the form of calcium caseinate. Rennin converts calcium caseinate into calcium and paracasein. Again it forms a smooth, soft clot of calcium paracaseinate which is non-dispersible. If milk is overheated it forms a weaker clot. Dried milk also forms a weak clot. Milk also contains lactalbumin, a simple protein of the albumin class. Prolonged and direct heating of milk also forms a weak clot. Milk also contains lactalbumin, a simple protein of the albumin class. Prolonged and direct heating of milk helps it to settle down at the bottom and sides of the container in which milk is heated. Use of double cooker rectifies this. The souring of milk is due to the presence of lactose, the carbohydrate. Lactic acid-forming bacteria use lactose as food to produce lactic acid in milk. Fat is present in emulsified form. Creamy layer of milk consists of fats. Milk contains potassium, sodium, calcium and magnesium chlorides and phosphates. On heating milk calcium precipitates on the sides of the container. Of all food materials milk is the best source of calcium and careless heating reduces its availability. Even though iron is present in minute quantities it is highly nutritional.

Processing of Milk

Pasteurisation of Milk

Milk is a favourable medium for bacterial growth. Louis Pasteur, the French scientist, developed the heat treatment of milk for inactivating disease-causing micro-organisms.

Milk-borne diseases are tuberculosis, typhoid, hoof and mouth diseases, undulant fever, scarlet fever, septic, sore throat, gastroenteritis and diphtheria. But pasteurisation destroys certain advantageous bacteria also. There are two methods of pasteurisation—the flash method and the holding method. In the flash method the milk is heated at a temperature of 160°F for 30 to 60 seconds and in the holding method the milk is heated to temperatures of 140° to 145° F and held there for at least 30 minutes. In both the methods, after the heat treatment, the milk is cooled quickly to about 45° F. Pasteurisation reduces the thiamine and ascorbic acid content whereas the nutritive content of other vitamins is not much affected.

Evaporated Milk

Evaporated milk is produced by evaporating 60 per cent of water from milk and the product is then sterilised and sealed in cans. To evaporate, the milk is heated at a high vacuum from 130° to 150° F. The concentrated product is homogenised to reduce the fat globules and then placed in cans, heated and sterilised at temperatures from 240° to 245° F for 15 minutes. Evaporated milk is fortified with vitamin D.

Condensed Milk

Evaporated milk is incorporated with 40 per cent carbohydrate to form condensed milk. Sucrose or dextrose or a mixture of these two is added.

Dry Milk

Whole milk or defatted whole milk is used in its preparation. From milk most of the water is removed. There are two methods applied to form dry milk-spray process and roller process.

In the spray process fresh milk is sprayed under high pressure into a drying chamber where dry air is passed. The current of dry air evaporates water and the dried solids settle to the bottom of the chamber.

In roller process fresh milk is spread over the surface of hot revolving metal rolls. The water evaporates and milk solids remain in thin sheets. If the fat is removed from whole milk the keeping quality is more. Dried whole milk does not keep so long because the fats tend to become rancid.

Milk Products

Cheese, yoghurt or curd, buttermilk, low-fat milk, non-fat milk cream and butter are the common milk products used.

Cheese is mainly from casein of milk with fat and a little whey. To precipitate cheese lactic acid or rennin are used. For commercial cheese making rennin is used and for homemade cheese lactic acid is used.

Cheese is rich in protein and fat and a considerable amount of lactose is also present. In homemade cheese calcium is less but other minerals like phosphorus are there in both. Compared to milk vitamin A content is the same but thiamine and riboflavin are dissolved in the whey. Cheese is used to spread in items like butter as it contributes flavour. In vegetables, fish and meat preparations and in custards and souffles cheese can be used. Low temperature is suggested for cheese cookery.

Buttermilk is prepared from curd; it is churned and the butter removed. Yoghurt or curd is a custard-like product prepared by fermenting milk. In commercial production streptococcus thermophilus is added to milk to ferment it. Low-fat milk is commercially prepared for people who prefer low calories from milk with a fat flavour. Non-fat milk is skimmed milk where the fat is removed entirely. Vitamin A and D are fortified in it. Creams with different levels of fats are commercially produced. The fat content ranges from 18 to 40 per cent. Cream combined with sugar, stabilisers and emulsifiers is often sold in cans. Commercially, cream is prepared by using a cream separator which enables the separation of fat at different levels. Whipped cream is an air-in-water foam in which fat globules are piled up in the film and it is used in salad dressings and in desserts.

Milk is used in many preparations for its solvent capacity and its nutritive contribution. Milk is used as a dispersing medium, especially in puddings and for scum formation with its coagulating property. Vegetables with tannin or acid cause milk to curdle. Scum formation and curdling occur when the protein in milk becomes insoluble in heat or in the pH change. Use of low temperature and short heating periods prevent scum formation. Acidity of the content produces curdling. Adding acid food towards the end and mixing it in low temperature reduce curdling.

Types of Milks in the Market

Homogenised milk, separated milk, toned milk, sterilised milk, separated milk (skimmed milk), recombined milk, filled milk and flavoured milk are the common fluid milks available in the market.

Homogenised Milk

In this, fat globules are broken up mechanically to less than one microne in diameter. It is easily digested but cream is not obtained on separation.

Separated Milk (Skimmed milk)

This is prepared by removing fat from milk in a cream separator. Very little fat is in it.

Toned Milk

Toned milk is prepared by mixing milk reconstituted from skimmed milk powder with buffalo milk which has 7.0 per cent fat.

Recombined Milk

It is a homogenised product prepared from milk fat, non-fat milk solids and water. It should be pasteurised.

Filled Milk

Filled milk is the homogenised product prepared from refined vegetable oil and non-fat milk solids and water.

Sterilised Milk

Standardised cow or buffalo milk is sterilised in bottles by heating to 115° C for 15 minutes.

Flavoured Milk

Chocolate, coffee, cardamom or any other edible flavours, colour and sugar are used to flavour milk.

Flesh of all edible animals including mammals and poultry is termed as meat. Meats of cattle origin, beef and veal, of hog origin, pork, sheep, lamb, mutton, flesh of partridge, duck and game birds are used commonly as food.

Muscle of meat is composed of 75 per cent water, 20 per cent protein and 5 per cent fat, carbohydrate and minerals. The composition of meat varies with its sources, season of the year and pH of the meat. Protein comprises about four-fifths of the solid material. True fats, fat-like substances called phospholipids, inorganic substances and vitamins are present in fats.

Veal is the meat from cattle slaughtered three to fourteen weeks after birth. Calf is from fourteen to fifty-two weeks old animal. Beef is from cattle over one year old. A heifer is a female cattle that has never borne a calf and a cow is a female cattle that has borne a calf. Meat has skeletal or muscular cuts and organ cuts. Skeletal or muscular cut has muscle, tissue, connective tissue, bone fats and nerve tissues. Muscle tissue and connective tissue supply the qualities of meat in cookery. Muscle structure is made up of bundles of muscle fibres called fasciculi. Connective tissues are scattered throughout the muscles where they play a connecting and supporting role. White fibrous and yellow elastic fibres with proteins like collagen and elastin are present in all muscles. Collagen contributes strength and elastin supplies elastic quality to meat. Collagen reacts with water in hydrolysis to produce gelatin and brings about a tenderising effect to the meat. But no such change is brought in elastin and if elastin is more in muscle fibres meat will be hard even after cooking. This can be remedied by chopping or grinding the elastin fibres.

Fats in meats are distributed between fasciculi. Fat is laid as a protective layer around the organs. The fat deposited with the muscle structure is known as marbling. Muscle haemoglobin is present in small amounts. Muscle cells of living animals contain glycogen which is otherwise known as animal starch. But immediately after the animal is dead glycogen is converted into lactic acid. The vitamin content of different meats varies. The B vitamins—thiamine, riboflavin and niacin—occur in significant amounts in all meats. The meat of hog origin is rich in thiamine. Liver is rich in vitamin A. Iron-containing substances and B vitamins are more in organ meats.

Rigor Mortis

After the animal is slaughtered certain changes occur in the meat and it stiffens. This process is known as rigor mortis. On slaughtering the animal adenosine triphosphate is synthesised from glycogen and lactic acid, ammonia and other products are formed from it. Myosin and actomyosin are found in contracted muscles and stiffening occurs to it. If the slaughtered animal has a high glycogen level, it produces a low pH and the quality of meat will be good with less rigor mortis. Fasting, exercise, nervous exhaustion or insulin injection cause low glycogen level and the carcass has a high pH. Undesirable dark colour and poor flavour and texture of meat result from this. Slow and long slaughter produce more adrenaline in the animals and this results in sticky, gummy and dark coloured meat. Rigor mortis reaches its peak within 24 hours and then the muscle softens.

Quality and Grading of Meat

Appearance, tenderness, juiciness and flavour of the meat decide the quality of meat. Good quality flesh must be firm, the fasciculi should be small and velvety in texture, with characteristic colour of the meat— bright cherry red for beef, pinkish-red for lamb, greyish pink for veal and pork; bone must be small, red and spongy in appearance and the fat must be white and firm. To grade the meat quality grades are given and they are prime, choice, good, commercial, utility and cutter and conner. For lambs and veal cull is the term used instead of utility. For pork grades of 1, 2, and 3 are used. Meat of top quality is more tender than lower quality grade. Tenderness of meat increases palatability and it varies according to the cuts of meat. The most tender cuts are from backbone and ribs. Less tender cuts are from the shank, shoulder, neck and under parts of the body. Under part cuts of beef are flank, plate and brisket. The same cuts from lamb and veal are known as breast.

Meat Cookery

Palatability, appearance and flavour are enhanced by cooking meat. Cooking also makes meat more tender and digestible. There are two methods generally applied to meat cookery—dry heat and moist heat methods. In all methods of cooking the interior of the meat changes. Heat penetration, substances added to meat and composition of the meat affect these changes. Mainly the method adopted for cooking depends upon the cuts of meat. Less tender cuts contain more connective tissues than tender cuts and so moist heat methods convert collagen to gelatin and it has a tenderising effect upon tissues. Roasting and broiling are the methods used to cook by dry heat methods and these methods can be applied to tender cuts of meat. For less tender cuts moist heat methods are used. Moderate temperature is recommended for this method. Water, juices and fluids are used for most heat methods. The addition of sodium chloride or sodium and potassium phosphate has been reported to increase the tenderness of meat.

Dry Heat Methods

Roasting: Roasting is cooking by means of radiant heat. Meat is roasted either in the open or in a closed tin in an oven. In covered roasting evaporation is diminished, and it cooks faster too. The water runs out of the meat instead of evaporating from the surface. An enclosed roast loses more weight and water than the open roast. Cooking to rare stage only increases the juiciness and flavour. If the pieces of meat lack fat, a thin layer of fat on top will be very effective. Water should not be added to oven roast.

Broiling and pan broiling: Slices from tender cuts of meat can be cooked rapidly without adding moisture or fat by radiant heat from a broiler or in an uncovered pan. The time required depends on the stage of cooking required and the size and shape of the pieces. This method gives a uniform result. The temperature should be higher than in roasting. It can be regulated either by changing the heat input or by changing the distance of meat from the heat source.

This method is suitable for cooking tender cuts of beef and lamb or ground meat on the pattern of ham, bacon and sausages.

Frying: Meat is fried when it is partly or completely immersed in hot fat during cooking. When the meat is completely immersed the method is called deep-fat-frying. When a small amount of fat is added it is called pan-frying or sauteing. The fat should be kept below smoking point. A temperature of 350° F for pre-cooked meat and 300° F for raw meat is usually satisfactory. This method is suited to lean meats such as liver or cooked steak.

Cooking by Moist Heat: The cooking medium is steam of water.

Braising and pressure cooking: Meat may be cooked in steam with or without pressure. When the meat is first browned in its own fat or a small amount of added fat and allowed to cook in its own steam without pressure the method is known as braising. Meat braised as a large piece is called a pot roast and that as small pieces, a fricassee. Braising is preferable to boiling for fresh pork, because it produces less hardening and drying of fibres when meat is cooked to a safe stage of cooking.

Stewing or simmering: Meat may be cooked by immersing it in water. To minimise the hardening effect of high temperature simmering is preferable to boiling. Vegetables are added to stews to enhance the flavour.

Generally shrinkage of meat cooked by moist heat method is greater than that in dry heat methods.

Tenderising Meat

Papain, an enzyme derived from papaya, tenderises beef. Solution of papain is often injected into the beef shortly before slaughter. Meat of old animals is tough and stringy and usually this meat requires tenderising. Tougher cuts of meat require a long, slow cooking period. Prolonged cooking changes collagen into gelatin in moist heating. Dry heat hardens it. Acid hastens this conversion of collagen into gelatin; tomato juice and vinegar tenderise meat. High temperature gives a tasteless dry-product-like quality to tough meat. Cutting the tough meat into smaller pieces enhances the flavour of meat. Mining, grinding or pounding of meat helps to break the muscle fibres.

Vitamin retention is more in dry heat methods. Roasting or broiling retains 65-70 per cent of thiamine whereas moist heat retains only 25 per cent of thiamine.

Gelatin

Gelatin is a protein obtained from collagen on hydrolysis. Connective tissues of cartilage, tendons, bones, skins and hoofs are used to prepare gelatin. After preliminary treatments a dispersion of collagen in water is obtained. And this dispersion is boiled for several hours. Water is evaporated and gelatin is obtained from collagen.

From the nutritional point of view gelatin is inferior because it is an incomplete protein. The property of gel formation is used in cookery. In desserts gelatin is used to provide a spongy appearance to the product.

Processing of Meat

Canned meat, cured meat, smoked meat, dehydrated meat and sausages are the common processed form of meat.

Canned-meat: The meat is cooked and filled in the can along with the gravy, leaving a little head space.

Cured-meat: Meat is pickled by the use of curing agents like sodium chloride, sodium nitrate and vinegar.

Smoked-meat: Smoking helps to preserve the meat and develop flavours in it. The temperature and period of smoking vary with the type of meat.

Dehydrated-meat: The meat is cut into pieces and cooked in steam for 30 minutes at 10 lb pressure. It is passed through a meat chopper and the chopped meat is dried in a drier.

Sausages: Cooked chopped meat is ground to a paste with seasonings and packed casings. It is available as fresh, cooked, smoked, cooked and smoked, dry, and semi-dry.

FISH

Fish is a very good source of calcium, protein, vitamins A, D and iodine. There are two main classes into which fish may be grouped as vertebrate fish or fin fish and shell fish. Cod, mackerel and salmon have backbones and fins, whereas a shellfish is more or less completely covered with a shell. Oysters, lobsters and crabs are examples of shellfish.

Protein is the main component in fish and its content ranges from 15 to 20 per cent by weight of flesh. The fat content in fish varies from 1 per cent to 20 per cent or more. Hilsa has a fat content of about 19.4 per cent. The fat content of shellfish is less than 5 per cent. Since the fats in fish are unsaturated fats even in therapeutic diets this can be recommended. The flesh of fish is devoid of carbohydrates except in the case of shellfish. The mineral content of fish is variable; 1 to 1.5 per cent of the flesh of fish is with mineral elements. Small fish which can be consumed with their bones are rich in calcium. Oysters and shrimps are rich in calcium. Most fishes are not very good sources of iron except oysters. Sea fish are high in iodine content. Oysters are also rich in copper. The flesh of most fish contains fair amounts of thiamine and riboflavin and some amounts of niacin. Fatty fish are rich in vitamins A and D. Fish livers are rich sources of these vitamins.

Freshness of Fish

Fish deteriorates quickly and so requires careful handling. The quality of freshness of fish is indicated by bright red gills, clear eyes, bright and slightly bulging but firm flesh when pressed with a finger, and elasticity. The fresh odour of fish suggests its freshness. Suggestion of putrefaction is easy to detect from its foul smell. The tail of a fresh fish is stiff.

Spoilage of Fish

Fish is highly perishable. The spoilage of fish is due to microbiological, physiological and biochemical changes.

Processing of Fish

Fish protein concentrates, fish meat, smoked and salted fish are the common forms of processed fish. Fish protein concentrate is used for supplementing diets.

Fish meals is not suitable for human consumption. It is used for poulltry and for animal ration.

Preservation of Fish

Cold storage, freezing, canning and drying are the common methods of preservation of fish. Salting before drying is essential.

16
EGGS

Eggs are used in many preparations due to the variety they provide to food. Eggs are important ingredients of recipes for breakfast, lunch or dinner for any person. Nutritive importance, flavour, pleasing colour, thickening power, foam-forming ability, emulsifying capacity, stabilising capacity and the binding property of eggs are utilised in menu planning.

An egg has two parts—outer egg-white and inner egg yolk. The egg is held in position in the shell by two membranes which lie close together. About 63 per cent by weight of an egg is made of egg-white. It has three layers—an outer portion of thin egg-white, a thick jelly-like layer and a thin portion which surrounds the yolk. The central part of the egg is the egg yolk, and the yolk is surrounded by a thin covering called vitellin membrane.

The egg-white is rich in protein. Albumin, globulin and mucin are the proteins in egg-white. It is easily coagulated by heat and it provides the jelly-like character of thick egg-white. Minute quantities of sodium, potassium, magnesium, calcium, chlorides and phosphates and riboflavin are present in the egg-white.

The egg yolk contains ovovitellin as the proteins and it is phosphoprotein, and it resembles the casein of milk. The egg yolk is rich in fat, that is, about one-third of the yolk is fat, especially of cholesterol and lecithin variety. The fats in egg are finely dispersed and are in emulsified forms. The mineral content is more in egg yolk compared to the white. Egg yolk is an important source of iron and it is also rich in sodium, potassium, calcium and magnesium. Lipovitellin and lipovitellinin are the lipo proteins in egg yolk which act as emulsifying agents. Egg yolk is rich in vitamins, especially thiamine, riboflavin, vitamins A and D and their content in egg depends upon the hen's diet.

The whole egg is a rich source of all nutrients except vitamin C. The protein in egg is considered as a complete protein because of its high biological value and digestability. It is often mentioned as reference protein. But a raw egg-white contains a protein known as avidin which renders the vitamins biotin unavailable to the body. Duck egg-white contains another substance known as trypsin-inhibitor which inhibits the action of trypsin on protein. Heating destroys avidin and trypsin-inhibitors.

Role of Egg in Cookery

Egg protein coagulates on heating. The coagulum formed is a smooth and jelly-like mass. It supplies a thickening effect to the products. If the temperature is high, the coagulum is toughened and it shrinks and water comes out of the product. This is called syneresis and it occurs in custards and scrambled egg preparations.

Egg is cooked in its shell, scrambled, poached, fried or used in the preparations of deserts, and cakes and other confectioneries. Egg is used in food mixtures to contribute flavour and colour to the products. Cakes and puddings owe their colour and flavour to eggs. In the preparation of mayonnaise the protein of egg stabilises the oil in water dispersion. The protein of egg stabilises the air in liquid dispersion. Egg is also used for thickening various desserts and creams and patties. Since egg is highly perishable the quality has to be judged by internal appearance flavour and external shell appearance.

Candling

Candling is used as a method to detect the interior quality of egg. In a closed box with a small opening a lighted candle has to be placed. The depth of air cell can be observed by placing the egg in front of the opening. In a fresh egg the white is stationary and slight movements of yolk are permitted by the white. Yolk is in the centre and it does not move nearer to the shell. In a poor quality egg the yolk moves. The shell of good quality egg is firm and not stained or cracked.

Formation of Dark Greenish Discoloration in Hard Boiled Eggs

When egg is boiled for more than 15 minutes a dark greenish colour may be formed on the surface of the egg yolk. This green colour is due to the formation of FeS on the surface of the yolk. Yolk contains more iron and the white has more sulphur in its amino acids. On boiling it yields H_2S. The H_2S combines with the iron of the yolk and it gives the dark green colour in the middle. In high temperature this change takes place immediately.

17

SWEETENING AGENTS

Sugar, sugarcane juice, jaggery, molasses, honey, saccharin and cyclamates are the common agents used as sweetening.

Sugar (sucrose)

Sugar is almost pure sucrose made up of glucose (dextrose) and fructose (laevulose). One gramme of sugar supplies 4 kcals and a teaspoonful (5 gms) provides 20 kcals. Brown sugar and white sugar are similar in nutritive value. Sweets made from sugar produce a sense of satiety and so they must be taken after a meal. If sweets are consumed at the beginning of a meal they reduce appetite. Sugar syrup is used as a preservative for fruits, jams and preserves.

Excessive consumption of sugar and sweets affects the teeth adversely.

Sugarcane Juice

The juice obtained by crushing sugarcane is a refreshing drink. Addition of sugar and lemon juice improves its taste and flavour. Sugarcane is good for hepatitis patients. Jaggery is produced by heating sugarcane juice. It has been reputed to be good for the heart. Molasses is a byproduct in the manufacture of sugar. Fermentation of molasses produce alcohol.

Honey

Honey is a golden-coloured syrup made by bees from the nectar of flowers. It is a mixture of glucose and fructose. The quality of honey depends on the flower blossom. Honey is a soothing drink for patients with pharyngitis and tracheitis. Honey contains 17.7 per cent water, 36.5 per cent dextrose, 40.5 per cent laevulose and 1.9 per cent sucrose.

Jaggery

Gur or Jaggery is obtained from sugarcane juice after processing. Palmyra palm, date palm, or coconut palm is also used for it.

Saccharine and Cyclamates

Saccharine and cyclamates are used as sweetening agents for calorie-conscious people. Saccharine was discovered in 1879. It is 350 times sweeter than sugar and has a bitter taste in concentrated form.

Cyclamate was discovered in 1937. It is 30 times sweeter than sucrose. Cyclamates are harmful to the body if consumed in large quantities. Malignant bladder tumours were produced in experimental animals. Excessive use of soft drinks with cyclamates produce renal tubular acidosis.

Leavening Agents

Leavening agents are substances which produce carbon dioxide in the product. This carbon dioxide contributes a porous appearance to the product as in bread, cake or in biscuits. Baker's yeast and baking powders are usually used as leavening agents. Baker's yeast, when added to the dough, ferments sugar and produces carbon dioxide and alcohol. This gives the characteristic structure to the product. Baking powders are leavening agents produced by mixing an acid-reacting material and sodium bicarbonate with or without starch. There are three types of baking powders—fast acting, slow acting and double acting based on their speed of action.

Flavour Components in Foods

Food industry is a fast growing field. Much progress has been made in understanding the chemical nature of flavours in foods. Many artificial flavouring materials are now avaiable in the market. The compounds which give the flavour characteristic in one food is given below:

Food		Main flavour compound
Banana	—	Isopentyl acetate
Lemon	—	Citral
Grape-concord	—	Methyl anthranitrate
Potato	—	2-Isopropyo-3-methoxy pyrazne
Beetroot	—	Geosmin
Apple	—	Ethyl-2-methyl butyrate

18

SPICES AND CONDIMENTS

Spices and condiments are accessory foodstuffs mainly used for flavouring food. Some condiments are good to fair sources of carotene. Red chillies and coriander are examples of this. Green chillies are rich in vitamin C. Turmeric and tamarind are fair sources of iron. Garlic promotes intestinal synthesis of certain vitamins. Among the spices and condiments fenugreek seeds have the highest amount of protein, that is, 26.2 per cent. Cuminseeds, dry chillies and coriander seeds have a protein content of 18.7, 15.9 and 14.1 per cent, respectively. Caraway has a protein content of 17.1 and fat content of 21.8 per cent in it. Coriander, cuminseeds and dry pepper have a fat content of 16.1, 15.0 and 6.8 per cent, respectively. Cuminseed is also rich in calcium. About 1.080 gm of calcium is present in 100 gms. Asafoetida and coriander are also good sources of calcium. Asafoetida, cuminseeds, cloves, fenugreek seeds, turmeric, tamarind and omum are good sources of iron. Cardamon, green chillies, coriander, cuminseeds, caraway and green pepper are rich sources of carotene. Dry chillies, nutmeg, cuminseeds, coriander and fenugreek seeds are good sources of thiamine. Even though these condiments and spices are rich in vitamins and minerals they are used only in minute quantities. Black pepper, coriander, cumin, ferugreek, mustard seeds, chillies, nutmeg, cloves, cinnamon and cardamom are used as spices in our country.

The popularity of spices is due to their stimulating effect on appetite next to its flavour. Certain spices and condiments have medicinal effect. Turmeric is believed to be anti-inflammatory. In anti-allergic drugs turmeric is used. Turmeric also reduces blood cholesterol level. Consumption of spices and condiments in large quantities produces irritation in the mucous membranes of the alimentary canal. Peptic ulcer is common among people who use condiments and spices liberally.

Herbs like curry leaves, coriander leaves, mint leaves and leaves of citrus fruits are used for preparing chutney powders and they are also used in many curries.

Gelatin Dishes

When the protein in connective tissues and bones—the collagen—is heated with water gelatin is obtained. To bring this change in collagen it has to be heated to 95°C. Some peptide bonds of collagen are hydrolysed to gel.

Commercially it is available in granulated, flake or sheet forms. It easily dissolves in hot water and on cooling it sets to a gel. Concentration of gelatin, cooling temperature, the presence of minerals like calcium and concentration of sugar affects the quality of the product. With a 2 to 3 per cent of gel concentration and at temperatures below 15°C a good gel is formed. Sugar in 6 to 10 per cent concentration enhances the speed of gel formation. If the gel is heated it melts and on cooling it sets again. Now vegetable gels are also available in the market.

Gelatin is used for decorating various types of desserts. For ice, souffles, baked ice-cream, or other creams, jelly trifles, caramel puddings, flans, milk puddings, sponge puddings, with stewed fruits, milk jellies, purees of fruits, junkets and with baked fruits gelatin can be used to make them more attractive. Gelatin acts as a stabiliser and reduces crystal formation of ice-creams.

Emulsifying and Stabilising agents

Substances which, when added to food, gives a uniform dispersion of oils and fats in aqueous media are called emulsifiers or stabilising agents.

In food industry it is often liberally used and they are harmful. Agar, edible-gums, brominated vegetable oils, gelatin, albumin, lecithin, starches, hydrolysed proteins and stearyl lastaric are some of the examples.

19

FATS AND OILS

Fats and oils are used in cookery to enhance flavour and taste of food. Moreover, fat gives much more energy to body; from every gramme of fat 9 calories are given. In India most of our fats and oils are extracted from vegetable oilseeds. A solid fat-like ghee has a decisive place in Indian cuisine and it is often substituted by vanaspati. Liquid vegetable oils are hydrogenated and converted to solid fats. Hydrogenated fat is incorporated with vitamins A and D.

Common oils used in cooking are groundnut oil, sesame oil, mustard oil, safflower oil, coconut oil, soyabean oil, cottonseed oil, palm oil and sunflower oil.

Choice of fat for cooking depends on various factors. Flavour, taste, saturation of fatty acids and presence of double bonds, melting points, smoking temperature and nutritive value are some of them.

Liquid oils rich in linoleic acid like safflower, cottonseed, and groundnut are good in suppressing the formation of scales on the walls of blood vessel. The characterisitc flavours of various oils are due to the presence of very small quantities of certain susbtances which have no nutritional qualities. Cooking in fat gives fullness of satiety along with taste to the dishes. Now most of the oils are refined to make them colourless and odourless.

Composition of Fats

Fats and oils are classified into two groups based on their origin as vegetable and animal sources.

Vegetable fats and oils are again broadly divided into three groups based on their composition. They are: Group I which has fatty acids with 16 or 18 carbon atoms; Group II has erucic acid; and Group III has short chain fatty acids. Groundnut oil, cottonseed oil, sesame oil, safflower seed oil, sunflower seed oil and soyabean oil are with 16 or 18 carbon atoms and they are termed as Group I. Mustard oil and rapeseed

Linoleic Acid Content of Some Common Oils

Oil	Linoleic acid content (%)
Coconut oil	2
Mustard oil	15
Ghee	2
Palmoil	10
Palmolein	12
Safflower oil	70
Cottonseed oil	50
Sunflower oil	50
Groundnut oil	40

oil have erucic acid in it and they are in Group II. Coconut oil and palm oil are with short chain fatty acids in Group III.

Animal fats are also classified into three groups based on their composition. Group I is milk fat which contains butyric acid and short chain fatty acids. Group II comprises animal body fat with fatty acids of 16 to 18 carbon atoms. Ox fat, pig fat and egg fat are examples of this group. In Group III fish oils with large amounts of polyunsaturated fatty acids are present. Herring, cod, halibut and sardine oils fall in this group.

Melting points of fats depend on the saturation of fatty acids. Solid fats like lard with high saturated fatty acids have high melting point and liquid oils have a low melting point.

The Smoking Temperature of Fats

When fats and oils are heated to a high temperature decomposition of fats occurs and at a point visible fumes are given off. This temperature is called the smoking temperature of fats. The smoking temperature of fat is low when amounts of free fatty acids are high.

Smoking Temperature of Some Fats and Oils

Oil or fat		Smoking temperature
Butter	...	208° C.
Cottonseed oil	...	322° C.
Coconut oil	...	138° C.
Lard	...	194° C.
Olive oil refined	...	234° C.
Groundnut oil	...	162° C.

Fat absorption is high if foods are cooked in fat with low smoking points.

Smoking temperature of fat varies depending on the surface area of oil exposed while heating. The penetrability of the produce to be fried also determines the fat absorption while frying.

Shortenings

Fat is used as a shortening agent due to its ability to give a soft crisp texture to fried or baked products. In bakery items fat plays a significant role.

In wheat products fat brings shortening of gluten strands and in other dishes shortening is through gelatinisation of starch. To bring shortening effect one fat or a mixture of fats is used. In biscuit-making plastic shortenings are used which contribute a white, opaque and creamy appearance to the shortening. Butter and ghee are generally preferred as shortening agents. In certain preparations fat blends homogeneously with non-fat substance to form an emulsion and examples of such preparations are sweets like halwa, mysore pak or cake.

Changes in Fats due to Heat

Changes in fat during heating are related to its smoking points. Free fatty acid is increased on heating. This is due to the change brought about by the moisture content of food materials. It hydrolyses the cooking fat and increases the free fatty acid content. Therefore, deep frying foods in fats with high smoking temperature is preferred. Ghee has a lower smoking point and therefore other oils or hydrogenated fat are suggested for deep frying.

When fat is used for deep frying, temperature control is essential. If high temperature is used to heat fat, it affects its nutritive value and in experimental cases it produced a toxic effect. Certain changes take place in fat during heating and this brings down the unsaturated fatty acid content. Repeated heating of fats brings chemical changes and results in poor absorption. It also increased blood cholesterol level in experimental animals. If the fat is heated too high, the food will char outside and remain raw inside. If the temperature of fat is too low the food will get soaked in it. In correct temperature food will be crisp and uniformly cooked. To get the best result fat must be heated to its smoking point. When fumes appear insert food material, fry and lower the heat. After frying the first batch allow the fat to heat to required temperature and add the second batch to fry. Absorption of fats by food materials varies depending on its smoking temperature. If fat with low smoking point is used to fry, more fat is absorbed and fat with high smoking point is required less to fry items. Food items with milk, sugar, or eggs require low temperature to fry them. If food items are fried at high temperature more fat is absorbed. If the food item has greater surface area fat absorbed is more and if surface area is small less fat is absorbed. The moisture content of food item also affects fat absorption. With more moisture content fat absorption also increases. Hard materials also take more fats.

Characteristics of Some Common Fats

Fat source	Polyunsaturated fatty acid	Saturated fatty acid	Mono-unsaturated fatty acid
Groundnut	31	19	50
Sesame	43	14	43
Safflower seed	67	7	26
Cottonseed	47	23	30
Coconut oil	2	92	6
Mustard oil	63	5	32
Butter	3	70	27
Soyabean	64	18	18
Lard	10	96	40

Salad Dressing

Fat is used as an emulsion in salad dressing. Along with fat, egg yolk, vinegar, salt, spices and starch are used in salad dressing. Mayonnaise, french salads and cooked salad dressing are the common methods used. Winterised oils are used in all these methods.

Mayonnaise

It is a semi-solid emulsion of vegetable oils, egg yolk or whole egg, vinegar and seasoning. Egg yolk functions as a seasoning agent.

French Dressing

Vinegar, oils (soyabeans, cornoil, seame oil or sunflower oil) and salt and spices are added. It is mixed vigorously. Mustard powder is also added.

20

BEVERAGES

Beverages are materials used as drinks for the purpose of relieving thirst and introducing fluid in the body, nourishing the body and stimulating or soothing the individual. Beverages are classified into four groups according to the reactions they produce.

(1) *Refreshing* to relieve thirst.

    (a) Plain or carbonated water.
    (b) Ginger ale and other bottled beverages.
    (c) Fruit juices and fruit-ades.
    (d) Iced tea or coffee.

(2) *Nourishing*

    (a) Milk pasteurised, skimmed, evaporated, dried, malted, buttermilk, and chocolate and cocoa.
    (b) Eggnog made with rum, whisky, brandy, fruit juices, coffee and chocolate.
    (c) Fruit juices with egg-white or whole egg.
    (d) Glucose lemonade or orangeade.
    (e) Tube feeding feeds.

(3) *Stimulating*

    (a) Eggnogs made with whisky, rum, brandy, tea or coffee, other alcoholic beverages.
    (b) Tea or coffee.

(4) *Soothing*

    (a) Warm milk.
    (b) Hot tea.

Coffee and tea have no food value unless served with cream and sugar. Cocoa in itself will increase the food value of the milk which is used in its preparation. Coffee, tea and cocoa, all have a certain amount of stimulating effect. Iced coffee, tea and cocoa are used all the year round between meals as a refreshing drink. Milk, eggnog and other cold beverages made with milk or milk and egg are valuable for serving between meals when the protein content of the diet needs to be increased. Wines and other liquors which are used occasionally to provoke appetite, or to stimulate or flavour furnish additional calories. Cold beverages may be used with meals or between meals. They are more appetising when chilled. The choice of the beverage will depend largely upon whether it is taken for its food value or merely as a refreshment. In any case a cold drink served between meals adds interest to the monotonous hours in the daily routine of a person.

Tea

Tea is obtained from the leaves and flowers of teabush, which grows in sub-tropical countries, such as China, India and Japan. The top tiny leaves and buds or flowers at the end of the shoot furnish the choicest and the most expensive brands designated as flowery pekoe. Orange pekoe is the most commonly marked tea which consists of the first and second leaves just below the buds.

The kind of tea is determined by its treatment. Subsequent to picking, the green tea undergoes no fermentation process and is light in colour and rich in tannin. Black tea is fermented to a dark colour and loses some of its tannin.

A good cup of tea will contain a high proportion of volatile oils and a minimum amount of tannin. Tannin is a stimulant and has approximately the same psychological effect as caffeine. Tea, which is allowed to stand too long in the container with the leaves, contains a considerable amount of tannin which causes the finished beverage to be bitter and unpalatable.

Coffee

Coffee is the beans of coffee plants which grow in tropical countries. It is tasteless in its green form. Roasting develops the volatile oils, specially caffenol which give the characteristic aroma and flavour to coffee. The typical individual brands depend upon the various types of coffee used and the length of the time of roasting. Bitterness is increased when combined with substances like chicory.

Coffee alone has no food value, but it does furnish a certain amount of stimulation of caffeine which raises the blood pressure and stimulates renal activity and momentarily masks fatigue. As a rule a cup of coffee contains from 1.5 to 2.5 grains of caffeine depending upon the strength of the brew. Tannin, another alcoholite present, interferes with digestion. The amount of tannin in coffee depends upon the method of preparation. Since it is soluble in hot water, the longer the coffee is brewed, the greater will be the tannin content.

Coffee beans are gound to increase the surface area for maximum extraction of the flavour. However, coffeole is rapidly lost, the loss being greater in freshly ground coffee. Ground coffee should be kept in a tightly covered tin in a cool place and should be used promptly after purchase.

Drip and vacuum coffee contains the least amount of tannin, caffeine and coffeole. Percolated coffee contains slightly more caffeine and less coffeole than drip and vaccum coffee. Boiled coffee should be strained. It contains more caffeine and tannin than either the drip or percolated coffee.

Instant coffee is made from pure coffee which has been pulverised. The extraction of caffeine and tannin is high, but the amount in the finished beverage will depend upon the amount used. Some instant coffees are mixed with malted cereals.

In decaffeinated coffee 75 per cent of caffeine is removed. It does not possess the stimulating property of coffee. Coffee substitutes are made from a combination of roasted grains and cereals.

Cocoa

Cocoa is the ground product of cocoa beans and often some of the fat has been removed. The cocoa beans are in fleshy pods. The well ripened pods are feathered and dried for 24 hours after which they are cut open and the beans are removed. The beans then undergo a series of processes like fermenting or sweating, removing the pulp, washing, drying and roasting. Chocolate and cocoa, unlike tea and coffee, have a high nutritive value. The roasted beans, likewise the bitter chocolate, contain approximately 50 per cent of fat, about 80 per cent protein, 10 per cent starch, and 7 per cent sugar. Like tea and coffee, they also contain a stimulant and tannin. The stimulant known as theobronine has approximately the same physiological effect, though not to such a marked degree. There is only a small amount of stimulant in one cup and the chief nutritive value of the drink lies not in the cocoa but in the amount of milk and sugar used in it.

Coconut water

Tender coconut water is high in sugar and electrolytes like Na and potassium.

Fruit Juices

Fruit juices in themselves are not only pleasantly refreshing but they are easily digested and especially useful in increasing the fluid intake. The citrus juices and tomatoes are excellent for the ascorbic acid content. Fresh, frozen and canned juices may be served plain or flavoured. They may be reinforced with egg white or whole egg. The following fruits include commonly used juices: (1) citrus—organge, lemon, grape fruit, lime; (2) Berries—blackberries, loganberries, raspberries, strawberries; (3) tree fruits—apple, apricot, peach, pear, plum, prune; (4) other fruits—grapes, pineapple; (5) vegetables—tomato; (6) Sugarcane juice, sweet toddy and coconut milk are some of them.

Milk

Milk is most of all liquid food since it has more nutritive value than any other beverage. Milk beverages add protein, calories, calcium and other nutrients to the diet. The milk flavour of food permits its use in a great number of ways. It may be plain, malted, or acidulated. It may be reinforced with egg and sugar depending upon the type of nutrient needed and it may be flavoured with chocolate and other flavouring extracts.

Egg

Eggs are specially useful for increasing the protein content of beverages. Eggnog in which whisky or other alcoholic beverages are used is the most important stimulating beverage. Eggnog made with strong coffee is only mildly stimulating but lends variety to the general liquid diets. Eggnogs contain egg, cream, and possibly milk and sugar in addition to fruit juice.

Sugar

Cane sugar, fructose and lactose may be used to sweeten beverages and to increase the caloric value.

Basic Rules in the Preparation of Tea and Coffee

Tea

The best tea produces a pale coloured infusion. Freshly infused tea has good flavour and it is harmless for digestion. Reheating or overheating of tea results in continued infusion and it extracts more tannin which gives a bitter taste to tea. Moreover, this is often harmful to the digestive system.

The quality of tea is an important factor in giving good taste to the product. Since tea leaves absorb water, they must be stored in airtight containers.

Water used for the preparation of tea also has the key role in producing good result. Water should be freshly drawn before it is used for tea. Previously drawn water and previously boiled water should not be used for preparing tea as it makes the tea insipid. To get the best flavour water should not be boiled before or after tea leaves are added. As soon as the tea leaves are added to boiling water it circulates from the bottom to the top and from the top to the bottom.

To prepare good tea, one teaspoonful of tea leaves for 1 cup is ideal. For one litre of water 15 gms of tea leaves are enough. It is always better to measure tea leaves to get good result. The vessel in which tea is being prepared must be warmed before making tea. Instead of adding tea leaves to water, pour boiling water into a warmed pot in which tea leaves are added. Do not disturb this for five minutes. Let the leaves infuse. If it is kept for more than five minutes, it gives a bitter taste and less then five minutes yields a weak tea.

Milk and sugar can be added according to individual taste. To get a good cup of tea, it must be served hot.

Coffee

There are different methods of preparing coffee. The pot method, the filter method, the urn brewing method and the vacuum brewing method are the common methods.

Coffee powder must be fresh to get the best flavour and taste. The quantity of coffee powder used must be just enough. For one cup of coffee 8.5 gms or 1/2 teaspoon of brewing coffee is required. If instant coffee is used one teaspoon is enough to make 1 cup of coffee.

Freshly drawn water must be used to prepare coffee.

Coffee is generally prepared by any one of the following methods:

1. The pot method.
2. Filter method.

3. The percolator method.
4. Instant coffee preparation.

The pot method: In this method an earthenware pot or jug is used to prepare coffee. Warm the earthenware pot or jug, put in 3 level spoons or 1 1/2 heaped teaspoons of fresh coffee powder (coarse grind) for an 8-ounce cup. Pour boiled water over the powder and stir. Cover the vessel and let it stand for 5 minutes. Strain the coffee through a fine meshed sieve or cloth. Add milk and sugar to taste.

Filter method: Stainless steel or brass filters can be used to filter coffee in this method. If brass filter is used it should be tinned properly to get good results. Put 2 to 3 level teaspoons coffee powder for 8 ounces water. Press the plunger down lightly over the powder and pour boiling water over the plunger in a circular motion. Allow to stand for 5 to 7 minutes. Pour out coffee from the lower vessel and add milk and sugar to taste.

The percolator method: Keep coffee powder in the middle of the percolator and pour boiling water through it to the upper section. Coffee is collected from the bottom section. It takes thirty minutes to percolate down. Vacuum coffee makers are also available in some places.

Instant coffee: Strong brew is made by percolation of roasted and ground coffee which is sprayed into fine atomised particles from the top of a chamber into a mass of very hot air. The flavour is retained through highly developed technology. It is quickly packed into airtight bottles. Varying degrees of chicory is mixed with coffee powder to give slight bitterness and colour to brew. Now mixtures of coffee soluble with solids and sugar in the form of thick pastes are also marketed. By adding hot water it can be used instantly.

Alcoholic Beverages

Beer, ale, toddy, wine whisky, gin, brandy, rum, vodka, arrack and cider are some of the alcoholic beverages. Beer is made by fermenting barley malt extract with yeast and ale is the same thing with more stimulation. Toddy is from fermenting sap of palm, coconut and palmyra or date palm.

Wine: Wine is prepared by the fermentation of grapes with yeast and cider is apple wine.

Whisky: It is an alcoholic distillate from a fermented mash of grains.

Gin: It is an artifical drink from diluted pure ethyl alcohol.

Brandy: This is made from fruit juices like grapes and apples.

21

METHODS OF COOKING

Basic Terminology in Food Preparation

Bake. Baking is a method of cooking by dry heat usually in an oven.

Barbecue. A preparation of meat where meat is basted with highly seasoned sauce.

Batter. A mixture of flour and liquid which can be used for coating or for frying.

Beat. Mixing any substance by vigorous motion wherein air is incorporated.

Blanch. Dipping any food article into boiling water for a few minutes.

Blend. Combining two or more ingredients.

Broil. To cook by exposing food directly to the heat or through a grill.

Browning. A substitute added to darken certain preparations.

Brushing. Thin coating of beaten eggs or milk to pies or any dish to provide a glossy appearance to the product.

Caramel. A brown product of sugar on heating, usually used for coating or decorating or flavouring dishes.

Caramelize. Heat sugar to brown colour.

Cisel. Finely chop vegetables.

Coat. To cover with a thin layer.

Concass. Chop roughly.

Condiments. Spices and seasonings.

Consistency. Texture of the mixture.

Cream. Beat fat with a wooden spoon until it is light and fluffy.

Croutons. Small diced bread pieces fried or toasted for decorating soups.

Custard. Steamed or baked mixture of milk and egg.

Cut and fold. Mix flour very gently into a mixture.

Cutlet. Minced meat shaped into small round or oval shapes which are usually baked, grilled or fried.

Dice. To cut into small even cubes.

Dough. Mixture of flour and liquid in a stiff form.

Dredge. Cover food with a thin sprinkling.

Dust. To sprinkle lightly with powdered sugar, milk or flour.

Escalopes. Fried sliced meat dipped in egg and bread crumbs.

Farce. Stuffing of any kind.

Fillet. Fish with bone removed or slices from the breast of birds.

Flan. A thin pastry case.

Flute. A long crisp roll of bread used for decoration.

Fondant. Sugar boiled to 234°F and smoothened into a sweet.

Fritters. Foods like meat, vegetables, fish or fruits first coated with batter and then fried.

Frosting. Icing or coating sugar for decoration.

Fry. Cooking food in hot fat.

Gelatin. A product made from cow's hooves and generally used for jellies. Now available from vegetable sources also.

Gild. Cover an object with beaten eggs.

Glace. Giving a glossy appearance for certain dishes with icing, frozen items or with jelly.

Hors-d'oeuvre. Small savoury tit bits used as appetizers before a meal.

Junket. Milk coagulated by the addition of rennet.

Kabab. Minced or small meat pieces braised or curried.

Knead. Forcefully mixing the flour using the knuckles of the hand.

Lard. Fatty substances of meat.

Macaroni. Paste of flour forced through a tube. Thus long strands are obtained which are known as macaroni.

Macaroons. Small cakes with coconut.

Marinate. Soak meat or fish in mixture of vinegar and spices.

Mask. Coat a dish with sauce or moulded jelly.

Mayonnaise. By mixing egg yolk, oil, vinegar and mustard a thick sauce is made which is used for dressing salads.

Mince. Finely slice or shred.

Muffin. Moulded baked batter used with butter.

Noodles. Flour paste in different shapes usually used for Chinese cooking.

Parboil. Partially cooked food.

Pare. To peel.

Pluck. Remove feathers from poultry.

Poach. Cooking on low temperature in hot liquid in an open pan.

Puree. Smooth mixture obtained by sieving cooked fruits or vegetables.

Raising agents. Substances which produce gas when acted on by heat. Examples are baking soda, baking powder and yeast.

Saffron. A yellow colouring removed from a flower used for appearance and flavour.

Sauce. A pouring mixture used for enhancing the flavour and taste of another dish.

Saute. Cook in shallow fat to brown.

Scald. Immerse food in boiling liquid.

Shortening. Fat used for baking.

Shred. Cut in fine strips.

Sift. Put dry ingredients through a sieve.

Simmer. Cook food in liquid on low temperature just below the boiling point.

Souffle. Lightly baked or steamed pudding puffed with egg whites.

Spaghetti. An Italian paste finer than macaroni and coarser than vermicelli.

Steam. Cook in steam.

Steep. Soak in liquid.

Stew. Cook by simmering in little liquid.

Stock. Flavoured liquid from meat, vegetables, fish or poultry used for soups, stews or sauces.

Weight and Volume Equivalents

Weight and volume equivalents are essential to work out new recipes. To scientifically impart the knowledge of cooking weights and volume equivalents are used. Some common weights and volume are given below:

1 teaspoon	...	5 millilitres
1 tablespoon	...	3 teaspoons or 1/2 ounce liquid
1 cup	...	16 tablespoons or 8 ounces or 235 millilitre
1/2 pint	...	10 ounces or 295 millilitres (approximate)
1 pint	...	590 millilitre (approximate)
2 pint	...	1.18 litre
1 ounce	...	30 grammes
16 ounce	...	455 grammes
1 pound	...	455 grammes
2.5 pounds	...	1 kilogramme
1 ounce	...	30 millilitre
34 ounces	...	1 litre

Aims and Objects of Cooking Food

1. Cooking partly sterilizes food. Above 40°C the growth of bacteria decreases rapidly and in general it ceases above 45°C. Non-sporing bacteria are killed at temperature above 60°C for varying periods of time. For instance, to make milk safe it is pasteurized at 62.8°C for 30 minutes. Boiling kills living cells, with the exception of spores, in a few seconds. Spore-bearing bacteria take about 4 to 5 hours boiling to be destroyed. To destroy them in a shorter time higher temperature must be used.

2. Cooking helps to make food more digestible. Complex foods are many a time split into simpler substances during cooking. This helps the body to absorb and utilise the food more readily than the raw food.

3. Cooking increases palatability.
4. Cooking makes food more attractive in appearance and therefore more appetising.
5. Cooking introduces variety. Many different types of dishes can be prepared with the same ingredients.
6. Cooking helps to provide a balanced meal. The different ingredients combined together in one dish make it easier to provide a balanced meal.

While the correct preparation of ingredients and correct mixing are necessary, greater skill is needed in the actual cooking of the food. The different methods of cooking are, roasting, baking, frying, boiling, poaching, steaming, stewing, braising, broiling, grilling.

Roasting

Spit Roasting

The food to be cooked is brought in contact with direct flame in front of a clear bright fire. The food is basted over with fat and is also turned regularly to ensure even cooking and browning. This method, known now as spit roasting, is little used as only good quality meats are suitable for this method. Roast meats, however, have excellent flavour and are still served in large hotels and in special restaurants and hotels, e.g., barbecued meat.

Oven Roasting

This has now taken the place of spit roasting because of its convenience, although only first class meat, poultry and vegetables are thus cooked. This is cooked in a closed oven with the aid of fat. The food is put into a fairly hot oven for 5 to 10 minutes and the temperature is lowered to allow the joint to be cooked. Cooking in a moderate oven for a longer time produces a better cooked joint than cooking at high temperature for a shorter period. Aluminium foil is now used in oven roasting. The joint is larded or raised with fat and cooked in the oven till done. The method is an improvement on oven roasting as the meat retains its moisture and flavour.

Pot roasting

This method is used to cook small joints and birds if no oven is available, but a thick heavy pan is essential. Enough fat is melted to cover the bottom of the pan. When the fat is hot the joint is browned. It is then lifted out and 2 or 3 skewers are kept at the bottom on which the joint is placed. This is to prevent the joint from sticking to the pan. The joint should just touch the fat. The pan is then covered tightly with a well fitting lid and cooked over a very low fire. The joint could be basted and turned occasionally to ensure even cooking. Prepared root vegetables and potatoes can also be cooked round the meat.

Baking

The food to be cooked is surrounded by hot air in a closed oven. The action of dry heat is modified by the steam which arises from the food whilst cooking. Bread, cakes, pastries, puddings, vegetables and potatoes may be cooked by this method.

Frying

This is a method of cooking whereby the food to be cooked is brought in contact with hot fat. Food cooked in this way is said to be indigestible but if the method be correctly and carefully carried out the food is quite suitable for normal people. The advantages of frying are (1) the food is very appetising, (2) it is a quick method of cooking, and (3) the keeping quality of food improves. For other foods and for reheating of food frying is a good means of providing variety.

There are two types of frying: (1) shallow fat frying, (2) deep fat frying.

Shallow Fat Frying

Only a little fat is used and the food is turned over in order that both sides may be browned. Generally this method is applied to precooked food unless the food takes very little time to cook (omelette, liver, etc.). Fat absorption is greater when food is shallow fried rather than deep fried.

Deep Fat Frying

The food is completely immersed in hot fat and therefore a large quantity of fat is required. The quantity of fat requires some time to heat. Special care must be taken to prevent overheating of fat as this spoils both the food as well as the fat. The fat decomposes at high temperature. If the fat is not hot enough the food breaks up and it absorbs extra fat thus making the product unfit for consumption.

Both sweets and savouries may be cooked by this method without the flavour affecting the fat or the foods, provided correct principles are applied. Food cooked by deep fat frying has a much better appearance than that cooked by shallow fat frying, as food is evenly browned.

General Rules for Frying

1. Have the fire clear and hot.
2. Make the food into suitable sizes and shapes and see that it is free from cracks as far as possible.
3. Apply the coating evenly. The breadcrumbs used should not be coarse. Remove any excess and press loose crumbs firmly on.
4. When frying chicken, dry off all moisture before dipping in flour.
5. Use fat with a high smoking point. The fat must be quite still and at the right temperature required, before the food is put in.
6. Do not put in too many articles at the same time as this will lower the temperature.
7. See that the temperature is not increased for increased output.
8. Follow a time and temperature chart.
9. Fry to a golden brown on both sides, turning over the food if necessary.
10. Drain well on paper and serve attractively.
11. Cover fats between frying periods when left in the fryer and maintain temperature not higher than 200°F.
12. Once fat has been used for frying, strain and store in cans in a refrigerator.
13. Replenish with fresh fat to original volume after each frying period.
14. Fat begins to thicken, getting to be what is known as gummy or syrupy, with container use. This condition is known as polymerisation.
15. Fats that are used for frying should have a high stability.
16. Darkening of the fat is caused by cooking at too high a temperature which carbonises loose breadcrumbs and small particles of fried food. Such fat should be strained and replenished with fresh fat before being used again.

Boiling

Food is cooked by surrounding it with boiling or simmering liquid (stock or water). Only sufficient liquid should be used to cover the article to be cooked.

Vegetables grown above the ground are cooked in boiling salted water and vegetables grown below the ground are started in cold, salted water with the exception of new potatoes and new carrots. Dry vegetables are started in cold water. Salt is added only after the vegetables are tender. Fish should be put into hot liquid and allowed to simmer.

Poaching

Poaching is cooking slowly in a minimum amount of liquid which should never be allowed to boil but should be just off boil. Fish, fruits and eggs are poached. When poaching eggs, a little vinegar and salt are added to the liquid to help in quicker coagulation and thus prevent disintegration.

Steaming

The food to be cooked is surrounded by plenty of steam from fast boiling water directly or by having the food in a basin or some other dish placed in steaming or boiling water. This is a slow process of cooking and only easily cooked food can be prepared by this method.

Advantages of Steaming

(1) Food cooked by this method is easily digested.
(2) All nourishment and flavours remain in the food.
(3) Food cannot be easily overcooked.
(4) Pudding basins and other containers need not be filled to the top, thus allowing room for food to rise, making food light.

General Rules of Steaming

(1) Prepare the vessel and have the water fast boiling.
(2) If a basin is to be used as a container inside the steamer, see that it is greased and that it is covered with a well fitted lid or with grease-proof paper. This is to prevent condensed moisture from falling on the food.
(3) Keep a kettle of boiling water handy so that the water in the steamer can be replaced as it evaporates away.
(4) Never allow the water in the steamer to go off boil, except when preparing dishes with eggs as the main ingredient as in custard.
(5) Dish out food quickly and serve hot. An appropriate sauce must accompany steamed food to make it appetising as steamed food is generally bland.

Stewing

This is a very gentle method of cooking in a closed pan using only a small quantity of liquid. The food should never be more than half covered with the liquid and the food above this level is thus really cooked by steam.

Advantages

1. Cheap cuts of meat, old fowls and tough or underripe fruits may be prepared by this method as the slow moist method of cooking softens fibres rendering them tender.
2. Meat and vegetables may be cooked and served together and so make an appetising dish while saving fuel and labour.
3. Food may be cooked in the oven after other food is cooked or it may be cooked on the side of the fire or on a very small gas or oil flame, thus again saving fuel.
4. All nourishment and flavour are retained and hence food is very appetising and healthy.

General Rules

(1) Have ready a pan with a well fitted lid.
(2) Prepare the food and cut into pieces conveniently for serving.
(3) Use tepid liquid and only sufficient to half cover the food.

Braising

This is a combined method of roasting and stewing in a pan with a tight fitting lid. The meat should be sealed by browning on all sides and then placed on a lightly fried bed of vegetables (generally root). Stock or gravy is added which should come up to two-thirds of the meat. The flavourings and seasonings are then added. The lid is put on and it is allowed to cook gently on the stove or in the oven. When nearly done the lid is removed and the joint is frequently basted to glaze it.

Broiling

Broiling is cooking by direct heat and is used synonymously with grilling. In pan broiling the food is cooked uncovered on hot metal grill or a frying pan. The pan or grill is oiled slightly to prevent sticking.

Grilling

Used synonymously with broiling. This is cooking by dry heat and is carried on an iron grill over the fire or on a grill placed in a tin under a gas or electric grill.

Over-heat

This is cooking on greased grill bars with the help of fat over direct heat.

Only first class cuts of meat, poultry and certain fish can be prepared this way. The grill bars are brushed with oil to prevent food sticking and can be heated by charcoal, coke, gas or electricity. The thickness of the food and the heat of the grill determine the cooking time.

Under-heat

Cooking is done on grill bars or on trays under direct heat. Steaks, chops and similar foods are cooked on the bars but fish, tomato and mushroom are usually cooked on trays.

Between Heat

Food is cooked between electrically heated grill bars.

Infra-red

This is cooking by infra-red radiation. This method reduces cooking time considerably, for instance, a steak can be grilled in one minute.

Microwave cooking

Microwave heating is used in cooking in all advanced countries. Since the heating is very quick it has its own advantages. A simple microwave oven consists of a metal cabinet into which a quick magnetron is inserted. A magnetron is a kind of electron tube within a magnetic field which generates high frequency radiant energy. Alongwith a magnetron a metal fan is also installed and the fan distributes the microwave throughout. Foods placed in the oven is heated by microwaves from all directions and it helps in easy cooking.

22

FOOD PRESERVATION

Food spoilage is brought about by the action of enzymes present in foods or due to the action of micro-organisms such as mould, yeast and bacteria or due to infestation with insects and worms. The environment unfavourable to the action of enzymes or to the growth of micro-organism is the main objective of food preservation. Natural and artificial methods are adopted for this purpose. Preservatives are also added to foods to preserve them. Various agents are used to bring either physical or chemical changes in food materials which are to be preserved.

As the principal spoilage agents are normally present in foods, destroying them or preventing their development becomes the chief problem of food preservation. Any condition opposed to the development of these organisms, whether by retarding their growth or by entirely destroying them, aids in the preservation of food. Methods commonly used to this end include common or cellar storage, refrigeration, canning, freezing, use of preservatives, drying and the exclusion of air. Although not a commonly used method at present, "cold sterilisation" or irradiation by beta and gamma rays to prolong the keeping quality of foods is being widely studied experimentally. The possibilities of this method of food preservation are great. When some of the major problems now limiting its use are solved, it is probable there will be radical changes in the present accepted methods of handling foods.

Refrigeration

Micro-organisms, although not readily destroyed by severe cold, are much less active at low temperature. Refrigeration is widely used both in homes and in commercial plants, as a means of maintaining the low temperature found satisfactory in the storage of perishable foods. Fresh milk, meat and similar foods are kept just above the freezing point.

Certain fruits and vegetables also keep better when cold, although as a rule they do not require low temperature for the limited time they are stored in the home as do the protein foods cited. Under-ripe fruits usually ripen rapidly at room temperatures. The keeping of cooked foods and leftovers is greatly facilitated by refrigeration, which is a more expensive but also a more efficient method of preservation than common storage.

Wrapping certain fruits and vegetables in paper or cellophane, or coating them with wax, improves the keeping quality. Pears and apples of high quality to be kept for winter use and oranges, lemons and grapefruit are often wrapped. The fruit or the paper in which it is wrapped may be treated to retard mould formation. Green peppers, tomatoes, oranges and other citrus fruits, cucumbers and cantaloupes are among the foods whose keeping quality is improved when they are coated with wax.

Heating

Food is commonly preserved through the application of high temperatures. A temperature considerably above that of the body may result in either a pasteurised or a sterilised product. Foods are commonly pasteurised by being held at a temperature of from 60° to 66° C., for thirty to forty minutes, during which time most of the organisms, although not all, are killed. Spores and some vegetative forms of bacteria remain, but as a rule those causing diseases are destroyed. This method is used for temporary preservation of milk, and for preservation of fruit juices and other fruit products of delicate flavour. Acid foods are rendered sterile by boiling for a comparatively short time.

Canning

If the effectiveness of pasteurisation and sterilisation is to extend over a period of time of practical significance, the material thus treated must be protected from fresh contamination by micro-organisms. The fact that in canning the sterilised or pasteurised food is afforded such protection accounts, at least in part, for the rapid growth in popularity of the process as a means of food preservation. The first foods preserved by canning were sealed in glass.

All prejudice which once existed against canned foods has been removed. Experiments have shown canned foods to be as wholesome as any form of preserved food. Often the canned food is found to be superior in food value to the freshly cooked. Canned foods are ready for use at a moment's notice. When food is to be kept over a long period of time, canned products are also most satisfactory and they do not require special temperatures or equipment for storage.

Freezing

Freezing, like cold storage, does not destroy the micro-organisms and enzymes present in the foods. It does render them more or less inactive, however, so that frozen foods, when held at the proper temperature, undergo change slowly. This applies to the nutritive value as well as to other chemical and physical characteristics.

Practically all common fruits are now preserved by freezing. However, the success with which the different fruits can be frozen varies. Most of the vegetables that are served cooked may be preserved by freezing. Scalding to destroy the enzymes is essential for successful preservation of almost all vegetables by this method. Hence vegetables to be used fresh and crisp in salads cannot be preserved by freezing. Fish, poultry and game, as well as beef, veal, pork and lamb are preserved by freezing. Frozen foods have little or no waste at the time of using and little time is required for preparation. However, time must be allowed for the thawing of fruits to be served raw, and the cooking period of frozen meats and vegetables not already defrosted must be sufficient to allow for both thawing and cooking.

Using Chemical Preservatives

Certain chemicals are helpful in preserving foods either by retarding or preventing the growth of micro-organisms. These may be either added to the product or produced in it by fermentation. Sugar, a common home preservative, is often used in such quantities as to increase the concentration of the food and make it an unfavourable medium for the organisms. Salt and acid, in the form of vinegar or lemon juice, are other substances added for their preservative action. Frequently, the fermentation process is used to produce, within the food itself, acetic or lactic that exerts the same preservative action as is obtained by the addition of vinegar. Salt is used as an aid in the preservation of vegetables by fermentation. It aids both in drawing out the juices and in delaying the action of certain spoilage agents. Formerly, spices were often used in such quantities as to have a definite preservative effect. Today the concentration in which they are used is usually less than that employed earlier and it is believed that only a few of them are of value as preservatives.

Certain preservatives such as borax, boric acid, sulfites, and formaldehyde, once sold as canning powders, are now considered injurious to human beings, and their use is usually prohibited.

Preserving and Pickling

Preserving and pickling are methods of preservation frequently employed. Long before canning was known as a means of preserving foods, the use of preservatives was practised. Salting of foods was an early method of preservation. Salt is a valuable preservative, both as an antiseptic and as an agent for removing water. Placing foods in brine of certain concentration promotes fermentation and the foods develop an agreeable flavour. Sugar in large amount is likewise a favourite preservative. Today, although practically every known variety of preserve and pickle is found in the market, the distinctive flavour of the homemade product is often preserved.

Drying

Removal of moisture is of benefit in preserving food. Although it is difficult to dry foods to the point of destroying micro-organisms, it is comparatively easy to dry foods so that no spoilage takes place. All organisms must have food on which to develop and grow and before the food is available to them it must be in a solution which is rather dilute. These micro-organisms obtain food by osmotic action. Drying of foods to prevent spoilage does not necessarily mean complete removal of the water, but it does mean concentration to such a point that the liquid is denser than the body fluid of the organisms. When the liquid outside the cell wall is more dense than that inside, the liquid within tends to be removed from the cell and the body processes are delayed or prevented. Hence, although the food is present it may not be available to the organism which might cause spoilage. Drying may retard enzyme action also, but in vegetables especially, the effect of enzymes is sufficient to cause comparatively rapid deterioration. Scalding to destroy the enzymes is highly beneficial in prolonging the storage life of dehydrated vegetables. Drying alters greatly the character of the food and requires some time for preparation both before and after the process.

23

NOVEL FOODS AND PROCESSED FOODS

Novel Foods

Food industry has brought out some novel protein-rich foods which can be used for combating malnutrition. Some of them are from unusual food sources which were never considered as consumable by our forefathers. Leaf and grass proteins, food yeast, algae and microbial synthesis of proteins from hydrocarbons are some of the novel food sources now available.

Leaf Protein Concentrates

Proteins from fibrous materials of leaf are separated and leaf protein concentrates with 30 to 35 per cent of the original nitrogen can be extracted from leaves. Outstanding work in this field has come from Pine et al in 1961. Leaf protein concentrates can be incorporated with milk or in common flours or dal powders for children's foods.

Food Yeast

Yeast is capable of converting carbohydrate to protein. About 16 to 33 per cent of this type of conversion is possible by yeast. Thus it can be incorporated at 5 to 10 per cent level in children's foods. Food yeast is a pale yellow product. It has a characteristic nut-like taste. This can be incorporated in low cost foods for infants. It can also be used for overcoming protein malnutrition among children.

Algae

A unicellular green algae chlorella contains a protein content of about 50 to 60 per cent. This can be incorporated with soups, noodles and in baked items. Even though it is nutritionally good, its acceptability is very poor.

Microbial Synthesis of Proteins from Hydrocarbons

Certain petroleum hydrocarbons can be converted to proteins through microbial use. Its utilisation for human beings is not established even though as an animal feed it is used.

Processed Foods

Modern technology has made many food sources into processed items. Food industry is developing in accordance with modern living. Almost all food groups are now processed into readymade or ready for table items. Pre-cooked or half cooked items are also available. Examples of some of these items are given below.

Cereals: Starch is a polysaccharide and it is used in cookery. It is manufactured from corn, potato, sweet potato and tapioca. In the market it is available as tapioca starch, arrowroot starch and starch products like sago or custard powder where cornstarch is flavoured with vanilla and edible colour and corn syrup.

Rice is available in processed form as instant rice or quick cooking rice. It is prepared by cooking rice and dehydrating the cooked rice so as to retain a porous structure.

Puffed rice from paddy and from parboiled rice is available in the market.

Cornflakes from corn can be used as a breakfast item.

Barley is processed into barley flour and pearl barley. Malted barley is breakfast item.

Oats is available as oatflakes in processed forms.

Breakfast cereals and infant foods are often prepared from cereals. Flaked items from all cereals, puffed wheat, rice, barley and corn are available in the market. Shredded breakfast cereals like shredded wheat is a pre-cooked item.

Infant Foods

Most of the infant foods contain both cereals and milk and these pre-cooked cereals are eaten as gruels with water or milk. Rice noodles are popular in some of the Far East countries. Sago or sabudana is made from rice, or other cereals. Biscuits and breads are also processed cereal products.

Pulses are processed into puffed grams. Now commercial instant mixes of cereal, dal, fermented products are also available. Ready mixes of South Indian dishes like idli and dosa are prepared by using baker's yeast or baking soda and acidifying agents like citric acid.

Puffed chickpeas and peas and canned dry peas are available as processed items.

Roasted groundnut and protein isolates from soyabean or peanut can be used in the production of toned milk and protein-rich biscuits or bread. Soyabean milk powder and butter are available in the market.

Milk powders, malted milk powders, various weaning foods, ice-cream mix, cream and condensed milk, cheese, khoa-based sweets, channa or paneer-based sweets like rasogolla and sandesh are some of the processed milk products. New milk-derived products like Miltone and Chai-sathi are available, especially in North India.

Fruits are processed into fruit juices. Today even bananas and guavas are used to prepare juice. Fruit juice conentrates and fruit juice powders are made from juices along with syrups or squashes. Cordials, ketchups, sauces, jellies, jams, marmalades, artificial syrups, dried fruit slabs, preserves, candies, glaced and crystallised fruits and fruit-cereal flakes are available in the market as processed foods.

Vegetables are processed into soups, purees, canned or frozen and dehydrated forms.

Egg powder, egg albumin powder, custard or caramelised custard powder and readymade puddings are some of the processed forms of egg available in the market.

Meat is processed into canned meat, cured meat, smoked meat, sausages, cutlets, soup powder and as dehydrated meat.

Strained baby foods with meat are being manufactured in some places.

Fish is processed into frozen, canned and dried forms. Fish protein concentrates and fishmeal and strained baby foods with fish are also available as processed items in developed countries.

All food items are processed in very many ways and they are marketed in various forms. Pickled and fermented items of innumerable sources are also available in the market.

24

FOOD, SANITATION AND HYGIENE

The word 'sanitation' is derived from the Latin word 'Sanus' meaning 'sound and healthy' or clean and whole. The modern interpretation of the term is broad, including knowledge of health and sanitary conditions as well as full acceptance and effective application of sanitary measures. The National Sanitation Foundation, a non-project, non-commercial organisation with headquarters in the School of Public Health at the University of Michigan, proclaims that sanitation is more than religious sanctions or a code of laws in these words:

> Sanitation is a way of life. It is the quality of living that is expressed in the clean home, the clean farm, the clean business and industry, the clean neighbourhood, the clean community. Being a way of life, it must come from within the people, it is nourished by knowledge and grows as an obligation and an ideal in human relations.

So, people need to be protected against food which has been contaminated by bacteria which are harmful. People also need to be protected against the sale of adulterated food, foods of inferior quality and false advertising. Some of these problems require government help; others depend upon individual understanding and vigilance.

Food is frequently subjected to chemical and biological contamination in a number of ways and this has a direct extensive and important bearing on public health. There is clear evidence now that a vast amount of human diseases and suffering is directly due to the consumption of infected and contaminated food.

'Food hygiene' means all measures necessary for ensuring the safety, wholesomeness and soundness of food at all stages from its growth, production, manufacture until its final consumption.

Diseases transmitted by contaminated foods are classifed as

foodborne infections and intoxications. Foodborne infections are usually gastro-intestinal disturbances caused by living organisms, while intoxications are diseases caused by chemical poisons in foods. Poisons may be microbial or non-microbial in origin. Some poisons are even naturally present in foods. Deliberate adulteration of foodstuffs and the use of an ever increasing number of chemicals in agriculture, dairy farming, storage and processing of foods is currently introducing a number of highly toxic substances into present day foods. A knowledge of the variety of toxicants found in foods due to lack of food sanitation and hygiene, faulty methods of cultivation, harvesting, transport, storage, processing, distribution and cooking, is therefore necessary for every consumer.

Freshness of Foods

The importance of an intelligent selection of fruits and vegetables for use in the home must not be ignored. This necessitates a knowledge of characteristics which denote good quality in the various products.

Fruits

Fruits such as apples, pears, peaches, plums and tomatoes should have full colour, a reasonable degree of firmness and an absence of surface defects such as scars and bruises.

Berries

Berries of all sorts and grapes should have full colour, should be firm and have a plump, fresh appearance. They should be dry, clean and free from foreign material, including sand and leaves.

Citrus

Citrus fruits should be well coloured and heavy for their size. They should have a fine-textured bright skin, russetting of the skin, if not extensive, need not adversely affect interior quality. Grapefruit should be flat rather than pointed at the stem end. Oranges should have the rough and loose skins which are characteristic of this variety of fruit.

Salad plants

Salad plants and greens which include spinach, should be of good colour, fresh, crisp, and tender. They should be free from wilted or yellow leaves. Headed types of salad plants like some varieties of lettuce should be fairly firm. Carrots and other root vegetables should be firm, of good shape, clean and fresh looking. The pods of lima beans, peas and all vegetables of similar type should be of a good green colour and well filled with seeds. They should be clean and bright in appearance and crisp and firm in texture. Snap beans should be of a healthy green or yellow colour according to the variety. The pods should be clean and fresh in appearance and firm, tender and crisp in texture. The enclosed beans should be small. Cauliflowers should be either white or creamy-white in colour. The head should be firm and compact, not open and loose, a condition which is indicative of growth of the flower clusters. Broccoli should be of a good dark green colour. The clusters of buds should be compact and should not show any of the purple or yellow colour of the flower. The stems should be tender, firm and crisp. Potatoes should be smooth, shallow-eyed and free from any green coloration. The colour of skin and the size and shape of this vegetable vary with variety. Onions should be dry, hard, bright and well developed.

Selection of Eggs

The shell of an egg may be either off-white or white in colour depending upon the breed of the hen producing it. But irrespective of colour, the shell of a fresh egg always has a delicate velvety appearance called "bloom" that is due to the protective mucous coating with which the shell is supplied when the egg is laid. The inner air cell of fresh egg is small. The egg contents, when broken out from the shell show an upstanding, well coloured yolk covered with a clinging layer of thick egg-white which, in turn, is surrounded by a relatively smaller amount of thin egg-white. The yolk may be either golden or light yellow in colour depending upon the amount of carotenoid pigments contained in it, and the white is practically colourless or possibly slightly opalescent. There is no odour other than that characteristic of an egg and upon being put to food use the flavour will be excellent.

Meat

Good quality requirements are as follows: The flesh must be firm, the fasciculi should be small, contributing thereby a fine grain and velvety texture to the lean part of the cut. The colour of the flesh must be characteristic of the animal origin—a bright cherry-red for beef, pinkish red for lamb, and greyish pink for veal and pork. The bone must be relatively small and when cut, must be red and spongy in appearance, denoting youth; this is in contrast to white, hard and flint-like bone which denotes age. The fat must be white and firm and there must be plenty of marbling. Finally there must be a relatively small proportion of connective tissues.

Fish

Fish is a food that deteriorates quickly unless handled with great care. When buying fish from the market the purchaser should be able to recognise the characteristics that indicate freshness of the product. Some of these are: Vertebrate fish: the gills should be bright red, the eyes clean, bright and slightly bulging. The flesh should be firm and, when pressed with a finger, sufficiently elastic to spring back into place. Shell-fish: those such as lobsters and crabs should be alive when purchased, shrimps should have firm not flabby bodies, oysters, clams and the like should be alive and their shells tightly closed or if relaxed they should be closed when the fish is handled. Always the odour of fish should be fresh with no suggestion of putrefaction.

Milk

The quality of milk is determined by the grades given to it. The criteria for grading milk as laid down by the Milk Ordinance and Code are on the basis of (1) the bacterial count per given volume of the milk as determined by laboratory investigation, and (2) whether the milk comes from daily farms which meets with designated requirements.

Certified Milk is milk which conforms to the requirements of the Medical Milk Commission and is produced under the supervision of the state or local board of health. It may either be raw or pasteurised. Such milk is the highest quality of milk obtainable and is often used for infant feeding.

Grade A Raw Milk must not exceed the limit of bacterial count permitted and it must meet the highest standards of sanitary production.

Grade A Pasteurised Milk must be of similar quality with these differences: Before pasteurisation the bacterial count may be higher than for raw milk of this grade; but after pasteurisation, it must be lower for grade A pasteurised than for grade A raw milk.

Grade B Milks, raw and pasteurised fall below the standards set for raw and pasteurised milk of grade A quality, but they must none the less meet specified criteria, both the limit of bacterial load and sanitary conditions of production that are permitted for raw milks of these grades.

Grade C Milks Raw and Pasteurised are products which violate the requirements for grade B products raw or pasteurised. Such milk should be used only for cookery purposes. This is especially true of the grade C raw milk.

Fats

Fats and oils may have one or more of five principal uses in the average institution food service. The uses may be as a spread on breads and toasts; flavouring or it may be an ingredient of a sauce or dressing for raw or cooked foods such as white sauce, mayonnaise, French dressing and tartar sauce. Another use is in frying, basting and other methods of cooking food. Lastly, for shortening, as in the making of doughs and batters. In each case, flavour, form and other physical and chemical characteristics, as well as food habits to which we are accustomed, influence the choice of fat and its use.

Colour, flavour, odour, consistency, keeping quality and nutritive value are important factors to keep in mind when selecting fat for the purpose of spreading or seasoning. Added to the above would be the emulsifying property and stability under heat for fats to be included in sauces and cooked foods. Oils are used in salad dressings and in browning and frying.

Fat for frying or shortening should be bland and should impart no flavour of its own to the fried food. It should resist rancidity and have a high smoking point, long frying life and low turnover or absorption by the food.

Cereals and Cereal Products

These include wheat, rice and corn in their various forms. The kinds of cereal grains are the dried fruits of grasses and although the seed structure varies characteristically with each kind, there are basic similarities among all of them. The first is the likeness of the kernel to a well-wrapped sealed parcel. If the package is broken, the possibilities of rancidity increase. Early measures taken to prevent rancidity in milled products include removal of the germ in the process of refining the cereal which reduces the national nutritive value of the cereal. Regarding rice, brown rice has a higher fat content and a high nutritive value.

Food Poisoning

Bacteria enter the body through either food or water from a contaminated source and cause poisoning which, in the majority of cases, turns out to be fatal. Practices to prevent food poisoning are:

1. Observe the rules of food hygiene at every stage in the handling of food. People known to be harbouring infections should not be allowed to handle foodstuffs in the critical stages of preparation and distribution.

2. Keep perishable foods under deep-freeze or refrigeration immediately after purchase to prevent multiplication of bacteria already present. The refrigerator should be kept clean and foodstuffs must be placed in it in such a way that cold air can freely circulate around different items. This is to make sure that the foodstuffs kept in the fridge are cooled rapidly and kept cold. No spoiled food should be placed in a refrigerator.

3. Cook foods for a sufficient length of time and at temperatures high enough to destroy the bacteria. Meat should be cut into small pieces to ensure thorough penetration of heat. If required in large chunks meat should be roasted or pressure cooked.

4. Do not keep foods exposed, especially after cooking. If the food is to be consumed later, it should be promptly cooled and put in the refrigerator.

5. If the food has been refrigerated for a long time, it should be reheated before consumption.

6. Foodstuffs such as custard-filled bakery products should be reheated in an oven at 200° C for 20 to 30 minutes before consumption.

7. Keep storage, cooking and service areas clean and free from insects and rodents.

Thus, careful selection of foodstuffs and observing certain food sanitation measures prevent all the food-borne infections and other diseases which are hazardous to health.

25

FOOD ADULTERATION AND CONSUMER PROTECTION

The practice of adulteration of foodstuffs and marketing of substandard or materials of poor quality is widely prevalent in our country. It has been roughly estimated that over 50 per cent of marketed foodstuffs available today are adulterated in one way or another. The percentage varies from region to region. It is an unpalatable fact for a nation to admit, but there is little doubt that the Indian consumer, unlike his Western counterpart, cannot take the purity of foodstuffs for granted. Despite the existence of legislation to prevent adulteration of foodstuffs, a very large number offered to the consumer today are injurious to health.

One of the causes of adulteration is that there is a wide gap between production and supply of food articles. The temptation for quick gain and easy profits amongst most merchants, slow action by the authorities, the poor enforcement of Prevention of Food Adulteration Act and leniency shown to traders in regard to the enforcement of the laws on food safety, lengthy procedural wrangles and delays, due to various loopholes in our legal system, contribute to the rampant adulteration of foodstuffs. The gullibility of the predominantly illiterate masses coupled with ignorance, apathy and indifference make for easy adulteration. In a developing country, the cost factor is the most crucial point for a large segment of the population, the cheapest product is preferred to the best. There are a large number of mushroom industries to cater to this section.

Almost all foods, milk, cereals, dals, spices, ghee, oils and beverages are adulterated. The adulterant used generally mixes well with the major food article in colour, shape, size and appearance. The more highly priced foods and those foods which are in great demand are the ones more often widely adulterated. By adulterating the foodstuffs, the merchant is benefited in many ways. First more weight is added to the commodity. Secondly, addition of colour improves the appearance of the product and hence substandard product can fetch higher price. Thirdly, new product when combined with the old one, lowers the quality and at the same time substandard commodity is sold at a higher rate. The ingenuity, imagination and initiative shown in adulteration make it difficult for an average buyer to detect it at first sight. Sometimes, it can be detected only in well-equipped laboratories. Besides the relatively harmless forms of adulteration like addition of water to milk, moisture to butter, mixing of edible oils with cheaper edible oils, many types of adulteration are positively injurious to health.

Rice and pulses are often polished with talc, a silicate containing asbestos fibre, which is not removed even after washing, cleaning and cooking. The Japanese have traced cases of stomach cancer to this practice. The other common adulterants used in cereals such as rice and wheat are clay particles, grit, soap stone and weed seeds. Most yellow pulses are adulterated either with kesari dal or by polishing with metanil yellow, a cheap soluble coal tar dye that makes the pulses deceptively brighter and cleaner looking. Metanil yellow is a highly toxic substance with accumulative tendencies, which over the years build up enough toxicity in the body to cause testicular degeneration in the male. When kesari dal is consumed continuously for a few months, it results in the development of lathyrism, a permanent paralysis of the lower limbs.

Spices, particularly because of their high cost, are the most adulterated item in food commodities. Turmeric is coated with lead chromate or metanil yellow to give a lustrous yellow colour. Black pepper is sometimes mixed with papaya berries. Foodgrains and pulses are often indiscriminately sprayed with insecticides to prevent infestation or to destroy pests; chillies are soaked in soluble coal tar dyes to give them a deeper hue, while sawdust, blackgram husk, and used tea leaves are utilised for adulterating tea dust/leaves. These are a few of the many common practices that are used today. Many cheap sweets, sherbets in variety of colours and ice fruits are adulterated with many non-permitted coal tar dyes. These undesirable colours can impair the liver and can be the cause of cancers. Similarly, lead chromate when added to turmeric powder can cause lead poisoning resulting in stiffness of limbs and paralysis. Mineral oils and other non-edible oils when mixed with edible oils can induce nausea, purging, impaired liver functions and cancer. Continuous use of mustard oil with more than 11 per cent argemone seed oil causes the disease 'epidemic dropsy' in people. Further, many mould-infested grains and oil seeds are further processed into flours and oils. Here the main danger is due to the mould growth which produces many hidden toxic substances called mycotoxins. These can cause various diseases and they act as nervous and neurotoxins impairing the general health. Some also have been found to be carcinogenic.

The menace of food adulteration exists all over the world. In developed countries, due to the implementation of food laws for the last few decades, there has been a significant improvement in the quality of food. But due to tremendous improvement in food industry and technology, various chemical substances like artificial colours, preservatives, antioxidants, emulsifiers, flavour and taste improvers are increasingly being used. Some of these pose a great threat to the health of the people. As against this, in developing countries adulteration is found to be rampant even in primary articles of food like milk, ghee, edible oils and foodgrains. Shortage of food and spiralling prices have aggravated the problem. Thus all countries in the world have to grapple in their own way with problems raised by food adulteration.

Food Legislation in India

In India, as early as in 1860, adulteration of food was dealt with in certain sections of the Indian Penal Code (Sec. 272, 273). Later it was included under the provisions of the Municipal Act. But as a comprehensive act, it was first promulgated in Bombay State in 1899. Subsequently similar acts were enacted by other states also. In the erstwhile Travancore State an Act—The Travancore Prevention of Adulteration Act—was enacted in 1931. Besides food adulteration, adulteration of other articles was also made an offence under this act. But then acts were not comprehensive in many ways. The punishment prescribed was not deterrent enough to prevent adulteration of food efficiently. There was no uniformity of standards prescribed for various food articles. The necessity of a comprehensive act applicable to all the states was felt. In 1938 the Central Advisory Board of Health was established. This Board in its report stressed the necessity for efficiently tackling the problem by all states. When the Constitution of India was framed the topic of prevention of adulteration of food was brought under the concurrent list and the P.F.A. Act was formulated in 1954. It was enacted on June 1, 1955. After about ten years of implementation of the Act, the position was reviewed and some amendments were made in the Act in 1964 to plug loopholes and to give more protection to the honest traders. Again in 1976 some other important amendments were made to the present act to make it more effective and purposeful. These amendments came into force from April 1, 1976.

Object of the Act

What the consumer wants is genuine, wholesome food, of nutritive value, free from any health hazard. He also expects that labelling must be truthful and there shall not be fraudulent claims of any kind by any statement, device or design. The interest of the trader is not only to sell the food articles to the consumers but also to make the maximum profit out of it. This conflicting interest of the consumer on the one hand and the traders on the other, lead to unhealthy practices in trade. It is to prevent such practices that the Act has been made. Though the consumer's interest is the foremost in the P.F.A. Act, that of the traders have also been accommodated reasonably as far as scientific grounds and consumers' interest permit.

Important Provisions of the Act

Food has been defined under the Act as articles other than drugs and water, which are ordinarily used as food or drink and all articles which enter into and are used in the preparation of human food. Another definition of 'primary food' has also been introduced by the amendment act of 1976. Primary foods are products of agriculture or horticulture in its natural form.

Adulterated Food

The term adulterated has been defined under Section 2 of the Act: An article of food will be deemed to be adulterated if it is not of the nature, substance or quality demanded by the purchaser and is to his prejudice or not of the nature, substance or quality which it purports to be; if an article is partly or wholly substituted by the cheaper substance; if any constituent of the article is extracted from it, if it is prepared or exposed for sale under insanitary and unhygienic surrounding; if it contains prohibited colouring matter or preservative or permitted colouring matters and preservatives in excess of the permissible limits; if it does not conform to the standards under all these conditions it will be deemed to be adulterated. (There is a provison that a primary food will not be deemed to be adulterated if it does not conform to standards due to natural causes beyond the control of human agency.) In short, anything which lowers the quality of a food article has been brought under the definition of adulteration.

Misbranding

Sale of food articles without proper labelling, imitation of other food articles and coating food articles to give improved appearance are brought under the definition 'misbranding'.

Prohibitory Section

Section 7 of the P.F.A. Act prohibits the sale of (a) any adulterated food, (b) any misbranded food, (c) any article of food for the sale of which a licence is prescribed except in accordance with the conditions of the licence, (d) any article of food and sale of which has been prohibited by the Food (Health) Authority in the interest of public health, (e) any article of food in contravention of the provision of the Act and Rules, and (f) any adulterant.

Crime and Punishment

Infringement of the provision of Section 7 is punishable under Section 16. Various offences and punishments for each have been detailed under these sections. This section has been amended by the amendment act of 1976. Non-graded punishment, depending on the nature of the offence has been laid down. For the sale of adulterated food the minimum punishment is six month's imprisonment and a fine of rupees one thousand. If the adulterant is of such a nature as to cause death or grievous hurt when consumed by a person, the punishment is imprisonment for a term of three years which may extend to life imprisonment and a fine which shall not be less than rupees five thousand. Punishment has been prescribed for sale of misbranded food and the sale of adulterant. Preventing a Food Inspector from exercising his powers and duties under the Act, using a report of the Public Analyst of Director of Central Food Laboratory for advertising purposes, not issuing warranty, issuing false warranty, tampering of seized food articles are all punishable under the law.

Protection of the Traders

Section 7 of the Act prohibits the sale of adulterated food or any consumable article, by any person either by himself or by any person on his behalf. Prima facie it may seem that an innocent person who buys a food article from a wholesaler or manufacturer and sells it without knowing that it is adulterated is punishable under the Act. Sections 14,

14A, 19(2) and 20A are meant to protect honest vendors of food articles. Section 14 lays down that no manufacturer, distributor or dealer of any article of food shall sell such article to any vendor unless he also gives a warranty in writing about the nature of substance and quality of such food to the vendor. Insistence of warranty at the time of sale by the manufacturer, distributor or dealer would make it easy to pin down the responsibility with the offender. The amendment of 1976 makes this easier by incorporating a provision that a cash bill can also be considered as a warranty. According to Section 14A, the vendor has to disclose to the Food Inspector the name, address and other particulars of the person from whom he purchased the food article. This helps the Food Inspector to proceed against the warrantor also. According to Section 19(2) of the Act, a vendor shall not be deemed to have committed an offence if he proves that he purchased the food article with a proper warranty, that he stored the article properly and that he sold it in the same condition in which it was purchased. Section 19(3) confers a right on the warrantor to appear in court and give evidence. The law thus protects the warrantor also against spurious warranties. When warranty is proved, the vendor can be exonerated and the warrantor can be proceeded against. As per Section 20A during the trial, when warranty is proved the court can proceed against the warrantor as though a prosecution has been launched against him.

Standards for Ensuring Quality of Products

There are two standards set up by the government to help the manufacturers, the traders and the consumers to ensure quality. They are 'Agmark' standard and 'Indian Standards Institution' mark.

Agmark Standard

The Directorate of Marketing and Inspection of the Government of India have set up this standard. This grades goods into (1) Special (Grade I), (2) Good (Grade II), (3) Fair (Grade III) and Ordinary (Grade IV). These standards also specify the type of packaging to be used for different products. An Agmark certificate is issued to traders and the mark on commodities provides assurance of the quality to the consumer.

Indian Standards Institution (ISI)

The ISI mark on food is a guarantee of good quality. This institution prescribes standards for various food items and issues certificates to traders.

Common Food Adulterants

Foodstuffs	Common adulterants
Milk and milk products	Water, removal of butter and addition of refined oil.
Milk, liquid	Fat addition of skimmed milk reconstituted from skimmed milk powder.
Milk powder	Starch, dextrins.
Cream	Other fats.
Ice-cream	Non-permitted colour, artificial sweetness, other fats and gelling agents.
Butter	Other fats.
Ghee	Hydrogenated fat.
Vegetables oils and fats	
Vanaspati	Animal fat and other high melting fats.
Vegetable oil	Argemone oil, mineral oil, orthotricresyl phosphate, cheap non-edible oils.
Spices and condiments	
Whole turmeric	Coating of lead chromate or coal-tar dyes.
Turmeric powder	Coal-tar colour, yellow earth, starch or talc coloured yellow by coal-tar dye.
Curry powder	Starch coloured brown by coal-tar dyes.
Coriander seeds	Other seeds coloured green.
Coriander seed powder	Powdered bran or sawdust coloured green with dye.
Chilli powder	Starch coloured red by coal-tar dye.
Mustard	Argemone seeds.
Cumin	Artificial jeera like product.
Black pepper	Dried papaya seeds.
Asafoetida	Resins and other plant gums.
Cereals	
Wheat and rice	Stones.
Wheat flour	Tapioca flour, talc.
Semolina	Tapioca semolina.

Foodstuffs	*Common adulterants*
Pulses	
Bengal gram dal	Kesari dal (Lathyrus sativus)
Red gram dal	Coloured yellow with coal-tar dye.
Bengal gram flour	Tapioca flour or starch coloured yellow with dye.
Sweetening agents and soft drinks	
Honey	Coloured canesugar syrup.
Soft drinks	Artificial sweeteners (Saccharin).
Beverages	
Coffee powder	Exhausted coffee powder, roasted husk or date seed or tamarind seed powder.
Tea	Other leaves with added colour, exhausted tea leaves.
Miscellaneous	
Processed arecanut (Supari)	Other seeds or nuts broken and coloured.

Consumer Protection

For consumer protection there are a number of laboratories in central and state level. They are set up to collect samples and to analyse it.

Some of the Government agencies are: (1) Municipal Laboratories in big cities. (2) Food and Drug Administration Laboratories of States. (3) Central Food Testing Laboratory of the Government of India, and (4) Laboratories of the Export Inspection Council.

Municipal Laboratories

In municipalities of big cities like Bombay, Delhi, Madras and Calcutta they have set up their own testing laboratories. According to the Prevention of Food Adulteration Act the Municipal analyst qualification must be scrutinised. Chemical and microbiological analysis of all kinds of foods are essential in the laboratory. Nutrient analysis like fat content of milk, contamination of water or pesticide residue in parts per million in foods etc. are some examples of the test conducted there.

These laboratories are under the Health Officer of the state. Health inspectors under him make periodical rounds of the various wards and collect samples of food suspected to be adulterated. Samples are sealed in the presence of the vendor and witness and sent to the municipal laboratory for analysis. The Health Officer can take action against the manufacturer of the food if he is found to be guilty. The manufacturer can defend himself in the court of law. Depending on the severity of crime he can be punished by a fine or imprisonment or both.

Food and Drug Administration

Some state Governments have laboratories throughout states. The Director of the Administration is empowered through his staff to collect samples which are suspected to be adulterated and have them analysed by the Health Officer of a municipality. The Food and Drug Administration has jurisdiction all over the state as compared to municipal laboratories which work only within city limits.

The Central Food Testing Laboratory

The Government of India has established a Central Food Testing Laboratory in Calcutta for carrying out analysis of all foods. These laboratories are very well equipped and carry out even sophisticated and sensitive analyses. These laboratories are the ultimate authority in determining whether a food sample is adulterated or not in cases of conflicting reports of analyses from two laboratories, the authorities concerned usually refer the case to this laboratory. Usually analysis carried out by these laboratories are accepted as the last word in analysis of food.

Export Inspection Council Laboratory

The Government of India has made it mandatory for all exporters to have their products analysed so as to ensure the quality of foods exported. Frozen food items like seafood, canned fruits and vegetables are also analysed before export. It also sees to it that all the foods exported conform to the minimum requirements as laid down by the council. The council has laboratories in all the major parts and the samples analysed. Without the council's certificate no food can be exported.

Voluntary Agencies

Quality Control Laboratories of Companies

Most of the companies which manufacture food products have well equipped quality control laboratories to check the quality of their products. The ingredients used for manufacturing and the products are examined physically, chemically and microbiologically. The taste, weight, volume, colour, keeping quality, packaging all these factors are checked.

In the dairy industry microbiological centre of the milk, are taken and the fat content determined, the former gives an idea of the sanitary condition under which the milk was collected, the latter whether any cream had been removed. Proper pasteurisation is also checked before supply.

In canning fruits and vegetables the fresh materials are visually inspected and all the bruised and spoiled ones removed. Oxidity of fruits like mangoes, cherries, tenderness of vegetables like green peas are determined to estimate duration of processing time, accelerated storage tests at higher temperature one conducted to ensure the keeping quality of the canned food.

In freezing, quality control checks at various stages of processing are carried out to see that the final frozen product conforms to the prescribed microbiological standards, weights after thawing and drying are taken to make sure that the customer gets the right weight. Biscuit, dairy, fruit and vegetable canning industries set up their quality.

Quality Control Laboratories of Consumer Cooperation

Apna Bazar in Bombay, Super Bazar in Delhi, Chinthamani in Coimbatore have criteria for selection of food items which they sell in their shop. If the qualities are not fulfilled they will not accept materials.

Testing Laboratories

There are a number of private testing laboratories which carry out tests of all food materials on payment. Government has recognised certain private laboratories and certificates given by them are valid for legal purposes.

Consumer Guidance Society

A consumer guidance society has been formed in India with Bombay as its headquarters and with branches in major cities. They create consumer awareness of the various forms of adulteration and develop consumer resistance to such adulterated food products through various communications and mass media.

26

FOOD GROUPS AND GUIDELINES FOR FOOD SELECTION

The ultimate aim of consuming food is to maintain health. There is no single foodstuff which can contribute all the nutrients needed by the body. Only a judicious selection can provide all the nutrients in required amount. In order to select the sources of all nutrients and that also in correct proportion one must know about the basic principles of food selection. The nutritionists and food scientists all over the world have put in a lot of efforts to formulate certain guidelines in these matters. Basic food groups suitable to different countries were evolved by the nutritionists.

The US Department of Agriculture suggested a number of food group plans like the Basic-4 food group.

The Basic-7 Food Group and the Basic-11 Group Plan

The Nutrition Expert group of L.C.M.R. (India) suggested a five-food group plan.

Based on their nutritive values foods are grouped into 11. They are:

1. Cereals and millets
2. Pulses (legumes)
3. Nuts and oil seeds
4. Vegetables
5. Fruits
6. Milk and milk products
7. Egg
8. Meat, fish and other fleshy foods
9. Fats and oils
10. Sugar and jaggery
11. Spices and condiments.

In an Indian diet this classification has great significance.

Cereals and Millets

They supply the major portion of calories (70%), more than 50 per cent of B Vitamins. In a poor vegetarian diet cereals supply more than 70 per cent of protein.

Rice and wheat are abundantly used as staple cereals in the world. In India rice is used mainly in the diet of South India, whereas wheat is the main staple in all other parts.

The major millets used are jowar, ragi and bajra. Though they are cheaper they are superior in their mineral supply and protein content. Ragi is a very good source of calcium.

Pulses and legumes are fair sources of proteins and they are good sources of B vitamins, especially thiamine and riboflavin. Quantitatively their protein content is high but qualitatively they are not as superior as animal proteins. But in an Indian diet cereals and pulses supplement mutually in their amino acid content and improve the quality of protein. Pulses and legumes are comparatively cheap sources of protein. Cowgram, horsegram, soyabean, dry field beans and dried peas are some of the cheap pulses.

Nuts and oilseeds are fair sources of protein. Coconut is a good source of energy. It has also fair sources of B vitamin. Vegetables are unique in their vitamins and mineral content. Vegetables are again grouped into yellow vegetables, leafy vegetables and as other vegetables. Yellow vegetables and leafy vegetables are rich sources of vitamin 'A' (carotene), calcium, iron, folic acid, riboflavin and vitamin 'C'. But the iron content in vegetables is comparatively poorly utilised by the body. Other vegetables are good sources of minerals like calcium, trace elements and vitamin 'C'.

Apart from these, vegetables have a high percentage of water in them. They contribute the alkaline ash and the bulk or cellulose to the body. Beetroot, carrot and ladiesfinger are high in sodium content. Fruits, especially citrus fruits, are good sources of ascorbic acid. Some starchy fruits are rich in fructose and dextrose; yellow fruits contribute carotene, the provitamin A. Fruits as a group supply water and electrolytes like potassium. Most of the fruits are rich sources of potassium and poor sources of sodium. Dates, dry raisins, grapes, peaches, lime and ripe papaya are very high in their potassium content.

Bananas are rich in starch content in the raw form and in sugar content in the ripe form.

Milk and milk products are the best sources of calcium and ribo-flavin and second to the meat groups in protein content. Except in iron and vitamin 'C' milk is good in all other nutrients. Milk products are high in biological value and milk cream is excellent in vitamin A.

Egg has biologically very good protein. Egg white is rich in protein and egg yolk is rich in fat, iron, sodium, potassium, calcium and magnesium. Vitamins like thiamine, riboflavin, vitamins A and D are also present in egg. It plays very many roles in cookery.

Meat, fish and other flesh foods rank first in protein content. They are also good sources of phosphorous, magnesium, iron, thiamine, niacin, B 6, and B 12. The biological value of meat protein is high. Fat is present in a good quantity in it.

Fats and oils contribute mainly calories and they are good sources of essential fatty acids and vitamins A and E.

Sugar and jaggery are the common sweetening agents in our diet. They are rich sources of carbohydrate.

Spices and condiments are necessary foodstuffs used for flavouring foods. Apart from these functions some of them contribute certain nutrients. Red chillies and coriander supply carotene; green chillies vitamin 'C', turmeric and tamarind iron; and garlic stimulates synthesis of certain vitamins.

Then food is classified into 11 groups for convenience in selection.

But in different countries different food group plans are followed by the nutritionists to formulate a balanced diet.

In India the nutrition expert group of ICMR suggested the five-food group plans.

They are given below:

Group	Nutrients
1. *Milk group*	
This consists of milk and milk products and protein-rich foods like pulses, nuts, meat, fish and egg.	This group supplies proteins, minerals and vitamins.

2. *Fruits and green leafy vegetables*

Fruits like papaya, orange, mango, Indian gooseberry, guava and green leafy vegetables like spinach, amaranthus, drumstick leaves.	Rice sources of vitamin 'C', vitamin A (carotene), minerals and roughage.

3. *Other vegetables*

Peas, beans, drumsticks, ladiesfingers, bringals, cucumber, bittergourd, ashgourd, plantain etc.	They are fair to good sources of minerals, vitamins and roughage and water content.

4. *Cereals, roots and tubers*

Rice, wheat, maize, ragi corn, tapioca, potato, sweet potato, yam, colocacia etc.	Rich sources of starch, fair to good sources of proteins and B vitamins. In an Indian diet this group supplies about 75-80 per cent of calories and 50-60 per cent of proteins.

5. *Fats and oils and pure carbohydrate foods*

Butter, ghee, vegetable oils, sugar, jaggery, honey, starch and egg powders, custard powders etc.	They are rich sources of energy, essential fatty acids, vitamins A and E and cholesterol.

When these food groups were suggested they were known as Basic groups. Basic-7 food group plan, Basic-4 food group plan, and Basic-11 food group plan of US Department of Agriculture was the first in these series. Basic dietary pattern and daily food guides were suggested by different nutrition boards. In India the National Institute of Nutrition of ICMR has done remarkable work in this field. Guidelines for a balanced diet, composition of balanced diet and balanced diet for different regions of India, viz., balanced diets for the eastern region, northern region, southern region and western region were suggested by the NIN and it was periodically revised based on their advanced research in this field. Guidelines for low-cost balanced diets were prepared by them for a student of nutrition. In our Indian background this has great significance.

27

MEAL PLANNING

Planning a balanced diet within the income level needs precise knowledge about the sources of nutrients, their requirements for various groups, seasonal availability of various foodstuffs and dietary habits of the group.

Blending these theoretical knowledge into a day's menu needs skill which has to be acquired through practice. There are certain basic principles which has to be observed while planning a balanced diet. As the name indicates a planned diet should be balanced. A diet is called balanced when all the nutrients required by the body are present in correct proportion. A judicious selection from the food groups will supply adequate nutrients for maintenance, repair and growth. Other factors to be considered are compositon of the family and the physiological phases of family members, dietary habits of the family, food budget of the family, variety in meal patterns, appearance, texture and taste of meals, selection of food for seasons (cold and hot climate condition) and nutritional balance.

While planning a diet, the composition of the family has to be considered. Infants, children, teenagers, pregnant and lactating mothers and geriaric people need food in different amounts. There are variation in their nutritional requirements and their digestive capacity. Quality and quantity and often the preparation need certain changes. A careful planning gives provisions for all these without making great changes in the preparation pattern of foods.

Dietary habits of the family also have to be considered while meal planning. Food habits are influenced by earlier experiences in life: sensory, aesthetic, economic, geographic, social and cultural factors. Often food habits change according to the new environment, new values and availability of items. When a child is exposed to group feeding practices slight changes in likes and dislikes of foods are common. Age and sex also influence food choices. The best example is an adolescent's dietary habits. There are vegetarian, non-vegetarian, lacto-aro-vegetarian and pesco-vegetarian dietary habits (plant foods and fish but no milk, egg, meat or poultry).

Food budget is a very important factor in meal planning. Money available to buy food items, time available for food preparation, job pattern, lifestyle of the family members, location of residence, and family values decide how much has to be spent on food. First of all to reduce food expenditure, one must have an idea about low cost nourishing foods for selection. Intelligent selection, good marketing, just enough bulk purchase, seasonal buying, food processing and preservation, better food preparation methods, avoiding more indulgence in ready-to-eat foods, fast foods, readymade food and hotel catering reduce food budget.

Variety in meal makes eating a pasure. The same meal, if repeated, creates monotonous taste and reduces appetite. Variety in choice of food items, methods of preparation in colour, texture and flavour induce appetite and provide satiety value to the meal. When food is prepared in a proper form with characteristic taste and flavour, it derives satiety value.

Above all these factors, a nutritional balance in each meal is essential. Successful meal planning principles suggest that each meal must be nutritionally balanced. One-third of the total nutrients must be in the lunch, one-third in the dinner and the remaining one-third in breakfast and teatime. Skipping a meal is not good. Many people often skip breakfast which is very bad as far as the body is concerned. Studies have showed that the performance of a person after mid-morning is very poor if they skip their breakfast.

Based on these principles, if a diet is planned it will be a balanced one. The Indian Council of Medical Research has suggested the amounts of various food items to make a balanced diet for various groups.

Some Clues for Different Balanced Diet

Low Cost B.D.

Millets, cereals, roots and tubers, pulses and leafy vegetables can be included liberally. Cheap seasonal fruits and salad vegetables lend attraction and freshness to the diets.

Balanced Diet at Moderate Cost

Balanced diets of middle income groups can include moderate amounts of protective and proteins-rich food. Milk, egg, fish and meat can be included in moderate amounts while pulses, nuts, fruits and other foods can be used in liberal amounts.

Balanced Diets for High Cost

In a high cost diet protective foods and protein-rich foods can be included liberally. Diet surveys in India have shown that malnutrition is prevalent among high class people also. B vitamins and certain minerals are not included in enough quantities in their dietaries. Over-nutrition due to high consumption of milk, meat, fats, ghee and sweets are common.

Part III
NUTRITION
IN
HEALTH

28

BALANCED DIETS

Everyone knows that good diet is needed to sustain good health. By health we mean the well-being of an individual in physical, emotional and social conditions. Just the presence or absence of a disease cannot label a person as healthy. Sound emotional and mental condition of an individual is contributed by good nutrition. A healthy person will have a positive attitude towards life. A good natured person full of life reflects his better health standards. A good or adequate diet is known as 'balanced diet'. A balanced diet yields daily nutrients in the proper amounts and proportion required by the body.

Nutritional requirements vary according to age, sex, physical activities and other physiological conditions. The National Institute of Nutrition is engaged in research work on the dietary pattern of Indians and their requirements of various nutrients. The Nutrition Advisory Committee of the Indian Council of Medical Research made recommendations in 1944 for all nutrients. They were revised in 1958 and 1968. In 1980 further recommendations were made by the Nutrition Advisory Committee and the latest requirements are available now for formulating balanced diets for various groups. A balanced diet must supply enough food to the body for deriving energy. Energy is simply expressed as the capacity to do work. For basic activities like heart beat, breathing and excretion energy is required. Energy is stored as carbohydrate in foods. Cereals like rice, wheat, millets like ragi or bajra contain much carbohydrates in the form of starch. Starchy fruits like banana and roots like tapioca, potato, yam, colocasia and sweet potato are rich in carbohydrates. Energy requirements for various age groups are given elsewhere and for an adult sedentary man 2,400 kcals are required and for a sedentary woman 1,900 kcals are recommended. In a balanced diet energy from cereals should not exceed more than 75 per cent of total requirements. Energy derived from fat or oil should not exceed 15 per cent of the total calories and from refined carbohydrates (sugar and jaggery) has been recommended around 5 per cent of the total calories.

A balanced diet must supply enough protein for building up our tissues in various parts of our body. When some tissues get worn out or used up proteins repair and replace them. Proteins are essential for the secretion of digestive juices and synthesis of enzymes and hormone production. Dietary proteins are used again for the synthesis of body proteins. Protein requirements must be met by dietary proteins. Usually protein requirement is in terms of body weight, that is, 1 gm of protein per kg body weight is the recommendation. Even though animal proteins are of superior quality it is not a practical suggestion to depend on them for dietary proteins. In an average Indian diet pulses are a very important source of proteins. When nutritional scores are given to various proteins egg has a high score of 90 per cent whereas vegetable proteins score only 45 to 50 per cent in the case of pulses and 45 per cent to cereals. But it can be improved by incorporating pulse and cereal proteins; 40 to 60 gms of pulses and 150 to 250 ml of milk can provide enough proteins in a vegetarian diet. For non-vegetarians 20 to 30 gms of pulses and one egg or 30 gms of meat or fish and 100 to 150 ml of milk provide the protein requirement. If no pulse is used non-vegetarians can take two eggs or 50 gms of meat or fish or 30 gms of fish or meat and one egg.

Fats and oils are other major nutrients in a balanced diet. Fats are concentrated forms of energy. Fat soluble vitamins are utilised only in the presence of fat. For males 40 to 65 gms of fat and for females 20 to 45 gms of fat must be included in a balanced diet. Vitamins are essential for the proper functioning of our body. Small quantities of vitamins show dramatic effect on our body. Organs like eyes, alimentary canal, skin and mucous membraneous structures depend on vitamins for their normal structure and functions. Leafy vegetables, other vegetables, yellow vegetables and roots and tubers provide almost all the vitamins required by our body. About a quarter kilogramme of vegetables is required in our daily diet to ensure vitamin supply. Raw vegetables or sprouted grams or fruits are essential to supply vitmain C. Minerals like calcium, phosphorus, iron and trace elements and salts are essential to maintain good health. Sodium chloride is essential to regulate water metabolism in our body. A balanced diet provides enough vitamins and minerals from natural sources. Tonics or supplements are not required for people who consume balanced diets. The Indian Council of Medical Research has designed Recommended Dietary Allowances for various nutrients. They have also formulated composition of balanced diet for various groups. These allowances are designed to serve as a guideline for planning diets. Suggestions are given for substituting foods for non-vegetarians and additional allowances during special conditions.

Recommended Dietary Intake of Nutri:mts: 1989 Revision

Body		Calories (Kcals)	Proteins (gm)	Calcium (gm)	Iron (micro gm)	Retinol (micro gm)	Carotene (gms)	Thiamine (mg)	Ribo-flavin (mg)	Niacin (mg)	Vit.C (ms)	Vit.D. (iu)
Male												
60 kg	Sedentary worker	2350	60		28	600	2400	1.2	1.4	16	40	400
	Moderate worker	2700		0.4-05				1.4	1.6	18	"	"
	Heavy worker	3200						1.6	1.9	21	"	"
Female												
50 kg	Sedentary worker	1800	50		30	600	2400	.9	1.1	12	"	"
	Moderate worker	2100		" "				1.1	1.3	14	"	"
	Heavy worker	2450	+15					1.2	1.5	16	"	"
	During pregnancy	+300	+25	1	38	950	3800	+0.2	+0.2	+2	"	"
	During lactation	+550	+18	1	30	950	3800	+0.3	+0.3	+4	80	"
	0-6 months			1								
	6-12 months	+440										

Recommended Dietary Allowances for Indians

Group	Particulars	Body Wt kg	Net energy KCal	Protein g/d	Fat g/d	Calcium mg/d	Iron mg/d	Vit A Retinol µg/d	Vit A B-carotene µg/d	Thiamin mg/d	Riboflavin mg/d	Nicotinic acid mg/d	Pyridoxin mg/d	Ascorbic acid mg/d	Folic acid µg/d	Vit. B$_{12}$ µg/d
Man	Sedentary work	60	2350	60	15	400	28	600	2400	1.2	1.4	16	2.0	40	100	1
	Moderate work		2700							1.4	1.6	18				
	Heavy work		3200							1.6	1.9	21				
Woman	Sedentary work	50	1800	50	15	400	30	600	2400	0.9	1.1	12	2.0	40	100	1
	Moderate work		2100							1.1	1.3	14				
	Heavy work		2450							1.2	1.5	16				
	Pregnant woman	50	+300	+15	25	1000	38	600	2400	+0.2	+0.2	−2	2.5	40	400	1
	Lactation															
	0-6 months		+550	+25	35	1000	30	950	3800	+0.3	+0.3	+4	2.5	80		1.5
	6-12 months		+400	18						+0.2	+0.2	+3				
Infants	0-6 months	5.4	118/kg	2.05/Kg		500				59µg/kg	71µg/kg	780µg/kg	0.3	25	25	0.2
	6-12 months	8.6	108/kg	1.65/kg				300	1200	54µg/kg	65µg/kg	710µg/kg	0.4			
Children	1-3 years	12.1	1125	23	20	400	12	400	1600	0.6	0.7	7.0	0.9	40	100	0.2-
	4-6 years	18.2	1600	31	15		18	400	1600	0.8	1.0	11				1.0
	7-9 years	25.2	1925	41	15		25	600	2400	1.0	1.2	13				
Boys	10-12 years	33.5	2150	53	15	600	28	600	2400	1.1	1.3	14	1.6			
Girls	10-12 years	35.0	1950	55	15		20			1.0	1.2	13				
Boys	13-15 years	46.8	2400	71	15	600	43	600	2400	1.2	1.4	16	2.0			
Girls	13-15 years	47.8	2050	67	15		28			1.0	1.2	14				
Boys	16-18 years	56.1	2600	79	15	500	50	600	2400	1.3	1.6	17				
Girls	16-18 years	49.7	2050	65	15	500	30	600	2400	1.0	1.2	14				

*On mixed cereal diet with absorption of 3% in man, 5% in woman and 8% in pregnant woman.
Latest Reference published by NIN in 1990.

To include the above nutrients in daily diet certain guidelines are suggested by the ICMR. Food items which contribute the same nutrients are grouped together and certain food groups are evolved. Foods are grouped into 11 groups based on their nutritive value. They are cereals and millets, pulses, nuts and oilseeds, vegetables, fruits, milk and milk products, meat, fish, eggs and poultry, fats and oils, sugar and jaggery and spices and condiments.

Cereals and millets constitute 70 to 80 per cent of calories and proteins of low income group. Except ragi all cereals are poor in calcium. Dried pulses are rich in proteins and a cereal-pulse combination is an excellent substitute for animal proteins—pulses are also good sources of many B vitamins and sprouting enhances the vitamin C content of pulses. Nuts and oilseeds are good sources of proteins, certain B vitamins, vitamin E and minerals like phosphorus and iron.

Vegetables are the storehouse of carotene, riboflavin, folic acid, vitamin C and calcium. Vegetables also supply water and roughage to the body. Leafy vegetables, other vegetables and roots and tubers are the different types of vegetables. Fruits in general are a good source of vitmain C. Milk is nature's best food as it is almost complete except for iron and vitamin 'C'. Like milk, egg also contains proteins of high biological value. Egg is a rich source of vitamin A and some B vitamins. Animal foods like meat, fish and poultry are rich sources of proteins and B vitamins. Fatty fish are good in fat, vitamin A and D and small fish with bones are good sources of calcium. Liver and other organ meats are good sources of proteins, vitamin A, B complex, B12 and iron.

Sugar and jaggery are good sources of energy and honey and jaggery contain minerals like iron. Condiments and spices are mainly used to enhance palatability.

For non-vegetarians pulses can be reduced to 50 per cent and instead of that, one egg or 30 gms of meat or fish can be included. If no pulse is taken two eggs or 50 gms of meat or fish can be included.

For planning a balanced diet for labourers, low cost nutritious foods must be included. Ragi, tapioca, sweet potato, clusterbeans, bittergourd, soyabeans, drumstick leaves, various types of leafy vegetables, cowgram, horsegram, groundnut, Indian gooseberry, guava, papaya, mango, cashew fruit and other seasonal fruits can be used liberally to make a low-cost balanced diet. Sprouted pulses and cheap vegetables that can be used as raw salads also must be included to meet the vitamin C requirement.

The ICMR Advisory Committee (1981)* recommended the composition of balanced diet and it is given below:

Food item	Adult man			Adult woman		
	Sedentary	Moderate work	Heavy work	Sedentary	Moderate work	Heavy work
Cereals	460 gm	520 gm	670 gm	410 gm	440 gm	575 gm
Pulses	40 gm	50 gm	60 gm	40 gm	45 gm	50 gm
Leafy vegetables	40 gm	40 gm	40 gm	100 gm	100 gm	100 gm
Other vegetables	60 gm	70 gm	80 gm	40 gm	40 gm	100 gm
Roots and tubers	50 gm	60 gm	80 gm	50 gm	50 gm	100 gm
Milk and milk products	150 ml	200 ml	250 ml	100 ml	150 ml	200 ml
Oil and fat	40 gm	45 gm	65 gm	20 gm	25 gm	40 gm
Fruits	60 gm	60 gm	60 gm	60 gm	60 gm	60 gm
Sugar and jaggery	30 gm	35 gm	55 gm	20 gm	20 gm	40 gm

For non-vegetarians pulses 50 per cent less + one egg or 30 gms fish or meat.
If no pulse, 2 eggs or 50 gm fish or meat

* *Recommended dietary intake for Indians.* Indian Council or Medical Research - 1984, p. 58.

A Sample Diet for a Sedentary Woman

Time	Meal	Menu
6.30 a.m. -	Bed coffee	
8 a.m. -	Breakfast -	Chapathi, Groundnuts-Tomato curry, Coffee
12.30 Noon -	Lunch -	Rice or Chapathi, Brinjal and horsegram curry Amaranth or spinach pugath, Lassi, Carrot salad.
4 p.m. -	Tea -	Vegetable vermicelli uppuma, Mint leaf chutney, Tea.
8 p.m. -	Dinner -	Wheat dosa or phulkas, Sprouted greem gram curry, Fruit cup.

Quantities of various food groups can be distributed according to the composition given by ICMR. This above diet provides:

Calories	-	2420 kcals
Proteins	-	53 gms

29

NUTRITION IN PREGNANCY

Pregnancy is a normal physiological phase where rapid growth takes place in the mother's body. The foetus in mother's uterus grows more rapidly than after birth. The zygote develops into a seven-pound baby within 9 months. At the time of birth, the infant is 9 months old. Optimum development of the infant is necessarily a function of parental diet. Inadequate maternal nutrition results in low birth weight of the infant and high depletion of mother's body reserves of nutrients. Premature death, maternal death and low vitality of the infants are due to poor nutritional status of pregnant mothers.

Before pregnancy a woman needs nutrients for growth and maintenance of her body. Good nutrition keeps her healthy. During pregnancy additional requirement for all nutrients occurs to enable the foetus to grow normally in the uterus. A full-term infant has about 300 ml of blood, 500 gms of proteins, 30 gms calcium, 15 gms phosphorus and about 300 to 400 gms of iron. Apart from these foetal reserves in the body, the pregnant mother needs nutrients for the development of the uterus, breasts, placenta, amniotic fluids and reserves for parturition. A full-term pregnant mother gains about 10 to 12 kg body weight and only an adequate diet can provide the nutrients for the normal weight gain. If the pregnant mother is underweight the infant born would be small in size and low in birth weight. Infectious diseases and infant mortality rate are common among such infants. Like underweight, overweight among pregnant mothers is not desirable. Overweight at the beginning of pregnancy or an excessive rate of weight gain during the second and third trimester results in pre-eclampsia and eclampsia. Correct weight gain during pregnancy is 1.5 kg in the first three months and 1.5 kg and a little more during the last two trimesters. Sudden changes in weight gain or weight loss are harmful.

Complications during Pregnancy

Nausea and Vomiting

Morning sickness like nausea and vomiting are common in early pregnancy. They may continue in some women till later stages of pregnancy. Even though the aetiology is not clear mental stress or emotional disturbance aggravate the situation. Diminished secretion of hydrochloride acid brings heartburn and gastric distress. Mild morning sickness can be controlled by consuming high carbohydrate foods such as biscuits or crackers. Small meals must be taken to help digestion. Fatty foods like sweets, fried items and strongly flavoured vegetables must be reduced, besides minimising coffee or tea.

Constipation

In the second and third trimesters constipation occurs among pregnant mothers. The amount of pressure exerted by the developing foetus on the digestive tract, lack of enough exercise and thiamine deficiency are the causes of constipation among pregnant mothers. Lack of fluid, fibre and bulk or cellulose also lead to constipation. If purgatives are used excessive potassium is lost and this can lead to constipation. Excessive use of irritating foods, fried items and emotional distress affect the normal bowel evacuation and result in constipation. Liberal intake of fruits, wholegrain cereals, leafy vegetables, other vegetables and fluids and a happy mental attitude are suggested to avoid constipation.

Toxemia

Toxemia occurs most commonly among patients who are overweight at the time of conception and during pregnancy. Pregnant mothers with underweight at conception and who fail to gain enough weight during pregnancy also manifest it. Excessive protein, salt and vitamin C metabolism in the body cause toxemia. Poor nutritional status also contributes to toxemia of varying degrees. During toxemia oedema, hypertension, albuminuria and convulsions occur. Kidney or heart diseases can manifest symptoms of toxemia. Sodium is restricted to 200 to 800 gms depending upon the condition and just enough protein is suggested.

Anaemia

About half the number of pregnant women in our country are anaemic. One out of every four maternal deaths are due to anaemia.

Complications of pregnancy, both foetal and maternal, can take place in an anaemic mother. The maximum rate of growth in a baby occurs before birth, in the fourth month of foetal life. Maternal malnutrition, especially anaemic conditon, affects the growth of the foetus. Foetus grows from 15 gms of its weight at 12th week to 3,200 gms around the 40th week. Infants of anaemic mothers are frequently born with a subnormal iron store. Still birth, premature birth, toxemia of pregnant mother and various infections and diseases of the newborn infants occur if the mother is anaemic. A pregnant woman is termed as anaemic if from 28th week onwards the haemoglobin level is less than 10 gms per 100 ml of blood. The normal haemoglobin level is 15 gms per 100 ml of blood. Even if it is above 12.5 gms per 100 ml of blood the person is not considered anaemic. Poor loss due to any cause can also result in anaemia. Apart from rich sources of proteins, iron, vitamin C, folic acid and B 12, copper and molybdenum, supplements of iron, that is, 30 mgs of elemental iron per day, after the first trimester of pregnancy prevent anaemia.

Diabetes in Pregnancy

A diabetic woman who is pregnant requires additional nutrients. So she has to adjust the insulin dosage. Glycogen depletion, hypoglycaemia, acidosis and frequent infections are the complications that occur in her. Milk secretion also fails in a diabetic mother.

Dietary Recommendations in Pregnancy

During pregnancy energy allowance should be increased so as to support the growth of the foetus, placenta, maternal tissues and for the increase in basal metabolic rate. During the first trimester 5 per cent BMR and during the second and third trimesters 12 per cent BMR increase takes place. For an Indian woman with 45 kgs weight the total energy cost of pregnancy is about 62,500 kcals. Some energy is deposited as fat during pregnancy for lactating period. Additional intake of 300 kcal/day during the second and third trimesters is the recommendation of the ICMR Committee in 1981. Besides, 35 gms of cereals and 10 gms of sugar or jaggery must be added to the normal balanced diet to derive the extra energy.

Protein intake must be increased for the development of the foetus and placenta and for accessory maternal tissue formation; 14 gms of protein along with the normal requirement will satisfy the demands of protein in the second and third trimesters of pregnancy. An additional quantity of 15 gms of pulses and 100 ml of milk along with the normal requirement will furnish the extra demands of protein.

Additional requirement of fat is not necessary during pregnancy. Since the foetal organs, especially the liver and brain, contain phospholipids rich in essential fatty acids, a normal balanced diet satisfies this demand.

During pregnancy minerals like calcium, phosphorus and iron are required more. A full grown foetus has about 25 to 30 gms of calcium. Most of the calcium deposition occurs during the last two months of pregnancy. The first set of teeth begins to form in the foetus in the eighth week. But its calcification starts just before birth—0.5 gm of calcium is recommended during the second half of pregnancy. Phosphorus allowance must be equal to that of calcium.

During pregnancy about 400 mgs of iron for haemoglobin formation and more than 240 mgs of iron for storage in the foetus are required. Loss of iron through the placenta and blood during parturition are about 90 mgs. To meet all this iron requirement during pregnacy 8 mgs of iron per day is additionally recommended. Iodine, an essential constituent of thyroxine, must be supplied in enough quantities to prevent goitre in infants and pregnant mothers.

All vitamins are required in additional quantities during the gestation period. But for most of the vitamins the exact amount needed in additional quantities is not known. Intake of 400 I.U. of vitamin D as against 200 I.U. of normal amount is recommended by the committee. If a well balanced diet is taken enough vitamin C and riboflavin will be supplied. Thiamine requirement is related to energy consumption and 0.5 mg per 1000 kcal is enough during pregnancy also. Based on the observation that urinary excretion of metabolites of tryptophan is higher in pregnant mothers it is assumed that conversion of the amino acid into niacin is more and 2 mgs more of niacin is recommended during pregnancy to about 200 mgs and it is difficult to supply it through food sources alone. So supplements with folate is essential. About 0.5 mg of B 12 a day is recommended during pregnancy.

The requirement of various nutrients during pregnancy is given along with balanced diets. Five or six small feeds are better than three or four meals so as to avoid fullness in the stomach. Leafy vegetables, fruits, other vegetables and fluids tend to maintain normal bowel evacuation. Rich, highly spiced and fried foods, heavy desserts, rich gravies and excessive amounts of salts must be avoided not to gain excessive weight. It is better to use jaggery instead of sugar as it contains more iron.

Due to tradition and habits many food fads are prevailing in our country. In the light of nutritional knowledge many of these food fads were proved to be prevalent without any scientific basis. Many mistaken beliefs still prevent pregnant mothers from consuming very useful foodstuffs. For example, in South India papaya, which is an excellent source of vitamin A, is avoided for fear of abortion. In the same way pumpkin and jackfruit which are good sources of carotene (vitamin A) are avoided, being classified as hot foods. In certain places, the quantity of food eaten during pregnancy is cut down stating that delivery will be difficult. Wheat, jaggery, meat, fish, eggs, mangoes, tea and coffee are also tabooed as hot foods. There is not scientific basis in such beliefs and a pregnant mother can consume all foods like a normal woman. The compositon of a balanced diet during pregnancy includes additional quantities such as 35 gms of cereals, 15 gms of pulses, 100 ml of milk or milk products and 10 gms of sugar or jaggery. For non-vegetarians some modification is normal.

A Sample Diet during Pregnancy

Time	Meal	Menu
Time 6.30 -	Bed coffee -	Coffee
8 a.m. -	Breakfast -	Chapathi, Dal curry, Soyabean milk, Guava
10 a.m. -	Mid morning -	Lime Juice
12.30 Noon -	Lunch -	Vegetable pulav, Sprouted green gram salad, Curry-leaves chutney, Lassi
2.30 p.m. -	Mid time -	Tender coconut water
4 p.m. -	Tea -	Tea, Moong dal laddoos
6 p.m. -	-	Amaranth soup
8 p.m. -	-	Chappathi, Liver-tomato curry, Cucumber salad, Fruit cup.
9 p.m. -	-	Milk.
This diet provides	Calories -	2,600 kcals
	Proteins -	62 gms.
	Calcium -	1.4 gms.
	Iron -	45 mgms.

Composition of Balanced Diet during Pregnancy
(Ref: ICMR-1984)

Items		Quantity	
Cereals	—	475	gms
Pulses	—	55	gms
Leafy vegetables	—	100	gms
Other vegetables	—	40	gms
Root and tubers	—	50	gms
Milk and milk products	—	250	ml
Oils and fats	—	40	gms
Fruits	—	60	gms
Sugar and jaggery	—.	40	gms

30

NUTRITION DURING LACTATION

The nutritional link between the mother and the child continues even after birth. The newborn baby depends for some period solely on breast milk for its sustenance. Unfortunately, most of the modern mothers do not want to breastfeet their children because they fear that they will lose their shape and charm. But breastfeed is not only the birthright of the baby, but proper emptying of breasts reduces the chances of mastitis and even of breast cancer. Studies have shown that mothers who have never fed their children have higher rate of malignancy. Nutritionists are of the opinion that there is no food equivalent to breast milk for a newborn baby. Nature has designed it to be a complete food for the first few months of a baby's life. Breast milk immunises the baby against infection also. To secrete enough milk for the baby the mother should have nutritious foods. Nutritional needs of a lactating mother are higher than that of a pregnant mother. The quality and quantity of breast milk depends on maternal diet. In an inadequate diet the quality of mother's milk is maintained by drawing the nutrients from her body reserves and from tissues and bones. That is why the milk secreted by poor women is equal in its nutritive content to that of lactating mothers from developed countries of the world. The diets consumed by many lactating mothers in our country are very poor. A lactating mother requires more calories so as to secrete enough milk and to meet the high BMR during this period. The ICMR recommends about 550 kcal/day additionally during the first 6 months and 400 kcal/day from 6 to 12 months for a lactating mother. An average of 600 ml of milk is secreted by a lactating mother in India. About 420 kcals are supplied through this milk. The efficiency of conversion of diet calories to human milk calories is only 60 per cent.

The human milk contains 7.2 gms of milk protein and 14.4 gms of protein is required to produce so much milk protein. Therefore, 25 gms of additional protein per day is recommended for a lactating mother during the first six months of lactation. The calcium content of breast milk of Indian mothers are about 30 to 40 mgs/100 ml and to meet the additional needs 500 mgs of calcium is recommended along with the normal requirements of 500 mgs. Thus 1 gm of calcium is recommended for a lactating mother.

The concentration of iron in breast milk is about 0.72 mg/600 ml. During lactation menstruation is not common, thus about 1 mg of iron is saved. So iron is not recommended by the ICMR committee for a lactating mother. But care must be taken to provide a balanced diet to meet the normal iron requirement. Since our Indian diets are predominantly based upon cereals, the high phytate content interferes with iron absorption. Good calcium and vitamin C ratio can minimise this phytate interference but our diets are again deficient in these nutrients.

The quantity of vitamin A in 600 ml human milk is 300 mgs and to meet this requirement 300 μgm (Microgram) of retinol or 1600 μgm carotene is recommended by the committee.

The quantity of ascrobic acid in human milk is only 15-30 mgs. ICMR committee recommended an additional 40 mgs of vitamin C per day. The thiamine content in breast milk is 60 μgms per 600 ml. Depending upon the energy requirements thiamine demand varies. The normal requirement of 0.5 mgm per 1000 kcals is applicable to lactating mother also. For riboflavin an additional recommendation of 0.3 mg/day is enough to meet the needs of a lactating mother. The niacin requirements during lactation is 4 mgms additional to normal requirements. Increased fluid intake is recommended during lactation period to enable the normal functions in the body. There are no foods which require restriction as it is customary in various parts of India based on food fads and fallacies. A lactating mother requires adequate nutrition for the proper development of the baby.

The composition of a balanced diet during lactation is based on the characteristic of a normal person. Additional requirements must be met by making slight variations in the intake of food groups. The ICMR committee of 1981 recommended an additional intake of 60 gms of cereals, 30 mgs of pulses, 100 ml of milk, 10 gms of fat and 10 gms of sugar. These additional quantities of various foodstuffs supply about 521 kcals besides 25 gms of protein and other requirements by the body during lactation. If such a diet is consumed, a lactating mother can produce enough milk for the baby without affecting her health.

Composition of Balanced Diet for a Sedentary Lactating Mother
(1984 - Revised ICMR)

Foodstuff		Quantities
Cereals	-	500 gms
Pulses	-	70 gms
Leafy vegetables	-	100 gms
Other vegetables	-	40 gms
Roots and tubers	-	50 gms
Milk and milk products	-	250 ml
Oils and fats	-	50 gms
Fruits	-	60 gms
Sugar and jaggery	-	40 gms

A Sample Diet for a Lactating Mother

Time	Menu
6 a.m.	- Coffee
8 a.m.	- Chapathi or idli, Dal-tomato curry or sambar, Orange
19 a.m.	- Spinach soup (Amaranth Soup)
12.30 Noon	- Rice or chapathi, Fish curry or cauliflower, Green peas curry Beans-carrot pugath, Curd Vegtable salad Fruit salad
2.30 p.m.	- Lime juice
4.30 p.m.	- Tea, Egg pakoda
6 p.m.	- Vegetable-dal stuffed, chapathi, Sprouted green gram, raita
9.30 p.m.	- Suji porridge

31

NUTRITION IN INFANCY

Nutrition during infancy lays the foundation for health. Growth is rapid and changes in body composition take place at this age. Chemical maturation of the body is accomplished and internal activities occur at a high speed. Basal metabolic rate is also high. Compared to an adult in terms of body weight, an infant needs all nutrients in more quantities. A healthy newborn baby doubles its birth weight by the fifth month and tribles by one year. The average birth weight of Indian infants is less than the average European infant. But the growth rate of Indian infants is on par with the developed countries in the first few months when it depends entirely on breast milk. A diet survey conducted in various parts of India shows that a lactating mother of lower socio-economic class consumes only about 1800 kcals and about 40 gms of protein which is much below to her requirement. Despite this, she is able to breastfeed her baby successfully during the first six months. Qualitatively her milk is not inferior to a well-nourished mother. But beyond three to four months, breast milk alone is not able to supply the needs of the infant. Supplementary foods are needed after three months. Sometimes breast milk is inadequate to meet the nutritional needs of the infants even up to six months. Continuous stress on the mother may result in her ill-health and reduction in the quantity of her milk. The nutrients from mother's body are withdrawn for milk production which leads to severe deficiency condition in her which in turn is reflected on the baby. Malnutrition impairs growth and development of the baby. Such babies have poor resistance to infection. Intellectual potentiality is impaired besides reduction in working efficiency in adult life. Studies conducted at the National Institute of Nutrition (1981) indicate that children from well-fed, well-to-do sections of the community are taller and heavier and their resistance power against diseases is far better.

Nutritional Requirement of the Infant

Infants in the age group of 0 to 3 months are mostly breastfed and lactating mothers of poorer section also secrete enough milk for their baby in the first three months. In our country, breastfeeding is traditionally prolonged and continues for one or two years. A well-fed mother secretes 850 ml of milk up to three months. Mothers from poorer sections secrete to an average of 600 ml/day. The energy requirements for infants of 0 to 3 months are 120 kcals/kg of body weight. If the mother secretes 600 ml of milk the infant gets 420 kcals per day.

Protein intake of healthy infants is found to be 2 gms/kg of body weight. Six hundred millilitre of breast milk supplies about 7.2 gms of protein for the baby. Fat content of breast milk is 3.8 per cent and about 24.8 gms of fat is supplied by the breast milk. Fat in breast milk supplies 50 to 60 per cent of energy; 100 mgs of iron and 0.5 mgm to 0.6 mgm of calcium per kilogramme of body weight is required by the baby. Calcium builds the skeletal structure of the baby's body.

Vitamins are essential for the rapid development of the infant. Breast milk supplies 140 gms of vitamin A during the six months of life. This is not enough when the requirement is 400 mgms of retinol during 0 to 6 months and 300 kcals gms from 6 to 12 months. They utilise the reserves in the body. Vitamin A deficiency is very common in our children. In India there is plenty of sunshine which is a rich source of vitamin D and 200 I.U. of this vitamin D is sufficient to meet the requirements and 20 mgs of vitamin C is recommended for infants. In 100 ml of breast milk 15 mgms to 20 gms of thiamine is present. Thus about 0.17 gms of thiamine is ingested through breast milk and the requirement is 59 mgs/kg of body weight, requirement of riboflavin is 0.25 gms/1000 kcals. Niacin requirement for infants is not studied and 780 mgms/kg of body weight is recommended by the committee. For infants recommended requirement of folic acid is 25 mgms and B 12 is 0./2 gm.

Recommended Dietary Intake of Nutrients for Infants (1981)

Group Infant	Calories Kcal/ kg	Proteins gm/ kg	Calcium mgm	Iron mg/kg	Retinol μgm	B1 mgm/ kg	B12 μgm/ kg	Vitamin C Mgm
-0-6 months	118	2-00	0.5-0.6	1	400	59	71	20
-6-12 months	108	1.7	0.5-0.6	"	300	54	65	20

Growth Rate of Infants

Infancy is a period of rapid growth and the growth rate is given below.

Age (Months)	Body length Male (cm)	Female	Weight Male (kg)	Female
At birth	47.5	47	3.1	3
1	50.6	50	3.8	3.7
2	53.7	53	4.8	4.7
3	56.8	56	5.2	5.1
4	58.8	57.9	5.8	5.2
5	60.8	59.8	6.4	6.1
6	62.8	61.7	7.0	6.6
7	64.5	63.4	7.4	7.1
8	66.2	65.1	7.8	7.5
9	68.9	66.8	8.0	7.7
10	70.2	68.1	8.2	7.9
11	71.5	69.4	8.4	8.1
12	72.8	70.7	8.6	8.3

Breastfeeding

Scientific studies have shown that the watery human milk is what the human infant needs. Cow's milk or buffalo's milk has the composition fit to match the rapid growth of its calves and not for a comparatively slow growing human infant. The nutritive value of breast milk is better than buffalo's or cow's milk. During the first two days after childbirth the yellowish fluid that is secreted is known as colostrum. This is very nutritious and good for the baby as it is a good source of vitamin A and contains substances which protect the baby from diseases. But many mothers do not feed the colostrum to the baby with the belief that it is not good for the child. The average quantity of milk secreted by an Indian woman is 600 ml or equal to four glasses of milk.

From the table, it can be seen that the protein content of cow's, buffalo's and goat's milk is three times that of human milk. The casein content is also more. In the stomach, hard curd is formed in children fed on animal milk. Fat content is almost the same except in the case of buffalo's milk where it is about twice as much as that in other milks. Minerals and vitamins are almost the same in all milks.

Advantages of using breast milk as an infant's food are many. No substitute has ever been developed that matches the numerous

Composition of Human, Cow's, Buffalo's and Goat's Milk (100 ml)

Nutrients	Human		Cow		Buffalo		Goat	
Proteins	1.2	gm	3.30	gm	3.8	gm	3.3 gm	
Fat	3.8	gm	3.7	gm	8.5	gm	4.1 gm	
Calories	71	kcals	69	kcals	100	kcals	76 kcals	
Lactose	7.0	gm	4.8	gm	4.4	gm	4.7 gm	
Calcium	33	mg	125	mgm	210	mgm	130 mgm	
Iron	0.15	μgm	0.10	μgm	0.20	μgm	0.05 μgm	
Vitamin A	48	μgm	47	μgm	60	μgm	36 μgm	
Thiamine	0.02	mgm	0.04	mgm	0.05	mgm	0.05 mgm	
Riboflavin	0.04	mg	0.18	gm	0.10	mg	0.12 mg	
Vitamin C	4	mgm	2	mgm	2.5	mgm	2 mgm	

advantages of this specific baby food. It contains various elements in the correct proportion required by the baby. Human milk is a dilute fluid which is easily digestible and it is the ideal starting food for the baby. Breast milk is readily available and it is very economical. By giving any food, breast milk can be produced in a lactating mother. No time is required for its preparation and the chances of contamination are nil. Artifical feeding requires complete cleanliness and in a country like ours where sanitary conditions are poor infections are more among artificially fed babies. Colic pain and respiratory diseases are common among such children. Polyomyelitis, influenza, mumps and infectious diseases are also common among artificially fed children because breast milk contains high concentration of antibodies which give resistance against infections. Milk allergy, constipation and fullness of the stomach, gas formation and gastro-intestinal discomforts are less among breastfed infants. A mother who is not feeding her baby due to some reason subconsciously feels guilty. The infant gets close physical relationship with the mother which provides emotional security and well being to the baby. Apart from these advantages, emptying the breasts reduces the chances of mastitis and cancer. Milk secretion is reduced if the secreted milk is not drained by suckling the baby. Only by emptying it further secretion is stimulated. Worry, tension, anxiety and emotional disturbances reduce the secretion of milk. Cleanliness of breast and nipple, care of inverted, fissured and cracked nipples are essential to ensure proper feeding. If the child is sick and is not feeding then the mother must empty the breast either manually or with the help of a breast pump. An infant must be fed at a breast for twenty minutes. An adequate diet, relaxed attitude, enough rest and willingness to breastfeed serve as the key factors to secrete enough milk by a lactating mother. Suckling position is also important. The mother should offer her whole breast to the baby rather than just the nipple, because the baby will not suck the whole milk secreted by the breast by sucking at the nipple. The feeding of the baby must be developed by every mother. Individual variations are there in this matter. For the first few days most of the babies are reluctant to suck as they are not very hungry. From the third day onwards the infant may want to feed as many times as it is fed. This may be to get the closeness and warmth of the womb from the physical contact in the new environment. From the second week onwards most babies can be trained to follow a routine of feeding.

In diseases like tuberculosis, typhoid, severe neurosis, psychosis, septicaemia and in eclampsia breastfeeding is not advocated.

Artificial Feeding

Industrial revolution, urbanisation and lifestyle of modern women, fast social life and employment status of mothers are some of the causes for the decline in breastfeeding. Commercial pressures from the advertisement of marketed foods, ignorance about the advantages of breastfeeding, misconception of the mothers that breastfeeding affects the figure, and lack of self confidence among lactating mothers are other factors which promote artificial feeding. Due to certain illnesses, some mothers are unable to feed their babies and they have to depend on artificial feeding.

Much care and awareness of the formulas are the factors to be considered when artificial feeding is opted for the new born to avoid complications. Preparation of a sterile infant formula is expensive and time-consuming. Morbidity and mortality rates are more among artificially fed children because the bacteriological safety of the artificial feed is inferior. A beneficial bacteria, lactobacillus bifidus, in the intestinal flora of the breastfed infants promotes better resistance to the infant.

If animal milk is used for infant feeding, adjustment of the fat content of the feed, sterilisation, dilution and addition of sugar are the factors to be considered seriously. Fat content of buffalo's milk is very high and it has to be adjusted. The animal milk has to be diluted with water after boiling it. Equal quantities of water and milk are enough for an infant of 1 to 2 months of age. Sugar at 5 per cent level is added. Gradually the quantity of water is reduced as the infant grows.

The number of feeds and dilution of milk vary according to the age of the infants. Seven feeds are enough for the first month. From second to seven months six feeds, and eight months to one year five feeds are recommended. From the third month onwards fruit juices and from the fourth month onwards cereals cooked in different forms must be introduced. From the sixth month onwards egg yolk, mashed vegetables, dals, vegetable soups and other forms of food can be introduced. This pattern is essential even for children who are breastfed.

For the first month dilution of milk with equal quantity of water may be done with the addition of 5 per cent canesugar. For instance, for the feed 400 ml milk, 200 ml water and 20 gms of sugar can be added. In the second month, 500 ml milk, 300 ml water and 30 gms of sugar are enough. From three months to 1 year 100 ml of milk is added and 100 ml of water is reduced and 10 gms of sugar is also added.

Formula for Infants from Animal Milk

Age	Milk (Cow's or buffalo's toned)	Water	Sugar	Feeds
0-1 months	400 ml	400 ml	20 gms	7
1-2 months	500 ml	300 ml	30 gms	6
2-3 "	600 ml	300 ml	40 gms	6
3-4 "	700 ml	300 ml	50 gms	6
4-5 "	800 ml	300 ml	60 gms	6
5-6 "	800 ml	300 ml	60 gms	6
6-7 "	900 ml	200 ml	60 gms	6
7-8 "				
8-9 "	950 ml	100 ml	60 gms	5
9-10 "				
10-11 "				
11-12 "	1000 ml	...	60 gms	5

Various processed infant foods are available in the market. The nutritive value of these infant foods is given on the container. Certain nutrients like vitamin D, iron, and other minerals are fortified in some foods. Dilution of these formulas must be done. Otherwise indigestion and other gastro-intestinal disturbances may occur. If the dilution is more enough nutrients will not be present in the formula and the baby will not show the normal growth pattern. Since vitamin C is absent in processed foods it must be supplemented.

For low-income groups, cheap nutritious substitutes can be prepared for an infant from groundnut or soyabeans. Instead of diluting the expensive artificial foods into watery milk these substitutes can be prepared at home.

Groundnut Milk

Select fresh groundnut, shrunken or shrivelled nuts are harmful. Shell and roast gently for 5 to 10 minutes. Rub off the pink skins and soak one cup of white nuts in clean water for 2 hours. Drain and grind the soaked nuts to a fine paste sprinkling with water. When the paste is ready dilute it with 5 cups of water and filter through a fine cotton cloth. Boil the milk for 10 minutes and keep it aside for 8-10 hours in a closed vessel. Afterwards remove the layer of fat from the top and the liquid can be used as a substitute for milk.

Soyabean Milk

Select fresh beans and discard discoloured or spoiled ones. Wash three times with water. For 1 cup of beans use 3 to 4 cups of water for soaking. Soak for 6 to 8 hours. Drain and throw away the water and rinse the beans with clean water. Grind them to a fine paste using 2 cups of boiling water and a pinch of baking powder of soda bicarbonate. Strain through a muslin cloth and add one more cup of boiling water. Boil this milk stirring constantly. Add 2 cardamoms to improve the flavour.

Children who are unable to tolerate animal food can be given these two types of milk. Artificial feeds must be given at body-temperature. The hole in the nipple should be just enough to avoid rapid flow of milk. If a large gulp is taken, air is swallowed along with it which causes discomfort and regurgitation. A small hole in the nipple provides very little milk and the baby may become exhausted by sucking. Along with the feed some air is swallowed, therefore the baby must be made to burp.

Sterilisation of bottles, nipples, bottle-caps, strainer, spoons and other equipment used is essential.

Other Requirements

Liquid and solid supplements, vitamins and mineral supplements are essential to meet the nutritional requirements of the baby. Juices of fresh fruits such as oranges, tomatoes, grapes, or soup of drumstick leaves can be introduced to meet the vitamin C requirement. One teaspoon of fruit juice can be given to the baby from the third week onwards. At this stage the fruit juice must be diluted with equal quantities of boiled water. This can be increased to about three teaspoons (without dilution) by 2 to 3 months. Boiled leafy vegetables, carrots and tomatoes can be introduced from the third month. After boiling, mash and strain the vegetables. Add salt and lime juice. Mashed banana, pumpkin, egg yolk, meat soup without seasoning, porridge, double-cooked cereals and pulses, roasted pulse-cereal powders sweetened with jaggery are the other items that can be introduced by the sixth month. Ripe fruits are also good for them. Only one food must be introduced at a time, though a variety of items can be given to familiarise with new tastes. Only a small quantity of food must be given to the baby in the beginning. Do not force the baby to take more, otherwise it will reject it in course of time. If the baby vomits or shows dislike for a food do not force him to eat it. After an interval start again and if the dislike persists substitute it with another food. Provide variety in supplementary foods because infants like older people prefer it. If proper supplementation is not provided to the infants its growth is retarded. Foods rich in proteins, calories and other nutrients must be supplemented to prevent malnutrition because the baby is growing vigorously at this stage.

Deficiency of protein leads to physical and intellectual dwarfism in the baby. Lack of adequate vitamin A in the diet results in poor vision even in the case of an infant because mother's milk and baby's store of vitamin A may not be enough. ICMR reports that about 12,000 to 14,000 children become blind every year. Deficiency of vitamin A is observed as one of the important causes for it. Deficiency diseases are not the only consequence of malnutrition but they again impair the power of resistance of an infant and expose them to a number of diseases. Respiratory diseases, gastro-intestinal disturbances and fevers are the common ailments during infancy.

Some recipes and their nutritive value are given in this chapter. These can be included in the diet of an infant to improve the nutrient intake. Green gram dal, kheer, rice wheat or ragi porridge, ragi milk, halwa, chandan kheer, idli, groundnut halwa, pongal, sweet kichiri, vegetable soup and fruit juices are some of the foods that can be given to a pre-school child.

Ragi, Wheat or Rice Porridge

Ragi flour	-	30 gms (2 tbsp) or any other flour.
Groundnuts	-	30 gms
Jaggery	-	50 gms
Water	-	2 glasses

Method: Mix ragi flour in a small amount of water and make it into a paste. Roast and grind groundnuts into a paste. Add ragi flour paste to boiling water and stir continuously. Crush the jaggery and dissolve in half cup water. Strain and add it to the ragi mixture. Add groundnut paste and allow the mixture to cook for five minutes and remove from the fire.

Nutritive value: This porridge supplies about 11.5 gms proteins and 225 kcals.

Ragi Milk Halwa

Ragi (grains)	-	100 gms
Milk	-	half cup
Jaggery	-	50 gms
Water	-	2 glasses

Method: Clean and soak ragi for 10-12 hours and grind into a paste. Dilute with water and strain the mixture through a thin cloth. Add milk and cook it on low heat. Stir to avoid lump formation. Add jaggery to the cooked milk.

Groundnut Halwa

Shelled groundnuts	-	100 gms
Jaggery	-	50 gms

Method: Soak groundnuts for 6 to 8 hours and grind into a paste. Add 20 to 25 ml of water to the paste and keep on fire. Add jaggery, allow to cook for 5 minutes and remove from the fire.

Pongal

Rice	-	20 gms (one fistful)
Dal	-	20 gms (2 tbsp)

Method: Cook dal, and a little salt, and mash it well with a ladle. Cook rice, add mashed dal. Add a little ghee to it. Serve this with a soup prepared from greens.

Nutritive value: 6.2 gm protein, 120 kcals (without ghee).

Kheer Pongal

Rice	-	50 gms (4 tbsp, heaped)
Amaranth	-	50 gms (one medium size bunch)
or any other greens		
Green gram dal	-	50 gms (4 tbsp)
Groundnut oil	-	10 gms
Salt	-	to taste
Cumin	-	a pinch

Method: Roast rice and green gram dal and powder them. Boil amaranth, mash and strain. Mix amaranth puree with rice and dal powders and make into a paste. Add this mixture to the boiling water. Fry cumin in oil and season the pongal.

Nutritive value: 4.0 gm protein, 100 kcals.

Low Cost Recipes

Chandan Kheer

Roasted bengal		
gram flour	-	25 gms (2 tbsp)
Milk	-	200 ml (1 glass)
Sugar	-	15 gms

Method: Add a little milk to the bengal gram flour to form a paste. Boil the remaining milk and add bengal gram flour paste to it. Stir continuously to avoid lumps. Allow it to cook for five minutes. Add sugar and remove from the fire.

Nutritive value: 4.0 gms protein, 110 kcals.

Sweet Khichiri

Wheat	-	45 gms (4 tbsp)
Roasted bengal	-	45 gms (3 tbsp)
gram dal		
Jaggery	-	50 gms (4 tbsp)

Method: Lightly roast wheat and bengal gram dal and powder them. Make into a thin batter. Add water to jaggery and make it into a syrup. Add jaggery syrup to the batter and allow to cook till there is no raw flavour.

Nutritive value: 5.0 gms protein, 150 kcals.

Drumstick Leaf or Spinach Chapathi

Drumstick leaves	-	25 gms
Onion (big)	-	15 gms
Salt and water	-	enough
Wheat flour	-	50 gms
Chillies (green)	-	1

Method: Chop onion and chilli. Clean and cut leaves into pieces and cook. Mix all three to wheat flour and make it into a soft dough. Divide into balls and make chapathi and cook it.

Nutritive value: 8.0 gm proteins, 196 kcals.

32

NUTRITION OF PRE-SCHOOL CHILDREN

The growth rate declines after the child is one year old, but the foundation of good health is laid during the pre-school age. In India about 20 per cent of the total deaths occur among toddlers in the age group of 1 to 4 years. A child who has failed to grow during this crucial period may not make up the loss in growth even with an excellent diet in later life. Deficiency of vitamin A which leads even to blindness and anaemia are common disorders found in children in the age group of 1 to 5 years. About 1 to 2 per cent of pre-school children suffer from severe deficiency diseases like kwashiorkor and marasmus. Studies in India have shown that the performance of children who had earlier suffered from malnutrition, was clearly inferior to that of children who had not gone through malnutrition. Their diets in general consist of cereals, roots, tubers and vegetables. Important items like pulses, leafy vegetables, yellow vegetables, milk and milk products and other protein sources and fruits, are consumed much below their requirement. Deficiency of protein calories, vitamin A and iron are very common among this group due to their inadequate dietary habits. Non-availability of protective foods, low purchasing capacity, illiteracy and ignorance about the importance of nutrition during this period, traditional habits, food fads and fallacies, insanitary living conditions and prevalence of infectious diseases are the main causes of malnutrition. Physical and mental retardation set in and high mortality takes place among infants. It has also been shown by studies that the measurement of head circumference usually indicates that the brain volume is less among malnourished children. Malnutrition reduces memory and hearing ability and impairs intellectual functioning.

Nutritional Requirement

Energy requirement varies according to age, activities, climate and the growth pattern. Proportionately, a child requires more calories per kilogramme of body weight compared to an adult person. This is mainly due to the high basal metabolic activities, extra physical activity of the child and extra energy needed for growth. The ICMR Committee (1981) suggested that the ideal weight chart must be consulted before recommending energy requirements.

Height and Weight of Indian Pre-school Children

Age Yrs.	Boy's Height	Girl's Height	Boy's Weight	Girl's Weight
		Cm.		Kg.
1-2 yrs	82.61	79.89	10.94	10.21
2-3 yrs	91.14	89.63	12.79	12.11
3-4 yrs	98.36	96.21	14.78	13.79
4-5 yrs	104.70	104.19	16.12	15.85

Energy Allowance for Children

Age group	Body weight	Energy requirement
1-3 yrs	12.03 kg	1220 kcals or 5.1 MJ
4-6 yrs	18.87 kg	1720 kcals or 7.2 MJ

Protein allowances for children of 1 to 3 years is 1.83 gms/kgs or 22 gms. For 4 to 6 year old, 1.56 gms/kgs or 29 gms to ideal weight is recommended.

From 1 to 6 years calcium requirement is 0.4-0.5 gms and iron requirement is 20-25 mgs. Retinol during 1 to 3 years 250 μgm and 3 to 6 years 300 μgm is enough. β Carotene is required 1,000 μgm and 1,200 μgm respectively. Also 0.6 mgm of thiamine and 0.7 mg of riboflavin and 8 mgs of niacin are recommended for 1 to 3 years. For both groups 40 mgms of vitamin C and 100 mgms of folic acid and 200 I.U. of vitamin D are recommended. All these nutrients are required for maintaining health and well-being of the growing child. Since childhood is the age of rapid growth, proteins of high biological value must be included in the diet. Iron deficiency is common among this group, food rich in iron must be made available in the diet. Low intake of iron was found in a high percentage of 1 to 5 year group which leads to iron deficiency anaemia. A study on pre-school children has shown that average per head intake of leafy vegetables is 4 gms aginst the recommendation of 40-50 gms per day. Intake of other vegetables is 14 gms instead of 30 to 50 gms. Only 7 gms of fruit is consumed by a pre-schooler as against a recommendation of 60 gms. For proteins 40 to 50 gms of pulses are recommended, but the average consumption is only

14 gms; 80 ml of milk instead of 200 ml of milk or milk products. Thus our pre-school children are exposed to an inadequate diet which is the major cause of malnutrition in them. The children often become victims of traditional beliefs and food fads and due to that many essential food items are forbidden to them. To an extent, malnutrition results from this. Cereals, pulses, other vegetables, leafy vegetables and cheap fruits are essential to provide energy, proteins and vitamins to the child. Milk can be substituted by giving other forms of milk like groundnut or soyabean milk. Composition of a balanced diet for a pre-school child is given below:

Balanced Diet for Pre-school Children

Age group	Cereals	Pulses	Leafy vege-tables	Other vege-tables	Roots & tubers	Milk	Fats & oil	Sugar or jaggery	Fruits	Egg	Non-vegetarian Meat or fish
1-3 years	175gm	35gm	40gm	20gm	10gm	300ml	15gm	30gm	60gm	1	30gm
3-6 years	270gm	35gm	50gm	30gm	20gm	250ml	25gm	40gm	60gm	1	30gm

If such a balanced diet is provided to the pre-school child, it will be reflected in normal growth pattern. An average of 12.4 cms height and 2.5 kgs weight is gained by a pre-school child during 1 to 2 years. The growth pattern of a pre-school child of 2 to 3 years is 8.9 cm height and 2.1 kgs weight per year. During 3 to 4 years there is a slight decline in the growth pattern, that is, 7.3 cms height and 2 kgs weight per year. Height gain of a pre-schooler of 4 to 5 years per year is only 5.6 cms and the weight is 1.8 kgs. Even though there are different factors which affect the height and weight gain of a child the proportionate rate has a pattern and marked variation in it must be taken seriously.

A Sample Diet for a Pre-school Child (1-3 yrs)

Time	Meal	Menu
6.30 a.m.	-	Milk
7.30 a.m.	Breakfast	Rava porridge, Sweetened chappati.
9 a.m.	-	Soyabean milk
11 a.m.	-	Biscuit
12.30 Noon	-	Rice pongal or stuffed chappathi Lassi, Carrot raita, Fruit cup
3 p.m.	-	Mango juice
4 p.m.	-	Horlicks, Spinach dal, Cutlet
7 p.m.	-	Idli or soft chappati Potato chips, Peas-tomato curry
9 p.m.	-	Milk

33

NUTRITION OF SCHOOL CHILDREN

Majority of our school children consume inadequate diet and so they are malnourished. School children usually skip their meals due to various reasons. Poverty, ignorance and disturbed emotional status due to maladjustment in schools are some of the factors which produce malnutrition among school children. Western countries have shown a general trend towards an increase in the average national height of the people with each succeeding generation. Better socio-economic condition and better nutrition contribute to this. But this is not true in our case. Diet surveys carried out in our country have shown that diet consumed by school children is deficient in calories, proteins, vitamin A, riboflavin, folic acid and iron. Deficiencies in the diet are both qualitative and quantitative. More than 50 per cent of our school children are anaemic. The growth rate is poor and they gain low body weight and height. Their capacity to put maximum effort for work is poor. They are unable to concentrate, their power of grasping is reduced and their learning ability is poor. Thus an undernourished child is hurdled in its physical and intellectual development. Periodical check-up of height and weight manifest if there is retarded growth.

Nutritional requirements of boys and girls are more or less the same till the first 9 years. After that there is variation in some nutrients. Recommendation of allowances of various nutrients for school children suggested by the ICMR is given below:

Recommended Dietary Intake of Nutrients

Age (Years)	Calories (kcals)	Proteins (gm)	Calcium (gm)	Iron (mgm)	Retinol (mgm)	β Carotene (mgm)	B1 (mg)	B2 (mg)	Vitamin C (mg)
1-3 years	1220	22.0	0.4-0.5	20-25	250	1000	0.6	0.7	40 mg
4-6 "	1720	29.4	0.4-0.5	20-25	300	1200	0.9	1.0	40 mg
7-9 "	2050	35.6	0.4-0.5	20-25	400	1600	1.0	1.2	40 mg

Recommended allowances of these nutrients can be derived from a balanced diet with the following composition:

Foods	Age group	
	1-3 years	4-6 years
Cereals	175 gms	270 gms
Pulses	35 gms	35 gms
Leafy vegetables	40 gms	50 gms
Other vegetables	20 gms	30 gms
Roots and tubers	10 gms	20 gms
Milk	300 ml	250 ml
Oils and fats	15 gms	25 gms
Sugar and jaggery	30 gms	40 gms

Among non-vegetarians 50 per cent of pulses can be deleted and instead 1 egg or 30 gms of meat or fish can be added.

A Sample Diet for a School-Going Child (4-6 yrs)

Time	Meal	Menu
6.30 a.m.		Proteinex
8 a.m.	Breakfast	Pancake, Mixed fruit jam, Milk
12 p.m.	Lunch	Vegetable pulao or stuffed sprouted green gram raita chapathi Vegetable salad, Fruit cup, Lassi
4 p.m.	Tea	Milk, Baked cutlet
6 p.m.	Mid time	Orange juice
8 p.m.	Dinner	Soft chapathi, Dal curry, Ragi porridge

Height and Weight of Indian School Children

Age (yrs)	Height (cm)		Weight (kg)	
	Male	Female	Male	Female
6	118.9	117.3	22.1	21.4
7	123.3	122.7	24.5	24.3
8	127.9	126.8	26.4	26.1
9	133.6	132.3	30.0	29.7
10	138.5	138.5	32.4	33.5
11	143.4	144.1	35.3	36.5
12	148.9	150.3	38.8	42.6
13	154.9	153.0	42.9	44.4
14	161.7	155.1	48.3	46.7
15	165.3	155.3	52.2	48.2

34

NUTRITION DURING ADOLESCENCE

Adolescence is a period of rapid growth after infancy. The rate of growth reaches its peak between eleven and fourteen years for the girl and between thirteen and sixteen years for the boy. Internal activities like secretion, hormonal reactions, basal metabolism and biochemical reactions are more during this stage. Pubertal growth demands more body-building substances and basal metabolic rate is increased which demands more energy. Since the period of adolescence is accompanied with considerable stress due to physiological and psychological changes attitude towards diet is often very unhealthy. Boys are usually well-fed in adolescence as they prefer to be tall and well built with strong muscles. Therefore, an adolescent boy is more receptive to form good dietary habits. Girls are often self-conscious of their figure and they avoid many foods labelling them as fattening. Complexion, pimples and other marks are often associated with certain foods and their consumption. Withdrawal attitude, a common problem of adolescents, is often taken on food. Weight control is another important problem with adolescent girls and they eliminate essential nutrients in this effort. Skipped meals, poor lunches, snacking in-between, munching in-between, consuming large quantities of soft drinks and salty tit-bits which reduce the appetite are the common unhealthy dietary habits observed among adolescents.

On the contrary, an adolescent girl requires all nutrients in good quantities not just for the rapid growth but also to obtain optimal storage for later requirements during pregnancy and lactation. Underweight is undersirable for them because it helps further susceptibility to infection. Studies on obstetric performance of adolescents have shown that high incidence of eclampsia, toxemia, miscarriage and premature deliveries occur among undernourished pregnant adolescent mothers.

Nutritional requirements for boys and girls differ at adolescence.

Requirement of Various Nutrients

Group	Age (years)	Calories (kacls)	Protein (gm)	Iron (mgm)	Retinol (gm)	β Carotene (mgm)	Thiamine (mg)	Riboflavin (Mg)	Niacin (mgm)	Vitamin C(mg)	Calcium (mgm)
Boys	10-12	2420	42.5	30.25	600	2400	1.2	1.5	16	40	0.4-0.5
Girls	10-12	2260	42.1	30.25	"	"	1.1	1.4	15	40	0.4-0.5
Boys	13-15	2660	51.7	25	750	3000	1.3	1.6	18	40	0.6-0.7
Girls	13-15	2360	43.3	35	"	"	1.2	1.4	15	40	0.6-0.7
Boys	16-18	2820	53.1	25	750	3000	1.4	1.7	19	40	0.05-0.06
Girls	16-18	2200	44.0	35	750	3000	1.4	1.3	15	40	0.05-0.06

The ICMR expert group suggested the following compostion of diet to derive the above recommended allowance for adolescent groups.

Composition of Balanced Diet for Adolescents

Group	Age (years)	Cereals	Pulses	Leafy vegetables	Other vegetables	Roots & tubers (Ml)	Milk	Oil & fat	Sugar and jaggery
Boys	10-12	420 gm	45 gm	50 gm	50 gm	30 gm	250	40 gm	45 gm
Girls	10-12	380 gm	45 gm	50 gm	50 gm	30 gm	250	35 gm	45 gm
Boys	13-18	420 gm	70 gm	50 gm	50 gm	30 gm	250	40 gm	45 gm
Girls	13-18	380 gm	70 gm	100 gm	50 gm	30 gm	250	40 gm	45 gm

Height and Weight of Adolescent Girls and Boys

Age years	Height (cm) Male	Female	Weight (kg) Male	Female
16 yrs	168.4	155.4	55.4	49.8
17 yrs	168.9	156.4	59.0	49.9
18 yrs	169.4	157.2	62.0	50.0

A Sample Diet for an Adolesent Girl

Time	Meal	Menu
8 a.m.		Coffee
8 a.m.	Breakfast	Idli or chapathi, Sprouted green gram curry, Plantain
12.30 Noon	Lunch	Soyabeans pulao or chapathi, Curry leaves chutney, Tomato salad, Curd, Fruit cup
4.30 p.m.	Tea	Vegetable cutlet, Grapes
8 p.m.	Dinner	Soft chapathi, Egg-green peas curry, Vermicelli kheer.
9 p.m.		Ragi malt.

35

NUTRITION DURING OLD AGE

Good nutrition throughout the life serves as a sound insurance for health for the years of old age. The process of aging brings about marked physiological changes in the body. Inadequate dentition, diminished sensitivity to taste and smell, diminished secretion of hydrochloric acid in the stomach and digestive enzymes, biliary impairment, if any, which interferes with fat digestion, irregular bowel evacuation, general ill-health, economic or emotional insecurity and unwanted feelings are some of the problems common among old people. Diseases of old age like diabetes, hypertension and other heart diseases also pose more problems to them. In modern society, with nuclear families, problems of old age are varied. In a joint family, old people are wanted and respected and they enjoy their position. But in our modern society old people often feel neglected and psychological problems created by this reflects as many ailments. Loss of appetite is a common complaint of old people.

Nutrition requirements of old change from normal adult requirements. The lowered metabolic rate reduces the caloric requirement by about 25 per cent compared with normal adults. Physical activity is also less compared to a normal person. If an old person has normal body weight adequate calories can be given. For obese people the calorie intake should be adjusted to reduce body weight whereas for underweight persons the calorie intake should be enough to bring them to normal weight. For a normal sedentary worker 2,100 kcals for males and 1,700 kcals for females are enough to maintain normal condition.

Protein deficiency is common among old people. Protein-splitting enzymes like pepsin, trypsin and erepsin are mild in their action and so protein is not digested properly. Absorption of nutrients is poor among old people due to changes in intestinal wall. Loss of appetite and difficulty in chewing and masticating food must be supplied to old people to provide 1.5 gms of protein per kg of body weight. Though pulses are rich sources of protein, they produce flatulence among old people. Cooking methods adopted for geriatric people must be like steaming or boiling, making food easily digestible. Fat digestion is difficult and delayed in old age. Moreover, cholesterol level could be high among old people and so it is better to avoid saturated fat from animal sources, coconut and palm oil. Vegetable oils reduce the blood cholesterol level and 40 to 50 gms of such fats or oils can be used.

Assimilation of minerals is poor in old people compared to a normal person. Osteoperosis and anaemia are common among elderly people. Poor absorption of minerals and hormonal imbalance, especially of androgen and oestrogen, produce osteoperosis in old people. About 0.8 to 1.00 gm of calcium and 30 to 40 mgms of iron are recommended for them. Chronic arthritis and hypoactivity of the thyroid diminishes the activity of bone marrow which results in anaemia. Generally vegetables, raw vegetables or fruits are consumed in less amounts by old people which produces signs and symptoms of various vitamin deficiencies. B complex vitamin deficiency is common and along with a good diet a multivitamin supplement is essential.

Fluid intake must be liberal so as to form 1 to 1.5 litres of urine daily. Since many renal diseases are common among old people proper urine output must be checked. Only proper urine formation eliminates the urea, uric acid and other metabolic byproducts.

Since constipation is a common complaint of this age bulk or roughage must be included in the diet. Too much of refined carbohydrate foods, sweets and juices lack bulk and produce constipation. Muscle tone of the intestine is reduced and physical activities are also less, so only roughage in the diet can stimulate the intestinal movements.

For non-vegetarians the amount of milk is reduced to 400 ml and pulses to 55 gms for males and 45 gms for females. One multivitamin mineral tablet is recommended for them. Individual variation is common among old people depending on their health status.

Nutrition of Workers

Requirement of various nutrients for labourers and industrial workers differ from normal adults. Calories, thiamine and riboflavin

Composition of Balanced Diet for Geriatrics Over 60 Years

Foodstuffs	Males	Females
Cereals	320 gms	220 gms
Pulses	70 gms	55 gms
Green leafy vegetables	100 gms	125 gms
Other vegetables	75 gms	75 gms
Roots and tubers	75 gms	50 gms
Fruits	75 gms	50 gms
Milk	600 ml	600 ml
Fats and oils	30 gms	30 gms
Sugar and jaggery	30 gms	30 gms

A Sample Diet for a Geriatric Person

Time	Meal	Menu
6.30 a.m.		Horlicks
8 a.m.	Breakfast	Pancake, Orange juice
10 a.m.	Mid time	Soup made from greens
12 Noon	Lunch	Lime rice or soft chapathi, Peas curry, Coriander leaves chutney, Potato-carrot raita, Bread pudding.
4 p.m.	Tea	Baked vegetable cutlet, Plantain
6 p.m.	Mid time	Mixed fruit juice
8 p.m.	Dinner	Rice gruel or wheat gruel, Fish molee, Tomato chutney, Ripe papaya.
9 p.m.	Bed time	Milk

requirements are high. Working efficiency of a person depends to a great extent on the pattern of diet consumed. To get the maximum output a labourer must have adequate diet. Manual work demands more energy and to assimilate energy sources properly B vitamins are essential. Energy requirement varies according to the climatic condition and pattern of work, that is, whether under the sun or inside a factory.

Protein requirement is not increased for labourers, but if the energy requirement is not met from energy sources proteins are utilised for energy purpose. Climatic conditions again affect the protein requirements, for, instance, about 50 per cent more proteins are required in cold climate.

Vitamins must be present in adequate amount in the diet. Thiamine is essential to maintain normal appetite because deficiency of it interferes with metabolism of carbohydrate. Therefore, 0.5 mg of thiamine per 1,000 kcals is the required amount. Riboflavin and niacin are also required in good amount to enable proper utilisation of energy.

Minerals like calcium, phosphorus and iron must be the same as in the diet of a normal adult. Adequate nutrition ensures working efficiency. Undernourished persons reduce their voluntary activity. An anaemic person cannot work hard or concentrate on anything. His output is low and this yields low income. Purchasing capacity of such people is low and as a result they buy foods insufficient for the family and consume inadequate diet. Inadequate nourishment brings ill-health and this cycle is continued. Low-cost foods can be substituted for high-cost ones. But often people are not aware of the cheap nutritious sources which can nourish them well. Nutrition education is essential to select low-cost foods like roots and millets like ragi or jowar, cowgram, horsegram, soyabeans, cluster beans, groundnuts, leafy vegetables, amla, papaya and locally available vegetables and fruits.

Compostion of Balanced Diet for Labourers or Industrial Workers

Foodstuffs	Male	Female
Cereals	630 gms	575 gms
Pulses	80 gms	60 gms
Green leafy vegetables	125 gms	100 gms
Other vegetables	100 gms	100 gms
Roots and tubers	100 gms	100 gms
Fruits	60 gms	60 gms
Milk	400 ml	400 ml
Fats and oils	50 gms	40 gms
Groundnuts	50 gms	50 gms

For non-vegetarians 60 gms of meat or fish or one egg can be included and pulses reduced to 55 gms and 50 gms for males and females, respectively.

A Sample Diet for a Labourer (Female)

Time	Meal	Menu
6 a.m.	Bed coffee	Jaggery coffee
8 a.m.	Breakfast	Wheat dosa, Soyabeans curry
12.30 Noon	Lunch	Rice or chapathi, Plantain stem-potato pugath, Dry fish curry, Mashed tapioca, Vegetable salad, Ripe papaya, Lassi
4 p.m.	Tea	Tea, boiled groundnuts
8.30 p.m.		Ragiputtu or chapathi, Drumstick leaf-mixed vegetable curry, Sprouted green gram curry, Gooseberry chutney, Cucumber salad, Ragi porridge.

This diet provides calories 3,100 kcals, proteins 58 gms.

Part IV
NUTRITION
IN
DISEASES

36

THERAPEUTIC MODIFICATIONS

"The best doctors in the world are Doctor Diet, Doctor Quiet and Doctor Merryman," said Jonathan Swift. Though it is an old saying it is very apt in the case of certain diseases. For, in certain diseases, dietary modification is more important than medical treatment. In some other diseases, diet therapy goes hand-in-hand with medical care. In deficiency diseases dietary modification alone is enough. Quantitative and qualitative modifications are done for various diseases. Elimination or addition of certain nutrients, or alteration in the normal pattern of diet and cooking methods are also employed in some conditions.

The main objectives of diet therapy are to maintain good nutritional status of a sick person, to correct deficiencies, if any, to restrict some nutrients, to change the cooking methods so as to give rest to digestive organs or to give rest to certain organs in the body, to reduce or increase the body weight whenever necessary.

There are certain principles in diet therapy. One important aspect is that all therapeutic diets are adaptations of the normal diet and skeletal structure of the therapeutic diets must be based on the requirements of a healthy person. The person in charge of dietetic planning also must consider the patient as a person and consideration must be given to the economic status, dietary pattern, likes and dislikes, family environment, preferences, religious status and availability of items. Dietetics must always give room for flexibility. Rapport with the patient is essential to make dietetic regimen a success. As a rule therapeutic diet must be easily digestible, soft, liquid, clear fluid or bland based on the conditions. Best sources must be selected to ensure maximum utilisation from the food consumed because as a whole a patient has poor appetite. Along with the discomfort of disease it is always difficult to implement a strict dietetic regimen. Confidence and cooperation from the patient are essential for the success of diet therapy. The patients must be educated on the importance of modification in the diet for quick recovery and the consequences of uncontrolled diet in special conditions. The dietetic history of the patient must be collected to know of any intolerance of food or allergic manifestation in the patient. Working conditions and dietary habits at work place also must be considered before dietetic instructions are given.

Common modifications in diet therapy are changes in consistency by adopting a full liquid diet, clear liquid diet, nasal feeding or tube feeding or soft diet. Changes in the preparation are made by avoiding all condiments and spices and suggesting bland diet which is chemically, mechanically and thermally non-irritant in nature. High calorie diets are also prescribed for underweight persons or in fevers or in hyperthyrodism. High protein diets are recommended for protein calorie malnutrition, cirrhosis of liver, peptic ulcer, tuberculosis, typhoid, nephrotic syndrome, celiac diseases and during pregnancy and lactation. Low-protein diets are suggested for hepatic coma or failure, kidney diseases like uraemia or nephritis.

Fats are restricted in a low-caloric diet, in liver diseases and in hypertension. Modifications are also necessary in fat in steatorrhoea, malabsorption syndrome and in undernutrition.

A mineral like calcium is essential in the treatment of rickets and osteomalacia and is restricted in renal calculi. Sodium is restricted in hypertension and in cardiac diseases. In kidney diseases also sodium chloride is restricted.

In all therapeutic diets high vitamin content is recommended. Restriction of various items in diet will result in deficiency or one or two vitamins and so their supplementation is essential.

Fibre content in the diet should be increased to remove constipation while it should be reduced in peptic ulcer, ulcerative colitis, celiac diseases, diarrhoea and dysentery.

Chemical constituents like purine are restricted in the treatment of gout and a low oxalic diet is prescribed for renal calculi.

Diet consistency is often modified depending upon the nature and condition of various diseases. Liquids are used for oral or nasogastric feeding. After surgery or in conditions where the patient has difficulty in swallowing foods or in inflammatory conditions of gastro-intestinal tract liquid diets are advocated. Soft and bland diets are given later on.

Liquid Diets

Liquid diets are suitable for post-operative diabetes mellitus, intragastric and jejunostomy feeding, constriction of oesophagus due to carcinoma or burns, fevers, acute diarrhoea.

If food is taken by mouth, wheat flour or the equivalent dry weight of other cereal may be given as thin conjee or gruel. This should be carefully strained in cases of constriction of the oesophagus and diarrhoea. If butter is prescribed, this may be added during cooking. Skimmed milk powder may be reconstituted with water or beaten into fresh milk. Tea, coffee or cocoa may be added as flavouring unless contraindicated.

Eggs may be given an egg flip. Fruit juice should be prepared fresh as required and carefully strained in cases of constriction of oesophagus and diarrhoea.

If food is required for tube-feeding, milk feeds may be prepared using proportionate quantities of foods prescribed.

Preparation of Milk Feeds

Mix wheat flour with cold water to a thin paste. Boil the milk and add it to the wheat paste, stirring continually, then return to the fire and cook for two minutes, stirring all the time. Add butter, if prescribed, and stir until melted and well mixed. Cool to near body temperature and beat in egg, skimmed milk powder, sugar and salt. Dilute if necessary to a consistency which will pass through the tube. Strain and administer at body temperature.

If using wheat flour, and the mixture is found to be too thick to pass through the tube, skimmed milk powder may be substituted, using the same dry weight. This will mean a decrease in the carbohydrate value of the total diet, but an increase in the protein value.

Liquid Diet 1000 kcals

Summary of Diet	gm C	gm P	gm F	kcals
Oranges 6 (juice only)	60	...	...	240
Sugar 4 ozs	120	...	...	480
Milk 16 ozs	22	14	16	288
	202	14	16	1008

Additional fluid as water or barley water may be used as desired unless fluid restriction is recommended.

Liquid Diet 1200 kcals

Quantities are the same as for the Liquid Diet of 1000 kcals, with the addition of one of the following:

Milk 10 ozs	giving additional 9 gms protein
Milk 6 ozs and eggs 2	giving additional 12 gms protein
Skimmed milk powder 2 ozs	giving additional 20 gms protein

Liquid Diet 1500 kcals

Summary of diet	gm C	gm P	gm F	kcals
Oranges 6 (juice only)	60	...	...	240
Sugar 2 ozs	60	...	...	240
Milk 30 ozs	42	27	30	540
Wheat flour 1 ozs	33	4	...	200
Eggs 3	...	10.5	10.5	135
Skimmed milk powder 2 gms	30	20		200
	225	61.5	40.5	1505

For tube-feeding, administer as follows:

Four feeds, each consisting of:
    Milk 7 ozs
    Skimmed milk powder 1 oz
    Wheat flour 1 oz (in each of three feeds)
    Egg 1 (in each of three feeds)
    Sugar 1 oz
    Salt (one) level teaspoon (unless restricted)

Orange juice and remainder of sugar should be given between the milk feeds during the day, with additional fluid (water or barley water) as desired.

Liquid Diet 2000 kcals

Summary of Diet	gms C	gms P	gms F	kcals
Oranges 6 (juice only)	60	...	...	240
Milk 40 ozs	56	36	40	720
Wheat flour 2 ozs	55	7	...	250
Eggs 3	...	10.5	10.5	135
Skimmed milk powder 2 ozs	37	25	...	250
Sugar 3 ozs	105	...	...	420
	313	78.5	50.5	2015

For tube-feeding, administer as follows:

Five feeds each consisting of:
    Milk 8 ozs
    Wheat flour 1 oz
    Skimmed milk powder 1 oz
    Egg 1 (in each of three feeds)
    Sugar 1 oz
    Salt, 1 level teaspoon (unless restricted)

Orange juice and remainder of sugar should be given between the milk feeds during the day, with additional fluid (water or barley water) as desired.

Liquid Diet 2500 kcals

Summary of diet	gms C	gms P	gms F	kcals
Milk 40 ozs	56	36	40	720
Wheat flour 2 ozs	57	7	...	250
Eggs 3	...	10.5	10.5	135
Skimmed milk powder 3.75 ozs	56	37	...	375
Sugar 4 ozs	120	...	...	480
Orange 3 (juice only)	30	...	...	120
Butter 2 ozs	...	...	48	432
	319	90.5	98.5	2512

For tube-feeding, administer as follows:

Milk 8 ozs
Wheat flour 1 oz
Egg 1 (in each of three feeds)
Skimmed milk powder 3/4 oz
Sugar 1 oz
Butter 1 oz (in each of four feeds)
Salt, 1 level teaspoon (unless restricted)
Orange juice and sugar should be given between milk feeds.

Liquid Diet 3000 kcals

Summary of Diet	gms C	gms P	gms F	kcals
Milk 40 ozs	56	36	40	720
Wheat flour 3 ozs	66	9	...	300
Eggs 3	...	10.5	10.5	135
Skimmed milk powder 6 ozs	90	60	...	600
Sugar 4 ozs	120	...	...	480
Oranges 3 (juice only)	30	...	...	120
Butter 3 ozs	...	...	72	648
	362	115.5	122.5	3003

For tube-feeding, administer as follows:

Six feeds each consisting of:
Milk 6 ozs
Wheat flour 1 oz
Egg 1 (in each of three feeds)
Skimmed milk powder 1 oz
Sugar 1 oz
Butter 1 oz
Salt, 1 level teaspoon (unless restricted).

Orange juice and remainder of sugar should be given between the milk feeds during the day, with additional fluid (water or barley water) as desired.

Liquid diets are usually used for relatively short periods. If liquid diet is to be used for prolonged periods supplementation of some vitamins and minerals is essential. The main purpose of liquid diets is to reduce effort for digestion and absorption and not to satisfy the requirements. All nutrient sources cannot be planned in a liquid diet satisfactorily. Enriched or pre-cooked infant cereal foods can be incorporated to contribute iron, thiamine and niacin.

Soft Diet

Soft diets are recommended for patients with gastro-intestinal disorders or in post-operative cases. In acute infection, where loss of appetite and vomiting persist, soft diets are recommended. The nature of the diet is soft but it is neither fluid nor a normal diet but in between these two. For patients who cannot masticate or chew, a soft diet is suggested. Soft diet contains no fried foods, strongly flavoured vegetables, raw foods, fibre, spices or condiments. Depending upon the disease condition, sources of nutrients can be selected. Milk and milk products, fruits, eggs and cereals can be incorporated with one another to give variety and good taste, since condiments and spices are used less in soft diet. Restrictions of various nutrients differ according to the symptoms of disease.

Characteristics of a Soft Diet

As a whole the soft food needs no mechanical action to digest it. Cereals as porridge, pre-cooked infant cereals available in the market or soft chapatis of wheat, rice, jowar or bajra, double-cooked rice and sweet cereal preparations are included in the soft diet. Rice flakes, puffed rice, noodles, strained oatmeal and macaroni are the other cereal items that can be included in a soft diet. Pulses can be included as dal soup or mashed dal. Vegetables are used as vegetable purees (cooked and mashed) or soups or boiled in various preparations. Meat or fish can be included in a soft diet as baked or minced items, strained unseasoned soup, broiled or roasted forms. Milk in any form is allowed. Egg as soft-boiled, scrambled, poached or in baked form is permissible. Fruits in the form of fruit juices and cooked or baked form are included in the soft diet. Steamed items are better digested.

Bland Diet

Bland diet is used for diseases of gastro-intestinal tract. In peptic ulcer and in gastric ulcer a bland diet is used. In this diet, mechanical, chemical and thermal irritations are avoided. Seeds, skin, peel, fibre and hard solid foods produce mechanical irritation. Chemical stimulation occurs on consuming meat extracts, condiments and spices, alcohol, acid-producing foods, strongly flavoured vegetables and fruits.

Muscular tone and motility of intestine are increased by hot and warm foods, liquid, fibrous or concentrated sweets. Cold foods, dry foods and low fibre foods reduce the motility of the intestine. Therefore, thermal irritation by cold or heat has to be avoided for gastro-intestinal disorders. Emotional attitude of the patient influences the enzyme production, muscle tone and motility and also affects digestion of food. Fear, anger, worry, pain and discontent have negative attitude in the patient towards food. Neurosis is to be handled first in the gastric diseases for effective dietary treatment.

Common diseases where dietetics plays an important role in the treatment can be grouped as (1) Deficiency diseases like kwashiorkar, marasmus, anaemia, (2) Gastro-intestinal disorders like peptic ulcer, ulcerative colitis, constipation, diarrhoea, (3) diseases of liver, biliary tract and pancreas like cirrhosis, infantile biliary cirrhosis, jaundice, and viral hepatitis, hepatic coma and coma, pancreatitis, (4) kidney diseases like nephritis, chronic renal failure or uraemia, calculi, (5) metabolic disorder like diabetes mellitus and obesity, gout and (6) heart diseases like high blood pressure and congestive cardiac failure.

37

DIET DURING DEFICIENCY DISEASES

Good wholesome food is essential for normal growth and development. Hippocrates, the father of medicine, used food as a remedial agent many centuries ago. Now it is an established fact that food is not only essential for growth but also required for preventing certain diseases. Inadequate intake of essential nutrients and improper utilisation of them leads to deficiency diseases. Body reserves of nutrients are depleted first and normal biochemical reactions are upset later on. Slowly automatic lesions develop and manifestation of malnutrition occurs. Functional disabilities are followed by fatal conditions in some cases. Deficiency may manifest within weeks to years. Children are more prone to develop deficiencies. If the signs of good nutrition are known it is easy to make a positive diagnosis of most nutritional deficiencies in early stages. Good nutrition is reflected not in the absence of disease alone but in proper physical, emotional and mental conditions of an individual. Well proportioned body with enough fat, proper height and weight for the age, well developed and firm muscles, smooth, clear and slightly moist skin, glossy hair which is neither too glossy nor brittle, smooth nails, clear eyes without dark circles under them, alert and pleasant facial expression, erect posture, broad chest, even shoulders, good natured attitude, sound appetite, digestion, good bowel movement and sleep are the signs of good nutrition. Well-fed people have a general feeling of well-being.

Loss of interest in and appetite for food, loss of weight, poor concentration power, insomnia, irritability, nervousness, frequent infections, sore tongue, mouth, dermatitis, and skin diseases, diarrhoea, constipation, muscular weakness, painful joints and muscles, deformities in the bone, difficulty in seeing in dim light, swollen or congested eyelids, dry eyes and poor general health and retarded growth are symptoms of malnutrition.

Common deficiency diseases are protein-energy malnutrition like kwashiorkor and marasmus, avitaminosis, ariboflavinosis and anaemia.

Protein-Energy Malnutrition

Deficiency of protein and energy during infancy is one of the most serious problems throughout the world. It leads to two clinical syndromes, kwashiorkor and marasmus. These two deficiency conditions are common among infants of lower income groups. It is a common problem of early childhood in India.

Kwashiorkor

This was first observed in 1930 in Asia and Africa. Kwashiorkor is an African word. It means, "the disease of the displaced child". It usually occurs in the first child when a second child is born. Dr. Cicely Williams reported it first from Africa. The disease is usually caused when the child is weaned from breastfeeding to foods. The foods given to a weaned child contain plenty of carbohydrates but little of proteins. Since growth is rapid and protein is essential to meet the requirement, retardation of growth occurs. Kwashiorkor is usually observed in infants between 1 and 3 years of age.

The first main symptom of kwashiorkor is lack of growth in children. Gastro-intestinal disturbances with anorexia, nausea and diarrhoea are common and enzymatic action of digestion is poor. Swelling of the body, especially on the hands, feet and face will be seen. The hair and skin show characteristc changes. Hair may be light coloured or dispigmented to reddish yellow and fall off in patches. Skin shows patches and becomes flaky and peels off. Hyperpigmentation and dispigmentation are common.

Changes occur in the structure and functional efficiency of liver. Liver may become palpable and soft. Fatty infiltration and enlargement of the liver, fibrosis and cellular necrosis are common. Due to liver disorder protruded bellies are common. Biochemical changes in the body fluids, in the compositon of blood, utilisation of amino acids, electrolyte imbalance and anaemia are common among kwashiorkor children. The child becomes apathetic and all functions of proteins are impaired. Pancreas shows atrophic changes and internal activities of the body are upset. Histological changes occur in the small intestine. The mucosa of the intestine become thin and villi is flattened; atrophy of villi is common. Enzyme activity in the intestine is diminished and disaccharides are not properly assimilated. Fat is not transported through the intestine which results in fat deposition in the cells. Triglycerides level in the blood is increased. Potassium is depleted from body fluids and muscles; magnesium deficiency is also common. Bacterial and viral infections occur in kwashiorkor children as their persistence power is low. Evidence of vitamin deficiency co-exists with protein deficiency condition.

The mortality is high in the absence of proper treatment. The rate of mortality depends upon the degree of fatty infiltration and degree of malnutrition in the child. Infections, other deficiencies, hepatic coma, low potassium level in the serum, or cardiac failure cause death. Though kwashiorkor occurs all over the country, the degree of severity is not the same in all places. It is mostly seen in the southern states of India.

Studies on protein calorie malnutrition by the National Institute of Nutrition has brought to light that the disabilities affected by it are not only on physical growth but also on brain development. Apathy, irritability, listlessness, psychomotor retardation, reduced attention and concentration, low decision-making and problem-solving capacity manifest poor brain development. Psychological development of a malnourished child is poor. Severe protein-calorie malnutrition during infancy can cause permanent and irreversible structural lesion in the central nervous system. Reduced brain size and weight decrease the brain cells. Language development is delayed and malnourished

A Sample Diet for Kwashiorkor Child

Time	Meal	Menu
6.30 a.m.		Milk (Skimmed Milk)
8 a.m.	Breakfast	Rava porridge, Boiled groundnut
10 a.m.	Mid-time	Ragi porridge, Gingelly seed laddu
12 Noon	Lunch	Dal rice or soft chapathi, Scrambed egg or egg curry, Vegetable puree, Guava.
2 p.m.	Mid-time	Tender coconut water
4 p.m.	Tea	Soyabean milk, Mixed flour biscuit
6 p.m.	Mid-time	Green soup
8 p.m.	Dinner	Soft chapathi, Fish molee
9 p.m.	Bed time	Milk

children show poor learning abilities and low scholastic achievements. Poor performance in intelligence tests is common. As the brain development is rapid at pre-school age protein malnutrition can cripple if enough of it is not given during infancy.

Marasmus

Marasmus is due to severe deficiency of proteins and calories in the diet. It is not due to calorie deficiency alone because marasmic children subsequently develop kwashiorkor. In both the cases protein and calorie deficiencies are present but the degree of protein or calorie deficiency results in kwashiorkor or in marasmus. The clinical picture of marasmus is basically due to lack of calorie intake though protein inadequacy is present. Loss of body weight and failure in weight gain and gradual emaciation occurs. Body fat is depleted, muscles are wasted. The child shows the appearance of a withered old man. Ribs and bones stand out and the abdomen may be distended or sunken. The body temperature is subnormal and the child may have starvation type of diarrhoea. The marasmic child is characterised by its thin, lean and skinny appearance whereas a kwashiorkor child is flabby with oedema.

Dietetic Treatment

Kwashiorkor is common among children from low socio-economic group. Prevention and cure include measures whereby highly nutritious low-cost diets are provided for them. Protein foods based on blends of soyabeans, groundnut, cottonseed, legume flour with cereal powders and protein-enriched cereals are recommended for practical purpose. A high calorie, high protein, high vitaminised and mineralised diet with high fluid is recommended for kwashiorkor child. The daily requirement is 90 to 100 kcals per kilogramme of body weight. In this 20 per cent of calories must be from protein sources. In hospitalised cases skimmed milk powder is used for the treatment of kwashiorkor as the main source of protein. Vegetable protein mixtures from various pulses, cereals or millet combinations are evolved by the National Institute of Nutrition (NIN) for the treatment of kwashiorkor. Groundnut milk, dried beans and pulses, small fish, organ meats like liver or brain can be used liberally in the diet of a kwashiorkor child. Ragi halwa, wheat kheer, bajra pongal, idli, uppuma, sweet potato or potato porridge, gram laddu, and green vegetable soups are some of the protein-rich low-cost items. Meal plan for an infant must have some form of milk on rising and cooked cereal pulse preparation for breakfast. Soft-boiled egg or fruit juice can be given to an infant at mid-time. This can be substituted by a millet-pulse porridge and green vegetable soup. For lunch, cooked cereals, or starchy vegetables or millets can be cooked. Boiled pulses, fish or minced meat or organ meats can be included depending upon the economic status. During mid-afternoon, supplements like fish liver oil or sources of vitamins and minerals from cheap sources can be included. For dinner, cereals like suji, broken wheat or ragi can be used as porridge. And before bedtime milk from any source or its substitutes can be given. Indian Multipurpose Food (MPF), malt food, Bal-ahar and supplementary foods are the commercial protein foods developed for kwashiorkor treatment by CFTRI, NIN and AHSCW (Avinashilingam Home Science College for Women). MPF is a blend of low fat groundnut flour and bengal gram fortified with vitamins A and D, thaimine, riboflavin and calcium carbonate. This formula contains 42 per cent of protein. Three different forms of MPF are available: one seasoned with masala which can be incorporated in curries or in soups, unseasoned which can be incorporated with flours and unseasoned with milk powder which is a substitute for milk. CFTRI has conducted studies with pre-school children and they have recorded highly significant improvement in the nutritional status of the pre-school children with the use of MPF.

Malt food: This is another product of CFTRI where a blend of cereal malt (40%) and low fat groundnuts (40%) and roasted bengal gram flour (20%) is fortified with vitamins and calcium salts. This provides 28 per cent good quality proteins and is comparatively cheap.

Bal-ahar: Bal-ahar is another product of CFTRI, a blend of whole wheat flour (70%), groundnut flour (20%) and roasted bengal gram flour (10%), fortified with calcium salts and vitamins. This contains about 20 per cent proteins. Vitamin A, riboflavin and calcium are present in appreciable amounts.

Supplementary foods: NIN has developed supplementary foods for the treatment of protein calorie malnutrition. Supplementary food is a blend of roasted wheat flour (30%), green gram flour (20%), groundnut (8%), and sugar or jaggery (20%). This supplement provides 12.5 per cent proteins and has proved effective in the treatment of kwashiorkor.

Sri Avinashilingam Home Science College for Women is engaged in extension activities among rural people. One of its projects is to impart nutrition education to rural women. They have developed a low cost supplementary food based on maize which is known as "Kuzhandai Amudhu". It is a blend of maize flour (30%), green gram flour (20%), roasted groundnut (10%), and jaggery (20%). This supplement supplies 14.4 per cent proteins and has brought significant improvement in growth rate and nutritional status of pre-school children.

A Sample Diet for a Marasmic Child

Time	Meal	Menu
6.30 a.m.		Milk
8 a.m.	Breakfast	Sweetened mixed flour chapathi, Soft boiled egg, Plantain
9 a.m.	Mid-time	Sago porridge
10 a.m.	Mid-time	Vegetable soup
12 Noon	Lunch	Soyabean pulao, Sprouted green gram raita, Fruit salad
2 p.m.	Mid-time	Ragi porridge
4 p.m.	Tea	Gingelly seed laddu, Ripe mango
6 p.m.	Mid-time	Groundnut milk, Carrot halwa
8 p.m.	Dinner	Wheat gruel, Green peas saute, Guava
9 p.m.	Bed time	Groundnut Milk

Prevention of Protein Calorie Malnutrition

Prevalence of malnutrition is due to various causes. Ignorance about the importance of pre-school nutrition and the non-availability of low cost nutritious foods are considered important reasons for kwashiorkor and marasmus. Nutrition education on these aspects assumes special significance in the prevention of malnutrition. Food fads and faulty food habits are stumbling blocks in improving the nutritional status of pre-school children. Prolonged breastfeeding up to the age of 2 to 3 years is common in rural areas. Proper emphasis is not given on weaning or supplementary foods for pre-school children. The infant is exposed to an adult diet and deficiencies are the result. Nutrition education must be related to supplies available in local conditions and dietary habits. Customs based on traditional habits are difficult to change. Only sincere efforts from various sources can bring gradual changes.

Anaemia

Anaemia is a condition in which there is reduction in the haemoglobin content of blood. This is due to a reduction in the number of blood cells or size of the red blood cells or due to defective maturation of the red blood cells. There is continuous degeneration and building up of blood cells in our body. The normal lifespan of a red blood cell is about 120 days. Building up of red cells and their maintenance require certain nutrients. Deficiency of any of these nutrients leads to anaemia. Iron, protein, B vitamins like B 12, folic acid, vitamin C and copper deficiency can produce anaemia. Diarrhoea, sprue or pellagra and low acidity of stomach glands affect the normal absorption and utilisation of iron. Malaria, hookworm infestation and other intestinal parasites or chemical agents like coal-tar products interfere with red blood cells concentration in the blood. Exposure to X-rays or radium, bone tumours, cirrhosis of the liver, carcinoma and leukaemias interfere with red blood cells formation. Haemorrhage due to extravascular blood loss from peptic ulcer, bleeding piles, excessive menstrual flow, aesophagal varies and hernia also can produce anaemia. Infancy, adolescence, pregnancy and lactation are special phases where anaemia is common due to rapid growth. Closely spaced pregnancies and prolonged breastfeeding may also result in anaemia. If phylates, phosphates and oxalates are present in the diet in large amounts they interfere with iron absorption which results in anaemia. Generally only 10 per cent of ingested iron is absorbed because of this.

Normally 100 ml of blood contains 14 to 15 gms of haemoglobin. When the haemoglobin content is below 12.5 gms the person is considered anaemic. About half the pregnant women in our country are anaemic and one out of every four maternal deaths is due to anaemia. In India 50 to 60 per cent of children and about 80 per cent of adolescents are anaemic.

Modification of the Diet

The cause of anaemia should be discovered before treatment. Diet alone is not enough as its causes are many. A well-balanced diet with high protein, iron, vitamin C and B complex must be accompanied with ferrous sulphate supplements. If diet is used as the only treatment for anaemia restoration of normal haemoglobin level it is a slow process. Since undernutrition is the cause of anaemia which is due to prolonged poor appetite, during treatment planning of diet must be from carefully selected best sources of nutrients. Sustained diet therapy is essential to regain normal health. Those who can afford organ meats can include it as they are excellent sources of iron. Liver, kidney and bone marrow in any form are the best sources to get iron. Dried fruits like raisins, currants, dates, dried figs, prunes and molasses, green leafy vegetables, drumsticks, green mango, solanum torvem, soyabeans, rice bran, gingelly seeds, watermelon, peaches, passion fruit and chiku fruit are excellent sources of iron. Egg is also a good source of iron and protein and can be taken by those who can afford it.

Pernicious Anaemia

Pernicious anaemia is not due to the deficiency of iron or other blood-cell-forming substances. This is caused by the lack of intrinsic factor in the stomach which is essential for the absorption of vitamin B 12 in the intestines. As a result red blood cells are not produced in the bone marrow after the old ones die.

In pernicious anaemia the red blood cell (RBC) count is low which is about 1.5 to 2.5 million per mm of blood where the normal count is 4.5 to 5.5 million of RBC. In pernicious anaemia the RBC are big in size and so it is also known as macrocytic anaemia. Haemoglobin content is as low as 7 to 9 per cent. The patient of this type of anaemia has lemon yellow pallor. Poor digestion and low hydrochloric acid secretion reduces the appetite and results in general weakness, sore tongue and glazed alimentary tract. If neglected, it will lead to numbness in the limbs and difficulty in walking. Slowly it progresses into anorexia or spasticity.

Dietary Modifications

A well balanced diet with B 12 supplementation is essential. Supplementation of liver extracts was found very effective in the treatment of pernicious anaemia. A high protein diet of 100 to 150 gms of protein with a high calorie diet is recommended. Fat content must be reduced because of the low hydrochloric acid secretion in the stomach. Liberal intake of minerals and vitamins and supplements of iron are recommended. Since anorexia or irritation of the gastro-intestinal tract and sore throat are present a soft or liquid diet is recommended. Refer to soft diet given earlier for meal planning.

Underweight

A person who eats little for a long period looks emaciated and shows underweight. Living habitually on an inadequate diet, especially of protein, results in low body weight. When food intake is 2/3 to 3/4 of the requirement among poor people the body weight is reduced up to 25 per cent. Underweight also results from debilitating diseases like tuberculosis, diabetes, malabsorption syndrome or cancer. Infections are common among them. Basal metabolic rate, resistance to infection and voluntary activities are reduced considerably, psychological efficiency as a whole is reduced and their power for concentration and decision-making and withstanding calamities are very poor. Internal structure and functional capacity of various organs is reduced due to deficiencies of essential nutrients. Extreme tissue wasting, depletion of adipose tissues, oedema, disturbed renal function and diarrhoea are common among such persons. Working efficiency is poor and the productivity is less. Lack of nourishment makes the worker inactive and weak. An undernourished person becomes weak and cannot work continuously for a long period.

Dietary Modifications

A high calorie, high protein, high fat diet with liberal vitamin intake is recommended. Depending upon the activities, the energy requirements vary. Along with the normal requirement an additional 500 kcals per day is recommended. Instead of 1 gm of protein 1.2 gm protein/kg of body weight is recommended. Good quality protein is completely utilised by the body and as far as possible best protein sources must be liberally included in the initial stage.

Even though fat content is increased, easily digestible fats are to be included. Fried foods are not suggested in the beginning as the patient may develop diarrhoea. Apart from this, fatty foods reduce appetite and so their intake is not advisable. High carbohydrate sources must form the basis of the diet. Dried fruits, sweets, nuts, desserts, preserves like jam, jelly, cereals, non-vegetarian foods and roots are rich sources of energy and these can be liberally included in an underweight person's diet. Since the persons were used to taking small quantities of food the number of meals has to be increased. Two-hourly feeds incorporating soups, juices or sweets in between major meals improve the nutritive value of the diet. Easily digestible forms are suggested for an underweight person. Porridge with milk and honey, cutlets, desserts, potato chips, high protein drinks like milk, punch, malted milk, eggnog, fruit punch, banana stew and enriched milk drinks can be used in the meal planning. Thick soups and fruit whips with honey are easily digestible and highly nutritious items.

Regular exercises enable one to stimulate appetite. Enough fluid must be taken so as to avoid constipation. Good dietary habits and healthy living promote weight gain. If there are any diseases or parasite infestation in the body they must be treated simultaneously. Synthetic drinks, saccharine, and salty tit-bits like popcorns, soft drinks, other aerated drinks, alcohol, too much coffee or tea and smoking reduce appetite and an underweight person must avoid all these. Emotional well-being is essential to have a good appetite.

A Sample Diet for an Underweight Person

Time	Meal	Menu
6 a.m.	Bed coffee	Coffee
8 a.m.	Breakfast	Poori, Egg-tomato curry, Apple, Tea
10 a.m.	Mid-time	Rava porridge or chapathi
12 Noon	Lunch	Vegetable pulao, fish cutlet, Sprouted green gram, raita ice-cream
2 p.m.	Mid-time	Green soup
4 p.m.	Tea	Tea, Egg pakoda, Grapes
6 p.m.	Mid-time	Groundnut milk
8 p.m.	Dinner	Chapathi, Vegetable kurma
9 p.m.	Bed time	Horlicks

38

OBESITY

Obesity or over-nutrition is a menace to health and it is a public health problem of the well-to-do people. Obesity is a condition in which there is excessive weight gain in the body. An increase of 10 per cent over the ideal weight or optimal weight is termed obesity. Excessive weight gain is mainly due to high intake of food. When more energy is taken through food and less is utilised through activities the excess energy is converted into fat which is deposited as adipose tissue.

Excessive weight is a predisposing factor for cardiovascular disease, osteoarthritis, diabetes, gout, liver and gall bladder disease and hernia. Surgery is always a risk with obese people. There is an old saying,"The longer the belt, the shorter the life". Modern medicine emphasises this statement. In obese persons physical activity is limited and fatigue, backache and foot aches are common after little exertion. Apart from physical handicaps it produces psychological setbacks. An obese person is very self-conscious and always lags behind in a group as the physical reflexes are slow. Their social involvements are poor because of overweight and its hazards.

Causes of Obesity

Obesity is mainly caused by excessive calorie consumption. If energy is not utilised for activities it accumulates as adipose tissues. If adipose tissues are formed even in early childhood they tend to produce obesity in later life. The number of fat cells will grow in size as the child grows and becomes obese. Thus over-nutrition in childhood has an influence over obesity in later life. Now a chubby child is not considered as a healthy child for this reason.

More fatty cells in the body need not always be due to high calorie consumption. Endocrine imbalance, and genetic factors often cause this peculiar phenomena in the body.

Excessive intake of calories can often be due to physiological or psychological causes. Through physical examination, dietary history, living habits and family and social set-up have to be investigated before dietetic planning. In the hypothalamus in the brain there are two parts in nuclei, median and laternal, which regulate appetite in a person. Lesion in median nuclei increases the appetite while a lesion in the lateral nuclei reduces the appetite. Another cortical centre of the brain controls hypothalamus.

Endocrine glands like thyroid, pituitary and in females hormones influence the appetite and weight gain. Obesity is common among women after pregnancy and it can be due to causes other than those connected with nutrition. But obesity resulting from disturbances of glands are less than 5 per cent and the remaining are due to too much eating. Labour-saving devices at home and in industry and modern comfortable living contribute to the high occurrence of obesity. Those who engage in strenuous physical activity are less likely to become obese. Since obesity is common among people after the age of 35, it is related with food consumption and pattern of work. When physical activities are reduced food consumption must be reduced. But the consumption pattern remains unchanged while activities are reduced which results in obesity. The role of heredity in obesity is not well understood. Dietetic habits of the family rather than hereditary factors are always responsible for obesity. Food habits are more or less the same from one generation to another and children imitate their parents' dietary pattern. Eating too much or eating fattening foods are thus handed over as food habits from generation to generation.

In middle age especially, women feel lonely and unwanted and they find solace in eating. A person who is bored, unloved or discontented with worry or sorrow indulges in overeating to escape from his problems. Like any other addiction overeating is also an addiction and treatment for this requires psychological approach. Such people derive physical pleasure by eating and thus an outlet of their emotional disturbances. A poorly adjusted person feels rejected and thus derives oral gratification through eating and this type of obesity is called psychological obesity. Psychological obesity is of two types: developmental and reactive. Developmental obesity develops from childhood onwards and it depends on food intake, both qualitative and quantitative and the pattern of living. Reactive obesity initiates with some upsetting experiences like homesickness, illness, separation or death of a dear person, and other maladjustment problems in life.

Treatment of Obesity

Losing weight requires careful planning in diet. Reduced food intake and reqular depletion of energy from the body for activities are the practical methods of reducing weight. Before reducing the weight one must know the ideal weight for various heights. For an adult, adjustment in the diet can be done based on body weight.

Standard Weight for Males and Females

Height in cms.	Weight in kg. (males)	Over-weight limit	Under-weight limit	Weight In kg. (females)	Over-weight	Under-weight
148	47.5	57.0	38.0	46.4	56.0	37.0
152	49.0	59.0	39.0	48.5	58.0	39.0
156	51.5	62.0	41.0	50.5	60.5	40.5
160	53.5	64.0	43.0	52.5	63.0	42.0
164	56.0	67.0	45.0	55.0	66.0	44.0
168	59.5	69.5	49.5	58.0	69.0	46.5
172	62.0	74.5	52.4	60.5	72.5	48.5
176	65.5	78.5	55.5	64.0	77.0	51.0
180	68.5	82.0	57.5	67.0	80.5	53.5

As the person grows old, a slight change in ideal weight is normal and that is why a limit is given for overweight. Gaining weight until late middle age is not physiologically necessary.

The treatment of obesity is a long range process and the patient's cooperation and efforts in dietetic discipline are the key factors in its success. It must be made clear to an obese person that obesity is less often due to what one inherits but due to what one ingests. Overeating becomes a habit and there is no mechanism other than strict control over diet which can reduce weight. All other efforts have little effect in reducing weight. Omission of one meal or the main meal has no advantage in weight reduction because it increases the appetite for the next meal. Usually obese people vehemently protest that they are not eating enough food, leave alone more food. The main meal may not be large in quantity but in between tit-bits or snacks or leftovers amount to a number of calories. To reduce weight one must be strict in the matter of food intake and energy output through work. Increase the physical activity through brisk walking, gardening, household chores like mopping, washing and ironing and cycling or swimming. Self-control in dieting and patience to do work for a prolonged period only can show results. Bringing about changes in dietary habits aim at depleting body fat for energy purpose. One gramme of body fat represents 9 calories. After comparing an obese person's weight with ideal weight a reducing diet has to be formulated. A determination to stick to a low calorie diet is an important factor in reducing weight. If 1,000 calories are reduced daily the weight reduction per week is about 770 gms, provided the person is active. Even this pattern will bring about reduction of only 3.1 kgs per month. One weeks's strict low-calorie diet pattern must be formulated in the presence of the patient and a strict follower of this regime can bring about weight reduction. Small helpings of calorific food in between definitely upsets the weight reduction pattern.

Keeping a weight chart and weekly recordings are very effective. Initial weight loss need not be from fat depletion. It can be from loss of salt and water. Motivation of the patient is essential to bear the initial problems.

Exercise in moderate form helps in losing weight. If cardiovascular diseases are affliciting an obese patient, exercises must be mild. As a rule obese persons cannot engage in hard exercise as they are less active. Massage or steam bath are not reliable or a permanent solution for obesity. Weight-reducing drugs or tablets can be harmful and only under medical supervision should a person consume them. Though formula diets with hydrophylic substances are effective a person cannot depend on them for ever. Fasting is not a healthy method for reducing weight because it affects the electrolyte balance, liver, hair and structure and functions of cardiac muscles. Nervous tissues are also affected which result in memory loss. Deviation of any form from a mixed diet is not advocated. Only restriction of certain nutrients is tolerated by the body. Even high reducing diets or rapid reduction in weight can produce hernia, gall-bladder diseases and peptic ulcer. Severe hunger or nervous exhaustion is not good for the body.

Dietetic Management

A reduction in diet aims at maintaining and restoring good nutrition along with gradual reduction in body weight. Low calorie foods must be included in the dietary pattern. An obese patient must be given information about low calorie items in the diet. A wide choice from daily food items provides confidence in following the dietetic instructions. About 20 kcals per kilogramme of ideal body weight is recommended for a sedentary worker and 25 kcals for a moderately active person. An obese person has to reduce the calories to an average of half of their requirements. Depending upon their body weight 800 kcals, 1,000 kcals, 1,100 kcals and 1,200 kcals diets are prescribed. Cereals and cereal products which make the main items of our meals have to be reduced considerably. Sweets, sugar, chocolates, jaggery, jam, honey, syrup, fruit preserves, cakes, pastries, puddings, fried items, roots like potato, tapioca, yam, banana, apple, whole milk, dried fruits, papad, chutney, pickles, nuts, alcoholic drinks and soft drinks, creams, coconuts and fatty foods and oils are avoided in the regime of low-calorie diet. Foods to be included are unsweetened lime juice, clear soups without seasoning, strained vegetable soups, all green leafy vegetables, carrots, onions, brinjals, drumsticks, tomatoes, bittergourd, pumpkins, cauliflower, ladiesfinger, ashgourd, cucumber, french beans, green mango, plantain flowers, snakegourd and prescribed amounts of cereals and pulses. An accustomed dietary pattern with less carbohydrate and fat but balanced in all other nutrients only makes it workable because reducing diet is used for a prolonged period. Judicious selection is essential. The patient must be educated on the calorific value of foods. For example, the breakfast items used in an Indian diet and their calorific value can be compared.

Food items	Calorie supplied
One thin chapathi	80 kcals
One slice of bread	60 kcals
One thin dosa	130 kcals
One idli	100 kcals
One bun	280 kcals
Two parathas (thin)	275 kcals
Two puris	245 kcals
Three tablespoon rice, cooked (60 gm)	70 kcals
Three tbs-uppuma (100 gm)	230 kcals
Rava puttu (100 gm)	230 kcals
One cup coffee with sugar	65 kcals
One cup coffee without sugar	25 kcals
One cup milk	100 kcals
1/2 cup sambar	105 kcals
1/3 cup dal (for chapathi)	92 kcals
One banana	153 kcals

From this any breakfast item can be selected but the calorific value must be adjusted. For lunch, tea and dinner, various familiar items in small quantities are practicable. Salads or steamed leafy vegetables can be liberally included so as to give bulk and fullness to the meal. Non-vegetarian items are rich in fat and so they must be included in small quantities in a reducing diet. Preparation of non-vegetarian dishes again contributes more calories compared to other food groups. Defatted skimmed milk can be included to provide protein and other nutrients.

One gramme of protein per ideal weight is essential to meet the protein requirements. Fat is restricted but vegetable oils other than coconut and palm supply essential fatty acids and little cooking fat is permissible.

One important aspect in prescribing low-calorie diet for an obese person is that the diet must provide satiety value or a sense of satisfaction and well-being to the patient. Reducing diet pattern should not be thrust upon him. He must wholeheartedly follow the regime. In a 1,000 kcals diet mineral and vitamin supplementation is necessary.

Sample Menu for an Obese Person (1,200 kcals-vegetarian)

Time	Meal	Menu
6 a.m.	Bed coffee	Coffee (without sugar)
8 a.m.	Breakfast	Dry Chapathi, Spinach Curry (50 gm), Coffee (without sugar)
10 a.m.	Mid-time	Buttermilk
12.30 p.m.	Lunch	Rice or chapathi (50 gms rice or flour), Beans pugath, Dal curry, Tomato-beetroot salad, Butter-milk
4 p.m.	Tea	Coffee (without sugar), Baked vegetable cutlet, Papaya
8 p.m.	Dinner	String hoppers or phulkas (50 gm), Cucumber salad, Fruit cup

The above diet supplies		
kcals	-	1,186 kcals
proteins	-	48 gms
fat	-	27 gms

39

GASTRO-INTESTINAL DISTURBANCES

The relation between nutrition and diseases of the stomach is complex. Modern medicine emphasises the fact that stomach is the seat of all diseases. Diseases of the upper gastro-intestinal cases interfere with the intake of food by reducing appetite, inducing nausea and vomiting, evoking pain or by producing obstruction. The intestinal tract, especially the small intestine, the site of digestion and absorption of nutrients, play an important role in maintaining the general health. Diseases of the intestinal tract impair the functions of intestinal tract and result in poor utilisation of ingested food.

Common disorders of stomach and intestine are:

> Gastric indigestion or flatulence or dyspepsia,
> Peptic ulcer,
> Ulcerative colitis,
> Diverticulosis or diverticulitis,
> Constipation,
> Diarrhoea,
> Dysentery,
> Malabsorptive syndromes,
> Tropical sprue, and
> Metabolic disorders—diabetes mellitus, phenylketonuria, galactosemia, Wison's disease.

Gastric Indigestion or Dyspepsia

Dyspepsia or flatulence is a common abdominal disorder. It is defined as deranged digestion when the functions of stomach are affected. Symptoms of this disorder are bitter taste in the mouth, heartburn, nausea, loss of appetite, distention, betching, anorexia, acrid eructations, epigastric distress or pain, discomfort or pain in the stomach, vomiting and cardiospasm.

The causes of dyspepsia are many. The presence of air or gas in the stomach or intestine interferes with the motility of the intestine. It occurs either during or after the ingestion of food. This disease can occur due to organic diseases of gastro-intestinal tract, cardiovascular or kidney disease or malignant diseases. Functional reasons of stomach also produce flatulence. In the absence of organic reasons rapid eating, inadequate chewing, swallowing air through food, ingestion of undercooked foods or fried foods, gas forming vegetables like onion, cabbage, beans, radish, cauliflower, pulses, starchy foods, protein-rich animal foods, absence of bulk in the diet can produce the presence of air in the stomach or intestine. A considerable amount of air is taken if we suck or chew food, and while smoking and chewing betel leaves. If fermentation of the food in the intestine takes place it produces gas. Enzyme deficiency like disaccharidase deficiency results in poor absorption of sugar and thereby in gas formation. Too many spices and condiments, high residue and infestation with worms and parasite also produce gas. Finally, the emotional state influences the stomach activity. Aggressive emotions like anger, rebelliousness and excitement increase the motor activity of the stomach while depressive states like worry, fear and depression delay contraction and emptying of the stomach. There is a saying that the abdomen is the sounding board of emotions.

Dietary Modifications

Dietary regulations bring marked difference in the occurrence of flatulence. But individual variations are here for its occurrence and so the cause has to be located. Treatment must be directed to the patient as a whole and not to the disease. Dietetic treatment aims to supply all nutrients. The person must be instructed to avoid excessive amounts of food, saturated fats, highly spiced and seasoned foods. Good eating habits must be developed. The food must be consumed in a relaxed manner. The patient must be advised to chew the food properly. Air swallowing should be avoided. Foul smelling, undercooked or overcooked foods, putrefied foods and fibrous vegetables must be avoided. Though condiments and spices are restricted, garlic is good for flatulence and it inhibits the growth of bacteria in the colon. Fluid intake must be increased but sucking through a straw or bottle increases air sucking.

Pulses and beans, raw vegetable salads, roots, sweets, dried fruits, bakery items except biscuits, nuts, condiments and spices, papad, chutney or pickles are better avoided or restricted. Dinner must be taken at least an hour before sleep. Meals should be taken in a pleasant and relaxed atmosphere. All forms of excitement are harmful to normal digestion. Nervous dispepsia must be treated psychologically.

Sample Menu for Gastric Indigestion

Time		*Menu*
6 a.m.	Bed Coffee	Milk tea
8 a.m.	Breakfast	Cornflakes or rava porridge in milk, Toast, Poached egg, Oranges or papaya
12.20 p.m.	Lunch	Chapathis or rice, Potato-peas curry, Fruit salad, Curd
4 p.m.	Tea	Tea, Sandwiches
8 p.m.	Dinner	Strained vegetable soup, Rice, Bread or chapathis, Brinjal curry or minced meat curry, Tomato saute, Lime pudding.

40

PEPTIC ULCER

Peptic ulcer may be defined as an open lesion upon the mucous lining of the stomach or duodenum. Discomfort and burning or gnawing sensation in the abdomen is the first sign of peptic ulcer. When the gastric juice comes in direct contact with the mucous membrane disintegration and necrosis of the tissue occur. Ulcers may occur in the stomach or in the duodenum. In India peptic ulcers are prevalent more in South India. Low-protein diet with high spices can be the special reason for their occurrence. Gastric ulcers turn malignant, whereas duodenal ulcers do not become malignant.

Aetiology

The exact cause of peptic ulcers remains unknown. Due to unknown reasons the mucosa of the stomach and duodenum become unable to resist the action of digestive juices and part of the tissue is digested and an ulcer develops. Irritation of the mucosa due to alcoholism or dietary irritation from various foods, fasting, mental stress or emotional upset causes peptic ulcers.

Heredity seems to have some influence on the occurrence of peptic ulcers. Blood group 'O' subjects are more liable to have peptic ulcer. Climatic conditions exert influence on the recurrence of peptic ulcer. Monsoon season records highest admission of peptic ulcer cases.

Normally gastric secretions are more if meat soups or extractives, condiments like chillies, pepper, ginger or strong tea or coffee or alcohol is ingested. Protein-rich foods as a whole induce secretions of gastric gland. Smoking appears to have an adverse effect. Ulcerogenic drugs such as aspirin and the various salicylates, conticosteroids, phenylbutazone, oxyphenbutaxone and resperine should be avoided. Mental stress in any form increases acidity. Irregular dietary hours and irritating foods aggregate the situation.

Dietetic Management

In no other disease does dietic treatment take such an important role as in peptic ulcers. A soothing diet gives symptomatic relief and an irritating diet produces sensitivity. Dietary habits must be set with a schedule. Persons engaged in certain occupations like busy executives, businessmen and professionals such as doctors are more prone to peptic ulcers and they have to set a time schedule for meals. Rushing before and after a meal should be avoided. Heavy meals should be avoided as distended abdomen causes pain in gastric ulcers and empty stomach causes pain in duodenal ulcer.

The objectives of the diet are to restore and maintain good nutrition to decrease secretion of gastric juices, to neutralise stomach acidity, to decrease gastric motility and to avoid irritation through mechanical movements on the lesion.

To fulfil the above objectives a strict dietetic regimen was set by physicians. The most popular regimen used for peptic ulcers was the Sippy diet. Though it was acclaimed in olden days now it is not practised as it poses problems of deficiency diseases. At present after the initial problems are removed a less restricted or regular diet is recommended.

Sippy's Diet

Every hourly feed consists of milk and cream in equal amounts. Between these feedings neutralising alkaline powders are given. The objective of this diet is to give maximum rest to the stomach. But Sippy's diet is not adequate for longer treatment.

Sippy's diet consists of different stages. In the first stage between 7 a.m. and 10 p.m. hourly feeds of milk and cream or olive oil with an antacid are given. In the second stage a milk-based diet with gradual introduction of solid foods is prescribed. In three weeks time the patient is exposed to a bland diet.

After the first stage of Sippy's diet lightly cooked egg, bread and well cooked cereals are recommended. In the third stage the quantity of cereal is increased and strained vegetable soups, purees, vegetables, jam, jelly, strained fruit juices are included. Three regular meals of cereals, steamed fish, minced mutton, chicken along with more milk are recommended in the next stage. A bland diet is suggested after this gradual modification. A bland diet is one which is mechanically, chemically and thermally non-irritating. Smooth consistency, bland taste and moderate temperature are the characteristics of a bland diet.

Foods Allowed

Foods allowed in a bland diet of a peptic ulcer patient are milk and milk products, weak tea, strained bland soup, white bread, soft chapathi of wheat, rice, ragi or maize, other soft breakfast cereal items and pre-cooked infant cereals. Fine cooked cereals, noodles, macaroni, potato, sweet potato or mashed yam, eggs in all forms except fried, baked or ground minced meat or fish, soft cooked mashed vegetables; carrots, peas, beets, strained tomatoes and all other vegetables except coarse fibre or overripe fruits without seeds are allowed. Mashed banana, cooked fruits, desserts, steamed or baked puddings are included.

Foods Avoided

Irritating and solid or hard foods must be avoided. It is better to avoid strong smelling vegetables and meat preparations. Carbonated beverages, cereals and cereal products with bran, fried foods, raw foods, and spiced items are not permitted. Sweets, sweet meats, papad, chutney, dried fruits, vegetable salads, are also avoided.

Sample Menu for a Peptic Ulcer Patient

Time	Menu	Meal
6 a.m.		
		1 cup of milk or tea with biscuits
8 a.m.	Breakfast	Egg sandwich, Orange milk shake
10 a.m.	Mid-time	Buttermilk or milk, Stewed apple or steamed banana
12.30 p.m.	Lunch	Double boiled rice or soft chapathi, Mashed dal or fish stew, Mashed potato, Lemon pudding
2 p.m.	Mid-time	Vermicelli kheer
4 p.m.	Tea	Milk and sweet chapathi
6 p.m.	Mid-time	Rava porridge
8 p.m.	Dinner	Soft chapathi, Vegetable purses with butter or butter with jam or arrowroot pudding
	Bed time	Milk

Strict dietetic regimen is essential to bring satisfactory improvement. The patient must be educated to live with the ulcers. The patient must accept the ulcer rather than resent it. A worrying patient with great mental stress must be admitted in a hospital.

A high calorie, high protein, highly vitaminised soft bland diet is recommended for peptic ulcers. One should suitably modify the work schedule so that there is not much stress or pressure on time. Surgical treatment may become necessary in severe cases. Even after surgery diet control is essential to avoid possible relapse of the condition.

41

CONSTIPATION

Constipation is characterised by infrequent and incomplete evacuation of the bowels. Hard, dried stools are difficult to pass. Autonomous nervous system normally controls the bowel movement. The type of food—high fibre or low fibre—also influences evacuation. For example, a vegetarian diet with increased roughage produces bulkier stools. Though most people have a bowel movement daily some people feel normal even with a bowel evacuation on every second or third day. Physical activity and ingestion of food provoke bowel evacuation. Fasting and inactivity produce constipation. Lack of exercise, poor personal hygiene in maintaining regular habits of evacuation, limited intake of fluids, consumption of concentrated foods, deficiency of fats and thiamine produce poor muscle tone and evacuation. Nervous disturbances like tension, anxiety, excitement of various forms and worry affect the normal muscular contraction and evacuation. Excessive use of laxatives and regular enemas deprive the muscles of the intestinal wall to have normal movements and develop constipation. Regular toilet habit must be inculcated from infancy.

Neglected constipation leads to piles and prolapse of the rectum. . .id it is dangerous for a heart patient to strain during defaecation.

There are three types of constipation—atonic constipation, spastic constipation and obstructive constipation.

Atonic constipation is more common among people. The main reasons for atonic constipation are lack of fluids in the body, especially after perspiration for stool formation, lack of roughage which contributes to the lack of cellulose stool formation, deficiency of B1 which produces poor muscle tone, lack of potassium which reduces muscle tone, irregular evacuation habits and use of purgation agents. Due to any of the above causes muscular tone of the intestine is affected and peristaltic action is reduced. Bacterial action on stagnated food is more and symptoms of constipation develop.

Spastic constipation, on the contrary, occurs due to excessive muscle tone of the colonic muscles. The movement of the food is very irregular and often causes pain in the lower abdomen. Irritating foods, excessive use of purgatives or mental stress produce this type of constipation. Spastic constipation occurs as a complication of some other disease. Excessive use of alcohol, tea or coffee also produce this.

Obstructive constipation is due to malignancy or stricture of the colon.

Use of castor oil or other purgatives in infancy is a common practice in our country. It contributes to constipation in later life.

Modification of the Diet

The objective of dietary treatment is to encourage bowel movement and improve bowel evacuation. A well balanced diet with high B group vitamins and liberal fluid intake is recommended. Fibre or cellulose content of the diet must be high. Bland cooking is preferred. In spastic constipation high roughage is harmful. A normal diet with light mental attitude and proper exercise or physical activity is recommended for a constipation patient. Potassium-rich vegetables must be included in the diet.

A high fibre diet is characterised with coarse cereals, wholegrain with bran, pulses, fresh fruits, salad, vegetables, fibrous vegetables like ashgourd, snakegourd, pumpkin, leafy vegetables, roots and tubers, dried fruits and fluids. Highly refined and concentrated items like maida, fried foods, excessive sweetened pickles and papads and chutneys are not permitted. A regular time for meals is very important. Relaxed living enables proper bowel movement in the body. Exercises also enable proper bowel evacuation.

For spastic constipation, a soft bland diet is recommended. Small meals prevent stagnation of food mass in the intestine. Vitamin B supplements are essential. Dialy 8 to 10 glasses of water must be ingested to help stool formation.

Constipation among Children

Continuous usage of castor oil or purgatives by infants and children to clean the bowels affects the muscle tone of the intestine. This leads to constipation. Instead of purgatives lots of water, fruit juices and fruits like banana, apple or guava or other fibrous fruits are better measures.

Sample Menu for a ConstipatedPatient

Time	Meal	Menu
6 a.m.		1 glass warm water. After some time coffee
8 a.m.	Breakfast	Chapathi from whole wheat flour, Vegetable curry with peas, Banana
10 a.m.	Mid-time	Fruit juice
12.30 p.m.	Lunch	Whole wheat chapathi or millet roti, Dal Curry with spinach or fish curry, Vegetable salad, Beans pugath, Buttermilk, Fruit salad
2 p.m.	Mid-time	Vegetable soup
4 p.m.	Tea	Tea, Boiled groundnut
6 p.m.	Mid-time	Sweetened lime juice
8 p.m.	Dinner	Wheat dosa, Sprouted green gram curry, Vegetable salad
	Bed time	Milk beverage

At least 10 glasses of water must be taken.

ULCERATIVE COLITIS

Ulcerative colitis is an intestinal disorder which is characterised by inflammation and ulceration of the colon or other parts of the intestine. In severe cases inflammation or ulceration leads to the appearance of blood and mucus in the stools. Intestinal allergy, especially cow's milk allergy, infections and psychogenic factors or nutritional deficiencies of multiple nature cause ulcerative colitis. No specific organism has been isolated for its occurrence.

The onset resembles an attack of dysentery but no organisms can be isolated. In the initial stage constipation, abnormal secretion of mucus or diarrhoea occur. In chronic ulcerative colitis, loss of appetite, nausea, fever, abdominal distention, flatulence, alternating diarrhoea or constipation and bleeding occur.

Dietary Modifications

An adequate diet with high protein and enough fat is recommended. Supplementation of vitamins and minerals, especially iron, is essential. Since significant nitrogen loss through urine makes the serum albumin level low, a high protein intake of 100 to 150 gms/day is required. Sodium and potassium loss is very high and supplementation is essential with a liberal intake of fluid. A bland high protein diet is essential to meet the requirements. If there is milk allergy soyabean milk can be given.

Cereal bran, raw vegetables, dried fruits, nuts, condiments and spices are avoided. If fat is not tolerated, only emulsified fats from egg yolk and butter are included. Small feeds are comfortable for the patient.

Psychological approach to the patient is essential and fatigue or emotional strain must be avoided.

DIARRHOEA AND DYSENTERY

Diarrhoea is a condition where loose or watery stools are passed frequently. In dysentery unformed stools are accompanied by the passage of blood and mucus. Diarrhoea can be functional or organic. Neuromuscular overactivity creates diarrhoea. Consumption of irritating foods, fermented foods, unhygienically handled food, stale food, besides allergy, achlorohydria, nervousness, uraemia, and endocrine imbalances are the main causes of functional diarrhoea. Nutritional deficiency like kwashiorkor or pellagra or vitamin deficiency produce diarrhoea.

Diarrhoea can be acute or chronic in nature.

Acute diarrhoea occurs mainly due to contaminated food consumption.

After an acute attack of dysentery or diarrhoea it may be repeated often. This can lead to chronic diarrhoea. Infestation with giardial-amblia is a common cause of chronic diarrhoea.

Nervous diarrhoea occurs to some people when faced with fear of an examination or an interview.

Diseases of small intestine, lack of hydrochloric acid in the stomach, malabsorption syndromes, malnutrition, vitamin A deficiency, niacin deficiency and protein deficiency cause diarrhoea. Tuberculosis also produces chronic diarrhoea.

Dietetic Management

A very low residue diet is recommended. Residue is the bulk remaining in the intestine after food is assimilated. Milk is a high residue diet. In acute diarrhoea the alimentary canal must get complete rest. If vomiting is present no food is allowed. Saline with 5 per cent glucose can be given. Electrolytes like sodium and potassium with high fluid are recommended. Apple, tender coconut water and fruit juices, rice gruel and thin porridges without milk are prescribed. Arrowroot and sago are excellent for diarrhoea. Strained fruit juices or soups are allowed. Jaggery and honey are also good. Leafy vegetables and green vegetables may be avoided. Overripe or fibrous vegetables are excluded. Biscuits, soft desserts without milk or with, if tolerating, skimmed milk and soft cooked eggs are permitted. Fried items, fat, pulses, beans, vegetable salads, seedy fruits, sweets, dried fruits, nuts, condiments and spices are best avoided. Only double cooked mashed vegetables are allowed. Once normal food is tolerated poached egg, cereal, porridge, fruit juice, baked non-vegetarian items, mashed potatoes or soups, biscuits and arrowroot drinks can be given in the menu. Since the food intake is low at first minerals like iron, calcium and all vitamins have to be supplemented. In acute stage 1,500 kcals and in chronic diarrhoea or dysentery 2,500 kcals are added. Liberal intake of proteins from permissible foods is essential. A fluid diet is modified into a soft bland diet as the condition of the bowel improves.

Sample Menu for an Acute Diarrhoea Patient

Time	Meal	Menu
Bed Coffee		
6 a.m.		Coffee (skimmed milk)
8 a.m.	Breakfast	Bombay toast, Barley water with milk (skimmed milk)
10 a.m.	Mid-time	Arrowroot porridge
12 Noon	Lunch	Rice gruel or soft chapathi, Mashed spinach, Dal or mixed potato mashed.
2 p.m.	Mid-time	Plain custard (skimmed milk)
4 p.m.	Tea	Salt biscuits, Tea
6 p.m.	Mid-time	Strained unseasoned vegetable soup
8 p.m.	Dinner	Soft chapathi or rice gruel, Mashed potato and peas, Apple
	Bed time	Sago porridge

Sample Menu for Dysentery Patient

Time	Meal	Menu
6 a.m.	-	Black tea
8 a.m.	Breakfast	Sago porridge with skimmed milk
10 a.m.	Mid-time	Lime juice
12 Noon	Lunch	Mashed curd rice or arrowroot porridge
2 p.m.	Mid-time	Orange juice
4 p.m.	Tea	Weak tea; Biscuits
6 p.m.	Mid-time	China grass pudding
8 p.m.	Dinner	Rava porridge, Mashed potato
	Bed Time	Rice water

44

MALABSORPTION SYNDROME

In malabsorption syndrome, adequate digestion or intestinal absorption of a number of substances like fats, proteins, carbohydrates, vitamins, minerals and water are disordered. Nutritional deficiencies develop in such a condition and normal life processes are affected. Chronic under-nutrition brings ill-health, anaemia, steatorrhoea, tropical sprue and celiac diseases. Fibrosis of the pancreas, chronic pancreatitis, carcinoma in the pancreas and stones in the duct of wirsung are other diseases due to malabsorption.

In all these diseases normal digestion and absorption of carbohydrate, proteins and fats are reduced. Enzymatic actions are very poor because some of them are absent in certain diseases. Stools are dry, bulky, pale and greasy and often frothy.

Tropical Sprue

The exact cause of sprue is not known. Supplementation of nutrients like folacin or B12 shows improvement in this disease. In sprue, normal absorption of glucose, fats and fat soluble vitamins is impaired. Symptoms of sprue are anorexia or vomiting, sore tongue, diarrhoea, abdominal distention, macrocytic anaemia, low prothrombin production, rapid weight loss and muscle wasting, excessive calcium loss, weakness and hyperpigmentation. It is also assumed that an infection factor may be the reason.

Dietary Modifications

Non-tropical sprue patients showed improvement in a glutengliadin restricted diet. A high carbohydrate, high protein, low fat, low residue, low fibre, bland diet is recommended. In a high carbohydrate diet glucose and sucrose sources produce discomfort. Fructose sources are better tolerated. Honey and fruits are the best sources of fructose. Mineral and vitamin supplementation is essential.

Foods included in a sprue diet are weak tea or coffee, non-fat milk like skimmed milk, double cooked soft porridge, infant foods, milled cereals, and their products, tender vegetables, ripe fleshy fruits like banana, papaya, mango, apple, baked or canned fruits without seeds and skin, fruit juices, strained vegetable soups without seasoning, mashed pumpkin, carrots, peas, beetroot, strained beans, custards and puddings with non-fat milk, white bread, sponge cake, honey, jelly, eggs and biscuits.

Foods avoided are cereals, bread with bran, fruits with skin, seeds, fats, fried and crisp items, puddings with whole milk or other milk items, confectioneries with cream or ghee, sugar and sweet items, preparations where spices are used, stimulants like alcohol, flavoured drinks, vegetables with fibres, skins, seeds, sprouts, strong flavoured vegetables like cauliflower, cabbage, cucumber, onion, dried peas, lentils, beans, leafy vegetables and hard sweets and raw vegetables.

Idiopathic Steatorrhoea

Steatorrhoea is characterised by loose motions containing large amounts of fat. The mucosa of the intestine is inflamed and the normal absorption of all nutrients is lowered. The cause of this condition is not identified clearly. Children with celiac diseases due to sensitivity of the intestine, especially gluten sensitivity, are prone to steatorrhoea in adult life. Family history also plays a role in its occurrence.

Treatment aims at removing irritation from dietary pattern. The faecal fatty acids are from fermented carbohydrates and unabsorbed dietary fat. Putrified foods, fried foods, and animal fats are restricted. Foods rich in fibres like whole cereals, millets and matured vegetables and spices are excluded in this diet. Diet prescribed for tropical sprue is given in this condition also.

45

DIET IN FEVERS

Fever may be defined as an elevation of body temperature above normal, i.e., 98.4°F and is the most important sign of an infection. Infection, inflammation or unknown causes manifest themselves as fever. Bacterial or fungi infections, antigen antibody reaction, malignancy or graft rejection are the main causes of it. When an exogenous factor causes fever it activates phagocytes in the bone marrow to release a fever hormone pyrogen. This endogenous hormone induces synthesis of prostaglandins which affect the thermo-regulatory centre in the anterior hypothalamus to increase body temperature. Drugs inhibit prostaglandis synthesis.

Fevers may be classified as (i) Acute, (2) Chronic, and (3) Recurrent.

The acute infections are of strong but short duration and they occur along with colds, pneumonia, influenza, measles, chickenpox, scarlet and typhoid fevers. All these diseases manifest fever as the first symptom. The duration of most acute infectious diseases is reduced by the use of antibodies.

Chronic infections may continue for months and stretch into years. Tuberculosis is an outstanding example. Fever accompanies it.

Recurrent fever is observed in malaria.

Metabolic Changes in Fevers

In most febrile conditions the metabolic rate is increased. The increase in metabolic rate is proportionate to body temperature and the duration of fever. An increase of 7-7.2 per cent in the metabolic rate per degree rise in Farenheit is observed. If the temperature is high about 40 per cent increase in metabolic rate occurs.

Glycogen stores are decreased. And catabolism of proteins is increased. This is very evident in the case of typhoid fever, malaria, typhus fever, polio-myelitis. Nitrogen waste is increased and it exerts a burden on the kidneys.

Water metabolism is also affected. Excessive perspiration and excretion of body waste increases the loss of body water. Electrolytes like sodium and potassium are also lost.

Accumulation of basic products in the body is another characteristic of fever due to infection.

Loss of appetite and nausea and vomiting are the other symptoms of fevers.

General Modification in Diet during Fevers

Dietary modifications vary according to the nature and severity of the fever and length of convalescence.

Energy utilisation is high in fevers due to the high metabolic activities. The calorie requirement is increased about 50 per cent. If loss of appetite, nausea and vomiting persist it will be difficult to administer a high calorie diet. High carbohydrate drinks and cereal gruels can be included in frequent small feedings to meet this demand.

In prolonged fever 100 gms of good quality proteins have to be included. Protein supplements can be incorporated in fruit juices. High protein beverages and soups are the other means of high protein liquid sources.

Glycogen stores are depleted and so a liberal intake of carbohydrate is recommended. Glucose can be used for sweetening beverages, starchy gruels also supply carbohydrates.

Even though fats are rich sources of energy, a judicious use of fat is essential as it may interfere with digestion.

Electrolytes, especially sodium choloride, have to be supplemented. Salty juices and soups can meet this demand. Even though potassium is abundantly present in most of the food items, limited food intake restricts its availability and so in prolonged fever it has to be supplemented. Fruits juices and milk beverages can contribute considerable quantities.

Vitamin requirement increases during fever. Vitamin A and ascorbic acid have to be supplemented; B complex vitamins intake have to be adjusted with calorie intake: 0.5 mgs. per 1,000 kcals is the correct requirement.

Fluid intake must be liberal so as to meet the additional loss during fever. At least 3-5 litres of fluid intake is essential.

Modification in food preparation is also necessary. Bland, easily digestible foods must be used for febrile conditions. If it is necessary, a full liquid diet is prescribed. Since it produces abdominal distension a soft diet is more appreciated.

Instead of a four-meal pattern frequent small feedings are recommended.

Typhoid Fever

Typhoid fever is an infectious disease caused by salmonella typhosa and is usually transmitted by drinking water or milk contaminated with intestinal contents or carriers. Improved hygiene and prophylatic public health measures have greatly reduced the incidence. The length of convalescence depends to a great extent on nutritional therapy.

The symptoms include severe headache, high temperature, acute stomach pain, diarrhoea, and peyers patches are found. The intestine is ii.flamed.

The body glycogen store is rapidly depleted and energy need is increased. Metabolic rate is increased by 40-50 per cent above the normal. Tissues protein breakdown is about 1/2 to 3/4 pounds of muscle per day. Nitrogen catabolism is three times above the normal.

Dietary Modification

A bland non-irritating diet, low in fibre content, should be given to prevent intestinal irritation. If diarrhoea is not present milk can be used on the basis of the diet. High fluid content is essential. About 3,500 kcals, 100 gms of protein, and 3,000 ml of fluid is recommended during the febrile period.

Foods Allowed

Milk with barley water and glucose, fruit juices with glucose, strained vegetable juices, milk puddings, cereal gruels, baked fish or minced meat, vegetable purees and thin dal curries are permitted.

A soft or fluid diet is suggested. Small feedings in more intervals are better. All irritating fibres, highly flavoured and spiced food items are harmful since the intestinal tract is inflamed.

Multi-vitamin tablet supplementation is essential. High carbohydrate, high protein beverages and puddings are ideal.

A Sample Menu during Typhoid Fever

Time	Meal	Menu
6 a.m.	-	Milk with Complan
8 a.m.	Breakfast	Milk, Poached egg, Bread, Fruit cup.
10 a.m.	Mid-time	Cornflakes in milk
11 a.m.	Mid-time	Orange juice
12.30 Noon	Lunch	Double boiled mashed rice or soft chapathi, Mashed carrot. Dal mashed, Biscuit pudding
2 p.m.	Mid-time	Eggnog
3 p.m.	Mid-time	Lime juice with glucose
4 p.m.	-	Egg and cheese sandwich, Tea
6 p.m.	-	Tomato juice
8 p.m.	-	Wheat gruel, Mixed vegetable puree, Soft chapathi, Pineapple cocktail.
9 p.m.	-	Complan

Tuberculosis

Tuberculosis is an infectious disease caused by the bacillus mycro bacterium tuberculosis. Usually lungs, lymph nodes and kidneys are affected.

Alimentary tract, lymph nodes of the neck, liver, spleen and bones and joints of children are more affected compared to adults.

Tuberculosis is a highly communicable disease. Congested dwelling and unhygienic living spread this infection. It takes years to manifest the symptoms after the initial attack.

Pulmonary tuberculosis is more common. Pulmonary tuberculosis is an inflamatory disease of the lung.

Symptoms

Wasting of tissues, exhaustion, persistent cough, expectoration and fever are the initial symptoms. Cough which persists for more than two weeks is the warning symptom. Loss of weight, pain in the chest, poor appetite, fatigue and blood-sputum accompany the other symptoms. The chronic phase of the disease is accompanied by low-grade fever.

The most important factor of treatment is complete rest along with drugs and diet. Antibodies are used as drugs.

Dietary Modification

A high calorie, high protein, high vitaminised and mineralised, high fluid soft diet is recommended. Easily digestible, good quality diet reduces strain on the body. Diet plays a key role in the treatment of tuberculosis.

About 500 kcals are required more during the illness. Good quality proteins of 75-80 gms help quick regeneration of serum albumin. Calcium is essential to promote healing of the tuberculous lesions. Iron is also required in high amount to increase the blood volume. Calcium, iron and phosphorus along with other minerals help the overall regeneration of cells, blood and fluids.

Vitamin supplements are also essential. Carotenoids are not converted to vitamin A very effectively. Vitamin C is also essential for many regenerative purposes. Prolonged administration of chemo-therapeutic agents in tuberculosis manifest antagonistic effect on certain B vitamins, especially on B6 folate. Inter-conversion of glycine and serine are also affected. Peripheral neuritis, characteristic of B6 deficiency, is common among tuberculosis patients. Supplements of these vitamins are essential.

Since most patients have very poor appetite small feedings with more intervals are recommended. Attractive, appetising meals induce appetite.

Milk and egg-based diet is better for a tuberculosis patient. Money cannot be considered as a criteria in the treatment. Liberal intake of citrus fruits and leafy vegetables and protective foods are essential in the dietary of a tuberculosis patient.

A Sample Menu for a Tuberculosis Patient

Time	Meal	Menu
6 a.m.	-	Milk
8 a.m.	Breakfast	Soft parathas or idli, Tomato-egg curry or groundnut curry, Poached egg, Complan
10 a.m.	Mid-time	Water melon juice, Bombay toast
12 Noon	Lunch	Soft chapathi, Dal curry, Fish molee, Rice, Curd, Fruit salad
2 p.m.	Mid-time	Grape juice
4 p.m.	Tea	Three-layered sandwich (with cheese, scrambled egg and coriander leaves chutney).
6 p.m.	Mid-time	Pineapple milk shake
8 p.m.	Dinner	Broken wheat gruel, Liver saute, Vegetable puree, Pumpkin chutney, Orange custard
10 p.m.	Bed time	Proteinex

46

LIVER DISEASES

Liver is one of the most important organs of the body. Liver secretes bile and takes part in metabolic processes. It manufactures many important substances. Digested amino acids are received and new proteins are synthesised by the liver. Many metabolic processes of protein take place in the liver. It also plays an important role in carbohydrate metabolism. Liver is the chief storehouse of carbohydrate and it regulates the blood glucose level by converting excess sugar into glycogen.

Liver has a prominent role in lipid metabolism. It converts absorbed fatty acids into circulating phospholipids. It also synthesizes cholesterol and converts it into bile salts. Fats in the liver are oxidized into energy. Again, protein, carbohydrate and fats are interconverted. Bile salts are essential for fat digestion and liver detoxicates poisonous substances from the body. Conversion of beta carotene into vitamin A and storage of vitamins A and D are other functions. Plasma proteins are also synthesised by the liver. Worn out red blood cells are broken down and the liver extracts useful substances. It also stores iron and copper. The intrinsic factor or the anti-anaemic factor is produced by the liver. There is no other organ in our body which takes part in so many vital functions. Thus, a healthy liver is essential for healthy living.

Disorders of liver are jaundice or hepatitis, hepatic percoma and coma, hepatic cirrhosis and fatty liver.

Dietary deficiencies produce liver disorders like fatty liver and cirrhosis of the liver. Protein deficiency, choline deficiency, cystine deficiency, methionine deficiency and B vitamin deficiencies produce either fatty liver or necrosis of liver. Liver injury occurs due to alcoholism. Acute hepatic damage and jaundice occur in malnourished alcoholic patients. Lipid metabolism changes in the alcoholics by enhancing fatty acid synthesis and decreasing its oxidation.

Triglyceride formation is stimulated by alcohol. Cirrhosis of liver occurs among chronic alcoholics.

Jaundice

Jaundice is a symptom which denotes abnormal liver function due to diseases. In jaundice the skin and mucous membranes show a yellow pigmentation due to rise in the serum bilirubin. Jaundice occurs from haemolysis of red blood cells as in yellow fever and pernicious anaemia. Obstruction in bile flow either through intra or extra hepatic obstruction results in jaundice. A malignant growth, stones or inflammation of the mucous ducts produce obstructive hepatitis. Hepatocellular jaundice results from damage to the parenchymal cells due to viral infection or due to toxic origins such as poison or drugs.

Viral Hepatitis

Viral hepatitis is otherwise known as infectious hepatitis. This is the common cause of jaundice. Through food or water the virus enters the body. Anorexia, fever, headache, rapid weight loss, loss of muscle tone and abdominal discomforts are the earlier symptoms. These develop into jaundice. The symptoms may continue for 4 to 8 weeks. If proper treatment is not given it leads to permanent liver damage. Living in crowded areas and living on an inadequate diet, especially on low protein diet, and consumption of alcohol while ill, produce complications. Recovery is possible even with restricted diet, rest and supplementation of deficient nutrients, especially vitamins. Prolonged convalescence results in relapse or fatal conditions because of liver cellular collapse. Mortality due to jaundice occurs mainly among malnourished people because an already damaged liver due to malnourishment is further affected by infection. Neglected hepatitis leads to cirrhosis of liver.

Dietetic Management

Modifications in the dietary treatment depend on the liver damage. Since anorexia is an important symptom, normal feeding is difficult in the initial stage. In hospitalised cases intravenous feeding with 10 per cent glucose solution is recommended. As soon as there is appetite simple foods of high nutritional quality can be given.

The objective of dietetic treatment is to avoid further injury and strain to liver, and provide nutrients for regeneration of liver tissues. A high protein, high carbohydrate, moderate fat diet is recommended. Small feeds of attractive meals at regular intervals are better tolerated.

In nasogastric feeding stage about 1,000 kcals are supplied for a person weighing 60 kgs. In severe cases 1,600 kcals to 2,000 kcals are suggested. Once convalescence stage is reached 45 kcals/kg body weight helps to regain normalcy.

Protein requirement varies according to the severity of the disease. With severe jaundice an intake of 40 gms of protein and in mild jaundice 60 to 80 gms of proteins is permitted. If hepatic coma or percoma accompanies it, protein-containing foods are not given as the liver metabolises the end products of intestinal protein. Cereal proteins are better suggested during this condition.

An average consumption of fat along with normal protein intake is recommended. In hepatic percoma and in coma, hepatic cellular failure takes place. Liver cells are not able to metabolise fats, therefore fat is restricted in such cases. In severe jaundice 30 gms of fat is permitted and 50 to 60 gms of fat in moderate jaundice.

High carbohydrate content in the diet is essential to supply enough calories so that tissue proteins are not broken down for energy purpose. For 1,600 kcals diet 300 to 340 gms carbohydrate is recommended.

Vitamins are essential to regenerate liver cells; 500 mgs of vitamin C, 10 mgs of vitamin K and supplements of B complex are essential to meet the daily needs. If anorexia and vomiting after consumption of these supplements are present intravenous administration is essential.

Mineral deficiency occurs if normal food consumption is not possible. Normal serum level of sodium and potassium must be maintained through supplements.

Foods Included

Foods included in viral hepatitis are cereal porridges, soft chapathis, bread, rice, millet preparations, milk, preferably skimmed milk, thin soups from tender vegetables, roots like tapioca, potato, sweet potato, yam, fruits and fruit juices, sugar, jaggery, honey, biscuits, soft custards without butter or cream and light non-stimulant beverages.

Foods Avoided

Foods to be avoided in the diet of a hepatitis patient are pulses, beans, meat, fish, chicken, eggs, soups, sweet preparations where ghee, butter or oil are used, backery products, dried fruits, nuts, spices, papads, chutney, pickles, alcoholic beverages, fried preparations, cooking fats, whole milk, cream, sardines, salmon, fried fish or fish rich in fat. Liberal intake of water is allowed.

The patient needs bedrest but slight movement in the room improves appetite. In moderate jaundice pulses or beans, meat, fish or chicken and eggs are allowed. Though fried foods are restricted cooking fat is permitted. Dried fruits, sweets without much ghee are included. Fruit juices, water and other beverages except alcoholic beverages are allowed.

Hepatitis in infancy and childhood is not complicated if the therapeutic dietary pattern is observed strictly. But hepatitis in pregnancy, especially in the second and third trimester, is harmful to the mother and child.

A Sample Menu for Hepatitis Patient

Time	Meal	Menu
6 a.m.	-	Coffee
8 a.m.	Breakfast	French toast, Coffee
10 a.m.	Mid-time	Orange juice
12.30 Noon	Lunch	Soft chapathi, Mashed potato and carrot, Curd (skimmed milk), China grass jelly
2.30 p.m.	Mid-time	Lime juice
4.30 p.m.	Tea	Strained ragi porridge
6 p.m.	Mid-time	Bread and honey, Strained vegetable soup
8 p.m.	Dinner	Rice noodles with boiled potato strips and carrot and scrambled egg, Tomato chutney, Fruit whip
	Bed time	Milk (skimmed milk)

Hepatic Percoma and Coma

Complications of viral or acute alcoholic hepatitis, accidental damage to the hepatic artery, anaesthetic agents and certain drugs, encephalopathy or surgery of the liver produce hepatic coma and percoma.

Common symptoms of these disorders are confusion, disordered consciousness, tremor of the outstretched hands, psychosis, apathy, and personality changes. Gradually these symptoms lead to death.

The exact cause is that the liver is incapable of detoxicating ammonia from bacterial decomposition of protein foods. In a healthy person's body, the liver converts ammonia into urea and excretes it through kidneys. In liver disorders or in hepatic surgery nitrogenous materials, especially ammonia, get into systemic circulation and reach the central nervous system. The blood ammonium ion level is increased in coma. Along with ammonia, indoles and phenols are also not detoxicated from the body by a damaged liver. There are many toxic products of metabolism in minute quantities which are detoxicated by a healthy liver. All these are accumulated in the body in the coma stage. Again urine is not eliminated properly which affects the concentration of waste products in the urine and in blood. Electrolytic balance is also upset.

Dietetic Management

For a coma patient 1,000 kcals are recommended. A low protein diet is prescribed for a coma patient. The endogenous breakdown of protein can be minimised by a high carbohydrate diet. An improvement in coma suggests 30 to 40 gms protein per day. In acute coma protein in the diet is withheld. As fats are not metabolised they are not given for a coma patient. Carbohydrate rich foods are included liberally as they prevent endogenous breakdown of protein. Glucose is recommended as it is easy to assimilate.

Vitamins and mineral supplementation is essential. Fruit juices, vegetable soups without seasoning, honey and barley water are fed to a coma patient. In most of the cases nasogastric feeding is carried out. The feed consists of

Orange juice	-	1,000 ml
Glucose	-	200 gms
Water	-	1,000 ml
		2,200 ml

A Sample Meny during Hepatic Coma

Time	Meal	Menu
6 a.m.	-	Apple juice
8 a.m.	Breakfast	Oats porridge
10 a.m.	Mid-time	Lemon juice
12 p.m.	Lunch	Cornflakes or rice gruel
2 p.m.	Mid-time	Orange juice

4 p.m.	Tea	Tomato juice
6 p.m.	Mid-time	Coconut water
8 p.m.	Dinner	Vegetable soup
9 p.m.	Mid-time	Water melon juice
10 p.m.	Bed time	Skim milk

Cirrhosis of Liver

Cirrhosis is a common disease of liver which usually affects alcoholics. Previous occurrence of hepatitis also causes cirrhosis of liver. Undernutrition causes necrosis of liver cells and fatty liver. Fatty liver produces cirrhosis of liver. Toxins of foods like aflatoxins and "bush tea" cause cirrhosis.

In cirrhosis of liver parenchyma is destroyed and it is replaced by fibrous tissues. Gradually all active parenchymal tissues are destroyed and liver function is seriously affected. Morphological changes occur and the liver is contracted and irregularly distorted. In advanced cirrhosis complications arise and one of the common complications is retention of water in the tissues due to hypoalbuminemia. Synthesis of albumin by liver is reduced in cirrhosis which leads to reduced osmotic pressure of the plasma. Due to high portal pressure, fluid is accumulated in the abdominal cavity and ascites occurs.

There are three types of cirrhosis: (1) Diffuse hepatic fibrosis which is also known as alcoholic cirrhosis or portal or Laennec's cirrhosis, (2) Post-necrotic scarring in liver, and (3) Biliary cirrhosis which occurs due to obstruction, infections or toxin. Wasting of tissues, low serum albumin, oedema, ascites and retention of sodium are some of the symptoms. Portal hypertension and lymphatic obstruction cause oedema. In infantile biliary cirrhosis diminished appetite, flatulence, liver enlargement and jaundice occur first. In later stages oedema and ascites occur.

Symptoms

Gastro-intestinal disturbances such as anorexia, nausea, vomiting, pain and distension of abdomen are common.

Dietary Regimen

A high calorie, high protein, high carbohydrate, low fat diet, with vitamins and mineral supplementation is recommended for cirrhosis patients. Calorie content of the diet for a cirrhosis patient is 2,000 to 2,500 kcals. Consumption of food is difficult because of anorexia and ascites. But the patient requires highly nutritious foods because of prolonged undernourishment.

The protein content of the diet varies according to symptoms. If hepatic coma accompanies, protein is restricted. Otherwise a high protein diet of about 2 gms of protein per kilogramme of body weight is advisable. Fat is restricted in cirrhosis of liver but 0.5 gm to 1 gm per kilogramme of body weight is harmless if enough protein is included in the diet.

Carbohydrate should provide more than 60 per cent of the total carlories so that liver damage is minimised.

Sodium is restricted in oedema and ascites. If there are no ascites very little salt is permitted. Potassium salt is administered for ascites and oedema to prevent hypokalemia. Anaemia is common among cirrhosis patients. So iron supplementation is essential. Vitamin supplementation, especially of B vitamins, is required to prevent anaemia. Choline and methionine are useful if fatty infiltration is present.

Foods included in a cirrhosis diet are cereals in any soft form, pulses, beans, meat, fish and chicken, soft cooked eggs, vegetables, cooked or pureed sweets, fruits, fruit juices and light beverages. Cooking salt is not added. Papads, chutneys or pickles are excluded in the diet of a cirrhosis patient. A smooth or liquid diet is suggested if there is difficulty in swallowing food. Fried items, rich desserts, strongly flavoured vegetables, nuts, milk, salads and seasoned gravies are avoided in a cirrhosis diet.

Composition of a Cirrhosis Diet

Foodstuffs in gms.	Vegetarian	Non Vegetarian
Cereals	250 gms	250 gms
Pulses	50 gms	50 gms
Milk and milk products (skimmed milk)	800 ml	500 ml
Cheese	50 gms	50 gms
Meat and liver	-	100 gms
Eggs	-	60 gms
Fats and oils	20 gms	20 gms
Vegetables	100 gms	100 gms
Fruit juices	500 ml	500 ml
Fruits	200 gms	200 gms
Sugar	60 gms	60 gms
Glucose	60 gms	60 gms

A Sample Menu for a Cirrhosis Patient

Time	Meal	Menu
6 a.m.	-	Milk (skimmed milk)
8 a.m.	Breakfast	Cornflakes or idli, Cheese, Milk, Sugar, Orange
10 a.m.	Mid-time	Guava-lime juice
12 Noon	Lunch	Soft chapathi, Egg-tomato curry, Rice, Baked vegetable cutlet, Curd, Fruit cup
4 p.m.	Tea	Green gram kheer
6 p.m.	Mid-time	Fruit juice
8 p.m.	Dinner	Mutton soup, Bread and liver-tomato saute, Plain custard with jelly
	Bed time	Skimmed milk

47

DIABETES MELLITUS

Diabetes is a chronic metabolic disorder that prevents the body from using energy from carbohydrate. This inefficiency of the body to utilise glucose may be partial or complete in a diabetic. When we eat carbohydrate, it is digested and absorbed as glucose. Glucose is stored in the form of glycogen which is otherwise known as 'metabolic fuel'. Glycogen supplies glucose to the cell when energy is required in excess or in fasting. Thus, excess glucose is converted to glycogen and glycogen is converted to glucose in a normal person's body. Insulin, a hormone secreted by islets of langerhans, which are spread out in the pancreas, regulates the chemical changes for the energy balance. Lack of insulin causes diabetes mellitus. In young diabetics, deficiency of insulin and in adult obese diabetics the overweight and in senile diabetics fibrosis in pancreas are the causes.

Diabetes, the Latin word, means 'flow through' and mellitus means "honey" and clinically it is manifested by the overflow of sugar or glucose in blood and urine instead of getting converted into glycogen.

Pancreatitis

Pancreatic disease may be due to congenital or inflammatory diseases, tumour or tracoma.

In pancreatitis the enzyme production is inadequate and this interferes with normal digestion. In pancreatitis undigested protein and fats are found in the stools. Some starch also may be present often.

These are two types of pancreatitis: Acute Pancreatitis and Chronic Pancreatitis.

Acute Pancreatitis

Inflammation of the pancreas takes place in this condition. The blood supply to the pancreas is poor and so the outflow of pancreatic juice is also less. Haemorrhagic necrosis of the pancreas and peritonitis are the other complications.

Aetiological factors are alcoholism, biliary tract disease, tracoma, virus infections, tumours, nutritional deficiency, certain vascular diseases, metabolic diseases or gallstone.

Symptoms

Sudden onset of severe upper-abdominal pain radiating to the back is the first sign of pancreatitis. Epogastric tenderness, distension, constipation, nausea and vomiting occur. Moderate fever, jaundice, high serum amylase and lipase, hyperlipermia, hypocalcemia are the other symptoms.

Treatment

Medical treatment for the control of pain and vomiting and to reduce pancreatic secretion and replacement of fluids are essential.

Dietary treatment consists of parenteral administration of 2,000-2,500 ml of glucose (10%) depending upon the blood sugar level. A diet of clear liquids or some synthetic fibre to a soft or bland diet depends on the condition of the patient.

Chronic Pancreatitis

This disease may be described as progressive fibrosis of the pancreas due to recurrent occurrence of pancreatitis. Periodic pain, recurrent attacks of burning, epigastric pain, especially after meals with fat, flatulence, anorexia, weight loss, nausea, vomiting, defective digestion of protein and fats are the major symptoms. Liver and gall bladder enlargement and jaundice may present chronic changes of pancreatitis, often lead to destruction of the islets of langerhans, fibrosis and pseudocyst and pancreatic calcification.

Dietary Treatment

A low fat, high carbohydrate, high protein diet is required. Alcohol should be completely prohibited. From carbohydrate and protein a diet has to be built. Skimmed milk can be included. Small helpings of low fat, lean meat, broiler chicken, small fish, fruit juices, semi-synthetic fibre-free diet are suggested. Pancreatic secretions are greatly affected and so easily digestible carbohydrate sources are recommended.

A Sample Menu for a Chronic Pancreatitis Patient

Time	Meal	Menu
6 a.m.	-	Milk (skimmed milk)
8 a.m.	Break fast	Bread or idli with jam or sugar, Orange juice
10 a.m.	Mid-time	Lime juice with glucose
12 p.m.	Lunch	Double boiled rice or soft chapathi, Vegetable puree, Baked chicken cutlet, buttermilk, Fruit cup
2 p.m.	Mid-time	Water melon
4 p.m.	Tea	Tea, Biscuits, Plantain
6 p.m.	Mid-time	Tender coconut water
8 p.m.	Dinner	Bread and jam or rice, Vegetable puree, Buttermilk, Lemon pudding (skimmed milk)
	Bed time	Rava gruel

Causes of Diabetes

At least two per cent of the world's population suffer from diabetes and the main causes are genetic, endocrine and others. Age, sex, heredity, obesity, virus infections, emotional stress and glandular disorders also cause diabetes.

Age is a factor because half of all cases occur in the age group of 50 to 60 and only five per cent of diabetics are under ten years of age.

Though the disease affects both the sexes, in younger group more boys develop diabetes and in the mature group more women develop it. On the whole men are more prone to diabetes.

Genetic factors contribute if the patient is below 40 years. But all children of diabetic parents are not affected. If both parents are diabetic one child out of four may be a diabetic. But others may have a tendency to develop it as they become old. If one diabetic marries a diabetic carrier half of their children will be potential diabetics. If a diabetic marries one who is neither diabetic nor a diabetic carrier none of the children will have diabetes.

Obesity is a strong predisposing factor in middle-aged diabetes. The percentage of obese people developing diabetes is greater than a normal person. Eighty per cent of the diabetics are obese. Middle-aged diabetes is due to increase in the size of fat cells and not the number. The insulin secreted by the body is not enough to convert it into glycogen. Normal amount of insulin is secreted in an obese diabetic patient also. In a juvenile diabetic body weight is often less and insulin secretion is also less. In adults diabetes commonly occurs among sedentary workers compared to labourers.

Latest researches have shown that virus infection may be a reason for diabetes because virus infections even could put strain on the body. But no clear evidence is yet found even though researches are diverted on this line.

Various emotional setbacks like worry, strain, rundown feeling, listlessness contribute to the physiological upsets in the body. In emotional disorders more adrenaline and cortisone are released which can lead to diabetes.

Glands like pituitary secrete growth hormones and over-secretion of growth hormone may overstretch the pancreas's ability to cope with the rapidly increasing size in the body.

Damage or tumours in pancreas, pancreatitis, and hemochromatosis and disorders of glands like acromegaly, Cushing's syndrome cause diabetes.

Symptoms

Disturbed metabolism of carbohydrates, protein and fat brings about many symptoms. Polyuria or frequent and large outflow of urine occurs because of the large amount of glucose content in the kidneys. Polydipsia or excessive thirst is another cause because of great loss of body fluids in the urine. Dehydration may occur if fluid is not taken in polyphagia or increased appetite results from the inefficiency of the body to utilise carbohydrate foods. General weakness and loss of body weight take place because of the depletion of body fat to energy purposes. Decreased resistance to infection especially staphylococcal infection, and tuberculosis, occur in poorly regulated cases of diabetes. Delayed wound healing occurs because of high blood sugar and oedema. Degenerative changes like peripheral neuritis, retinitis, diseases of coronary arteries and arteriosclerosis are symptoms of advanced cases or poorly adjusted diabetes. Ketosis or acidosis is another symptom because of high depletion of fat from the body.

Urine changes show certain biochemical indices. Glycosuria and ketoneuria are common. In glucose urea sugar is found in the urine. Glucose tolerance test, a test used to diagnose diabetes, must be done before confirming diabetes by glycosuria because sugar occurs in urine due to other causes also. Pentose uria takes place in the inefficiency of body to use pentose and lactose uria in lactating mothers. In ketoneuria ketones like aceto acetic acid are present in urine. Hyperglycaemia is another symptom when blood sugar level is above 120 mg per 100 cc of blood.

In a national survey it was found that only in 30 per cent of those diagnosed as diabetics had hyperglycaemia. So the confirmation of diagnosis of diabetes depends on urine test and blood examination in the fasting state. Glucose tolerance test is used to detect diabetes.

Glucose Tolerance Test

The test is performed after a fast of 12 hours or more. Dissolve 100 gms of glucose in 250 ml of water. Take a blood sample of the patient before giving the known sample of glucose. Again blood samples are taken to test content at the end of 1/2, 1, 2 and 3 hours after giving the glucose.

The blood sugar rises 1/2 to 1 hour after taking glucose even in normal persons. After one hour it falls down. By the end of the second hour, normal sugar level is obtained in a normal person. In a diabetic person maximum sugar concentration reaches by the second hour and falls down very slowly. Elevated blood sugar level is accompanied by glycosuria.

Metabolism in Diabetes

Diabetes is also known as a disease of metabolism because normal metabolism of carbohydrate, proteins and fats is affected in this condition.

Carbohydrate Metabolism

The body converts the ingested food into carbohydrates and fats. Glucose is formed not only from carbohydrates but from proteins and fats also. Amino acids from protein foods are used mainly for tissue building and maintenance. The amino acids remaining in the amino acid pool are deaminised by the liver. Some portion of this deaminised molecule of amino acid is left out which is oxidised to glucose and fatty acids. Thus, on a low carbohydrate diet glycerol function of the fat molecule and amino acids are used for energy.

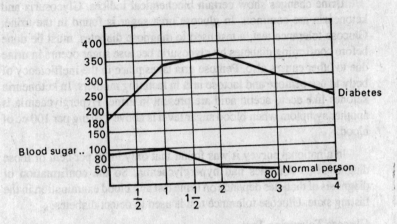

Glucose Tolerance Curve

In a diabetic patient, due to deficiency of insulin, the metabolism of carbohydrates is disturbed. Decreased oxidation of glucose in the tissue results in high blood sugar level and glycosuria.

Sorbitol, a hydrogenated sugar, is less sweet and is absorbed slowly by the intestinal tract. This is due to its conversion into fructose by the liver before converting it into glucose.

Protein Metabolism

The breakdown of protein is more in a diabetic patient due to reduced carbohydrate utilisation. Nitrogen excretion is more and negative nitrogen balance is common. So protein requirement is high in a diabetic to ensure essential amino acid supply.

Fat Metabolism

In a diabetic patient glycogen is not synthesised and so fatty acids are metabolised by the liver for energy purposes. End products of fat metabolism are released by the liver into the bloodstream. Acetone, acetic acid and beta-hydroxybutyric acid are the end products of fat metabolism and together they are known as ketone bodies. Due to excessive release of ketone bodies in the blood the acid base equilibrium is disturbed and gradually acidosis develops. This condition can lead to dehydration and coma. Acetone is a volatile substance which is excreted through lungs and so it gives out a characteristic odour to breath.

Clinical Types of Diabetes

Dietary modification suggests three categories of diabetics: juvenile diabetics, adult diabetics and senile diabetics.

Juvenile Diabetes

This occurs in children below the age of 15 years. Acute symptoms occur. Insulin production is minimal with the tendency to develop ketosis. Most of the juvenile diabetics lose weight because of abnormal carbohydrate metabolism. Dietary habits of the child and at times of the family have to be changed. Information regarding selection of food and substitutes should be known to the child because complications are more in this age group.

Adult Diabetes

Usually obese people are diabetic. Middle-aged diabetics show increase in the size of fat cells and glucose deposition is not possible in cells as there is no space there. Insulin secretion in an obese diabetic may be normal but because of lack of available space for conversion of glucose to glycogen, its storage is affected and hyperglycaemia and glycosuria occur. Insulin therapy is not necessary for an obese diabetic. Weight reduction often corrects the disease in them.

Senile Diabetes

This occurs among elderly people. This is mainly due to diminished insulin production by the pancreas in fibrosis or in tumours. These subjects require more insulin to bring their blood sugar to normal.

Dietetic Treatment

Dietetic treatment aims at bringing the blood sugar level to normal along with proper health of the patient. Intake of calories are an important yardstick in bringing the normal blood sugar level. Body weight has to be watched carefully. Weight check-up and urine examinations are indispensable in the treatment of a diabetic. Calorie distribution in various common food items must be made clear to a diabetic, so that they can adjust their intake by themselves in course of time. The ideal body weight of the patient must be calculated and known to the patient.

The calorie content of the diet must be calculated to the ideal weight. If the actual weight is more, calories must be reduced to bring

Height and Weight for Indians

Males (weight in kilogrammes)

Height (centimetres)	Age (years)						
	20	25	30	35	40	45	50
148	42.7	44.2	46.2	47.6	48.8	50	50.9
150	43.6	44.9	46.9	48.5	49.7	50.8	51.5
153	45.4	47.0	49.0	50.4	51.7	52.3	53.5
155	46.3	48.1	49.9	51.1	52.7	53.5	54.2
158	48.6	50.0	52.0	53.5	54.5	55.7	56.3
160	49.7	51.1	53.1	54.7	55.6	56.7	57.4
163	51.1	52.7	54.9	56.3	57.6	58.5	59.4
165	53.1	54.7	56.9	58.5	59.7	60.6	62.0
168	54.0	56.3	58.1	60.1	61.5	62.4	63.7
170	56.5	57.9	60.3	62.2	63.7	64.7	65.8
173	58.1	60.1	62.2	64.0	65.8	67.0	68.3
178	61.9	64.0	66.3	68.5	70.6	71.9	72.4
180	64.0	66.2	68.5	71.0	73.3	74.4	75.1
183	66.0	68.5	71.0	73.3	75.6	77.1	77.8

Females (weight in kilogrammes)

Height (centimetres)	Age (years)						
	20	25	30	35	40	45	50
148	38.6	41.0	42.6	44.0	45.1	46.3	47.1
150	40.3	41.6	43.5	44.8	46.0	47.0	47.7
153	41.9	43.5	45.3	46.4	47.9	48.4	49.5
155	42.8	44.3	46.2	47.7	48.8	49.5	50.1
158	44.9	46.3	48.1	49.5	50.4	51.6	52.1
160	46.0	47.3	49.1	50.6	51.5	52.4	53.0
163	47.3	48.8	50.8	52.1	52.2	54.1	54.9
165	49.1	50.6	52.6	54.1	55.3	56.0	57.3
168	50.0	52.1	53.8	55.6	56.8	57.7	59.0

down the body weight by breaking the body fat. Calorie intake also varies depending upon the type of activities the patient is engaged in. A sedentary worker requires 30 kcals per kilogramme of body weight whereas a moderate worker needs 40 kcals and a heavy worker 50 kcals per kilogramme of body weight, respectively. Once the weight is reduced by an obese person enough calories must be supplied to keep the body in normal condition.

Dietary instructions given to a diabetic must be simple. The National Institute of Nutrition has classified all foodstuffs into exchange groups for the benefit of a diabetic's selection. With careful selection from this exchange group a diabetic can consume any item within the limits. The aim is to select a low carlorie diet and items rich in carbohydrate are better restricted for wide choice. The exchange list is given below.

Vegetable Exchange-A

These vegetables may be used as desired. Carbohydrates and carlories are negligible.

Leafy vegetables	Other vegetables
Amaranth	Ashgourd
Bathua	Bittergourd
Brussels sprouts	Brinjal
Cabbage	Calabash cucumber
Celery	Cauliflower
Coriander leaves	Chow-chow (Marrow)
Curry leaves	Cucumber
Fenugreek	Drumstick
Lettuce	French beans
Mint	Knol-khol
Rape leaves	Ladiesfingers
Spinach	Mango, green
Soya leaves	Onion stalks
	Parwal
	Plantain flower
	Pumpkin
	Radish
	Rhubarb stalks
	Ridgegourd
	Snakegourd
	Tinda
	Tomato, green
	Turnip

Vegetable Exchange-B

Carbohydrates - 10 gms, Calories - 50 kcals.

Root vegetables	Quantity (gms)
Beetroot	75
Carrot	105
Colocasia	45
Onion, big	90
Onion, small	75
Potato	45
Sweet potato	30
Tapioca	30
Yam (elephant)	60
Yam	45

Other Vegetables	Quantity (gms)
Artichoke	60
Broad beans	90
Cluster beans	90
Double beans	50
Jack, tender	105
Jackfruit seeds	30
Leeks	60
Peas	45
Plantain, green	75
Singhara	45

Fruit Exchange

Carbohydrates - 10 gms, Calories - 50 kcals.

Fruit	Quantity (gm)	Approximate number or size
Amla	90	20 medium
Apple	75	1 small
Banana	30	1/4 medium
Cape gooseberry	150	40 small
Cashew fruit	90	6 medium
Custard apple	45	1 small
Dates	15	2
Figs	60	4 small

Grapes	105	20	
Grapefruit	150	1/2 big	
Jackfruit	60	3 medium pieces	
Jambu fruit	50	10 big	
Lemon	90	1 medium	
Loquat	105	6 big	
Mango	90	1 small	
Mangosteen	75	2 medium	
Melon	270	1/4 medium	
Orange	90	1 small	
Papaya	120	1/4 medium	
Peach	135	2 small	
Pear	90	1 small	
Pineapple	90	1 $1/_2$ slice (round)	
Plum	120	4 medium	
Pomegranate	75	1 small	
Strawberry	105	40	
Sweet lime	150	1 medium	
Tomato	240	4 small	
Water melon	175	1/4 small	

Cereal Exchange

30 gm provide 100 kcals, carbohydrates 20 gms, protein 2 gms

Bajra	Barley	Bread*	Cholam (Jowar)
Cornflakes	Maize, dry	Oatmeal	Ragi
Rice	Riceflakes	Rice puffed	Sago**
Samai	Semolina (Suji)	Vermicelli (Sevian)	
Wheat flour	Wheat, broken (dalia)		White flour

* To meet carbohydrates and calories requirement add 5 gms sugar.
** Requires supplementation with other high protein foods, when used.

Legume and Pulse Exchange

30 gm provide - 100 kcals, carbohydrates - 15 gms, protein - 6 gms

Bengal gram	Bengal gram, roasted	Besan (Bengal gram flour)
Black gram	Cowgram	Green gram
Horsegram	Kabuli channa (White gram)	
Lentils	Moth beans	Peas, dried
Rajmah	Rawan	Red gram

Flesh Food Exchange

Calories 70, protein 10 gms, fat 5 gms

Food	Quantity
Beef	60 gms
Crab	120 gms
Egg, duck*	2 gms
Egg, hen*	2 gms
Fish, big	60 gms
Fish, small	60 gms
Fish, vajra	60 gms
Fowl	60 gms
Liver, sheep	60 gms
Mutton muscle*	60 gms
Pigeon	50 gms
Pork	60 gms
Prawn	60 gms

* Provides 100 calories

Milk Exchange

Calories 100, protein 5 gms, fat 5 gms

Food	Quantity
Buttermilk	750 ml
Cheese	30 gms
Curd	210 gms
Khoa	30 gms
Milk, buffalo	90 ml
Milk, cow	180 ml
Milk, skimmed*	260 ml
Milk, skimmed, powder*	3 gms

*Provides 10 gms protein.

Having gained an elementary knowledge of the calorie content of various foodstuffs from the exchange list one can select a low calorie diet. In our country 60 to 75 per cent of the total calorie intake is from carbohydrates and so in a reducing diet or in a low calorie diet the amount of carbohydrate has to be reduced. Places where roots like tapioca (cassava) are used as the major source of carbohydrate, incidence of diabetes is more. In South India, especially in Kerala, pancreatitis or pancreatic diabetes is very common.

Fat Exchange
Calories 100, fat 11 gms

Food	Quantity (gms)
Almonds	15
Butter	15
Cashewnuts	20
Coconut	30
Ghee	11
Groundnuts roasted	20
Hydrogenated fat (vanaspati)	11
Oil (coconut, mustard)	11
Pistachio nut	15
Walnuts	15

There is no other disease in which diet takes on a greater role as in diabetes. The patient must actively cooperate for the management of dietary treatment. Even though there are many complications of diabetes like paralysis, coronary thrombosis, blindness and coma, diabetes is no more a dreaded disease. A well managed diabetic with diet control, insulin therapy or oral drugs, weight check-up, urine and blood examination has a good expectancy of life. On the contrary negligence of the condition causes irreparable damage to the arteries, gangrene, coronary infarction, kidney diseases or other complications of diabetes. Success or failure in the treatment of a diabetic patient depends on dietary regimen. Optimum nutrition is essential to lead a healthy life but it must be judiciously selected. Normal nutrition, normal weight, normal blood sugar level and minimum complications are the objectives for the treatment of diabetes.

Distribution of calories in terms of carbohydrates, proteins and fats is the first step. The total calorie requirement for the ideal weight has to be calculated in terms of activity. In an obese diabetic 10 kcals per kilogramme of body weight is reduced, as also for a sedentary and moderate worker, and 5 kcals per kilogramme for a labourer. In an underweight diabetic 5 kcals per kilogramme of body weight is increased for all three groups.

Caloric distribution for the total diet is 60 to 70 per cent from carbohydrate, 15 to 25 per cent from fats and 15 to 20 per cent from proteins. These calories are distributed as 1/5th of the total for breakfast, 2/5th for lunch and 2/5th for dinner.

Calorie distribution can be calculated by another method. Total calories for ideal weight of a normal, obese or underweight person can be calculated based on their activities. For example, for a normal sedentary man with an ideal weight of 65 kilogrammes the total calorie requirement is 65 x 30 kcals = 1950 kcals. Protein requirement for him is 1.2 gm/kg body weight; for 65 kg weight = 65 x 1.25 gm = 81.25 gm.

Protein calorie contribution 81.25 x 4 kcals = 324.8 kcals.
Non-protein calorie contribution 1950-324.8 = 1625 kcals
Non-protein calories have to be divided
     between carbohydrate and fat
Calories from: carbohydrate 1625/2 = 812.5 kcals.
Amount of carbohydrate in diet 812.5/4 = 203 gms
Calories from fat 812.5 kcals
Amount of fat 812.5/9 = 90.15 gms

Therefore the ration in grams of carbohydrate, protein and fat in the diet is 203 : 81.2 : 90.15.

Once the calorie distribution from carbohydrate, protein and fats is calculated, using an exchange list items can be selected for various meals by a diabetic patient. In the exchange list amounts of food groups are given. The availability of local foods and their preparation vary a great deal in each part of our country. Practical suggestions considering locality, availability, economic status and dietary patterns are more useful. Calorific value of common items must be made clear to them. For example, one cereal exchange of 30 gms contributes 15 gms carbohydrates, 2 gms protein and 70 calories. One thin chapathi requires 20 gms atta, and so 1 chapathi makes 1 cereal exchange. Therefore, 3 tablespoons of cooked rice, one idli, one slice of bread, one medium potato, 3 tablespoons cornflakes, 3/4 cup cooked porridge, 3 Marie biscuits and 1 tablespoon ragi are equivalent in its carbohydrate content with one cereal exchange. For a thin diabetic when 2 chapathis are recommended, for a person with normal weight or an obese diabetic one chapathi is enough. Among diabetic people there is a wrong notion that wheat products like chapathi or brown bread, millets like bajra or jowar or rava can be eaten in any quantity without harm. They believe that only rice is restricted for them. In fact, all cereals and millets more or less provide the same amount of calories. Since wheat is better in its protein content it is recommended instead of rice to rice-eaters. For a thin or underweight diabetic one exchange of rice can be taken daily. For other groups who prefer rice, two chapathis can be substituted for

1 cereal exchange gives 15 gms carbohydrate - 2 gms protein and 75 kcals

1 1/2 thin chapathis - 30 gms
3 tbsp cooked rice - 30 gms rice
1 idli
1 slice of bread
1 boiled potato
3 tablespoon cornflakes
3/4 cup cooked porridge
2 Marie biscuits
1 tbsp ragi - All are equivalent to 1 cereal exchange.

Calorie Content of Some Common Items

Food	-	Calories
1 idli	-	75 kcals
1 dosa	-	130 kcals
1/3 cup oatmeal (27 gms)	-	110 kcals
1 cup cornflakes (25 gms)	-	95 kcals
100 gms uppuma	-	230 kcals
2 parathas	-	275 kcals
1 cup rasam	-	12 kcals
1/2 cup sambar	-	105 kcals
1 egg (hens)	-	50 kcals
1 cup cow's milk	-	100 kcals
1 cup buffalo's milk	-	115 kcals
1 cup skimmed milk	-	45 kcals
1 cup toned milk	-	100 kcals
1 tbsp. condensed (20 gm) milk	-	64 kcals
1 glass buttermilk	-	25 kcals
1 glass curd	-	60 kcals
1 cup kheer	-	178 kcals
1 cup ice-cream	-	205 kcals
100 gms tapioca	-	157 kcals
100 gms potato	-	97 kcals
100 gms groundnut	-	560 kcals
1 meat puff	-	200 kcals
1 vada	-	200 kcals
100 gms tapioca chips	-	500 kcals
100 gms halva	-	570 kcals

30 ml. brandy	-	73 kcals
43 ml. rum	-	105 kcals
1 cup of coffee (1 ounce milk)	-	65 kcals
without sugar	-	25 kcals
1 cup of tea without sugar	-	65 kcals
	-	22 kcals
10 gms Horlicks	-	41 kcals
10 gms Ovaltine	-	38 kcals
1 tbsp. pickle	-	65 kcals
1 fried papad	-	43 kcals
1 grilled papad	-	25 kcals

three tablespoons of cooked rice. For a thin diabetic, if vegetarian, 1 cup thin dal is allowed per meal which supplies 100 kcals per cup. If egg, meat or fish or milk is used for non-vegetarians 200 kcals worth exchange can be included. Leafy vegetables can be included liberally in a diabetic diet. Dates, bananas and dried fruits like raisins are rich in calorie content. Groundnut has high fat content; 100 gms supplies 560 kcals. One cup of coffee with 1 oz milk and sugar supplies 65 kcals, whereas without sugar it has only. One cup of tea with sugar and 1 oz milk has 62 kcals whereas without sugar it has only 22 kcals. Pickles and papads are rich in energy.

Foods to be Avoided and Allowed

In a diabetic diet sugar, pastries, rich sweets, cakes, candy, dry fruits, fats and oils, fruit juices, in-between snacks, coconut, groundnut, fried items like pickles, papads and thick soups are restricted. Salads from raw tomato, cucumber, cabbage, capsicum, green chillies, radish and lemon, sprouted pulses are recommended liberally. Salad dressings are not allowed. Root vegetables are also restricted...

Regular exercises like walking rapidly, running, cycling, household work and light games are good. Exercises helps improve the function of cardiorespiratory organs.

Diabetics with Pregnancy

Complications are common among diabetics with pregnancy. Toxaemia and placental dysfunction can occur. Normal delivery is often difficult and Caesarean operations are necessary. Newborn babies may have congenital malformation and respiratory problems. Jaundice is also common among newborns. A diabetic mother must be under the care of the physician throughout pregnancy. Insulin treatment is preferred to oral drugs. Nutritional requirements are the same as that for a non-diabetic woman. Additional calorie requirements should be evenly distributed to all meals so as to avoid hypo or hyperglycaemia. The insulin intake must be adjusted. All other nutrients recommended for a non-diabetic pregnant mother are advised for the diabetic also. Weight gain of the pregnant mother must be periodically checked because unusual increase in weight during early pregnancy may be due to prematurity of the foetus and excessive weight gain in the third trimester is associated with toxaemia. High calorie items like ghee, nuts, dry fruits, sweets, dal preparations, and coconuts are restricted because they are calorigenic foods. If the dose of insulin is not regulated complications occur in pregnancy and such cases must be hospitalised. Infections during pregnancy in a diabetic mother are a serious complication and emergency treatment is essential. Since diabetes increases the hazards of pregnancy due to dangers of glycogen depletion, hypoglycaemia, acidosis and infection, regular obstetrical supervision is very essential. Early detection of any complaint prevents complications with critical conditions like proliferative retinopathy and nephropathy. Abortion may threaten a diabetic pregnant mother. A diabetic mother may not be able to secrete enough milk and so breast-feeding should not be encouraged in such cases. Often a diabetic pregnant mother is induced even if there is no complication in pregnancy by 36 to 38 weeks of gestation. Usually obstetricians admit their pregnant diabetics three months earlier, to observe the health of the mother and the child.

General Complications in a Diabetic

As a rule, even though diabetics are not more prone to infections compared to a normal person, if they fall ill complications are more in them. Cold, pneumonia or vomiting or diarrhoea upset their carefully set balance. Any illness increases the body's need for insulin. Urine and blood tests are necessary to check their sugar level and sometimes two to three times daily checking is necessary. Organs that are mainly affected by diabetes are kidneys, blood vessels, nerves and skin. Often due to excess work the kidney is damaged. Blood pressure may rise because blood vessels, especially arteries, are affected. Arterial walls become thickened and later hardened. Angina and heart pains are more common in diabetics and lead to coronary thrombosis or heart attacks. Blood pressure must be checked periodically. In senile diabetes the circulation of blood in the legs and arms may be reduced. Foot care is very essential in old people because damaged toe nails lead to infection. If abrasions, injuries, cuts, sores or corns occur, they are difficult to heal

d may lead to gangrene. Small blood vessels in the eye are damaged
d retinopathy in diabetes is common. Blood circulation to nerves
ffers due to thickening of small blood vessels in the brain. Sensitivity
1 skin's perception capacity are affected and often the skin may
:ome insensitive. Nerve sensation impairment, on and off pains,
icks of "pins and needles" in the legs, feet, arms or hands are
nmon. Warm clothing helps to relieve these conditions. The skin of a
betic is liable to infection. Sugar content in the urine often causes
gus, skin infections around the genital, especially in women. So
sonal hygiene is very important in the case of a diabetic.

48

DISEASES OF THE CARDIOVASCULAR SYSTEM

A healthy human heart is an extremely efficient muscular organ contracting and relaxing 1,00,000 times per day. A person is said to be as old as his arteries because once the arteries of the heart, kidneys or brain show degenerative changes these organs suffer. The heart pumps the blood and pushes it through the body.

The arteries branch into smaller capillaries and supply nourishment and oxygen to each and every cell in our body. The veins collect the impurities and impure blood from the cells and bring it back to the heart. This is how complete circulation takes place in our body. The force exerted by the heart as it pumps the blood into the large arteries creates a pressure within the arteries. The pressure depends on various factors and the most important of them is the size and nature of the arterial walls. They have high elasticity so as to dilate and constrict on pumping of the heart. The more constricted the arteries the higher the pressure tends to be. Thus it is the amount of constriction which determines the level of blood pressure rather than the force of the heart's pumping. Indirectly this affects the force of pumping. Narrowing, hardening and degeneration of arterial walls produce high blood pressure and coronary heart diseases. Atherosclerosis, a progressive vascular disease, reduces the elasticity of arterial walls and causes degenerative changes. Ninety-five per cent of coronary heart diseases are due to coronary atheroma and arteriosclerosis. No doubt cardiac diseases are a menace to health because kidneys, brain, lungs and extremities are affected due to cardiac upset. The diseases of the heart may be classified as functional or organic. The pericardium, endocardium or the myocardium are the different parts of the heart. Any of these can be affected and at times blood vessels within the heart or leaving the heart or the valves can be diseased. Enlargement of the organ also brings disorder. When the heart is not able to maintain the normal function heart failure occurs. Weakness, pain in the chest, dyspnoea on exertion, loss of appetite and digestive disorders manifest as the first symptoms of heart diseases. Atherosclerosis and hypertensions are the common heart diseases.

Hypertension

High blood pressure, commonly known as hypertension, is not a disease but only a symptom indicating that some underlying disease is progressing. Cardiovascular diseases, renal diseases like glomeulonephritis, polycystic renal disease, pyelonephritis, tumours of the brain, or adrenal glands, hyperthyroidism or diseases of ovaries and pituitary may cause hypertension. However, the majority of patients with high blood pressure are grouped as patients with "essential hypertension" for which the cause is unknown.

Predisposing factors of hypertension are heredity, stress, obesity, smoking, high viscosity of the blood due to too many red blood cells in the circulating blood, narrowing of the main blood vessels near the heart or aorta due to congenital malformation and excessive hormone secretions especially cortisone, aldosterone, adrenaline and non-adrenaline.

Studies conducted on parents and their children and siblings showed that there is a strong tendency for hypertension to run in families. Hypertension is often mentioned as a disease of modern living because city dwellers are more prone to it compared to rural people. Usually a villager leads a quiet life whereas a city dweller leads a mechanical life with various stresses and strains. People who are usually tense show high blood pressure as compared to a normal person. Overwork, unhappy home, marital disharmony, financial worries, and generation problems can create continuous stress. If the cause of stress is isolated half the problem is over. People who cope with their problems quickly worry less and produce less pressure compared with a person who always broods over a problem.

Obesity has a tendency to increase blood pressure. When the weight is brought down pressure usually falls. People with sedentary work suffer more from hypertenison in contrast to a moderate or a hard worker.

Smoking of cigarettes causes rise in blood pressure. Nicotine in the tobacco causes the release of adrenaline and non-adrenaline from the adrenal glands which increases blood pressure. Atheroma, a condition where deposits of fatty materials line the blood vessels which later break up causing blood clots, is more common among smokers. Coronary thrombosis occurs more among hypertensive patients who smoke.

Symptoms of Hypertension

Mild and moderate hypertensions usually produce no symptoms. The first symptom may be, if any, headache towards the back of the head and neck on walking. All headaches need not be related to hypertension. Giddiness, unexplained tiredness, change in eyesight, especially a blind spot when they look in one or another direction and shortness of breath, are signals of rise in blood pressure. Acute attacks of breathlessness in the night are very harmful. Reduced blood supply due to constriction of arteries, especially coronary arteries, makes the heart work hard and this may cause angina pectoris, a discomfort of pain usually felt in the centre of the chest. If a coronary artery is completely blocked the condition is known as thrombosis. And it is often referred to as 'heart attack'. Hypertension patients are more prone to coronary and cerebral thrombosis. Cerebral thrombosis is one of the causes of a 'stroke'. Depending upon the site and position of the blockage in the artery the patient may become unconscious and go into a coma. Cerebral haemorrhage also causes a stroke. In this condition, an artery may rupture and the blood flow thus destroys a part of the brain. This stage is mentioned as 'apoplexy'. Therefore, hypertension can produce such complications if neglected.

Dietary Treatment

'Kempner's rice-fruit-sugar diet' is very effective in severe cases. It provides about 2,000 kcals, 5 gms fat, 20 gms protein, 150 mgs sodium and 200 mgs chloride. It consists of boiled or steamed rice, 250 to 350 gms (dry) in weight. Rice is cooked in water or in fruit juice. No salt is added. Fruits may be eaten raw or stewed with sugar or as fruit juices. Free fluid should be limited to 700 to 1,000 ml only as fruit juice. Vitamin supplements other than vitamin C are essential; 5,000 I.U. of vitamin A and 1,000 I.U. of vitamin D, 5 mgms of the amino chloride, 5 mgs of riboflavin and 25 mgs of niacinamide are essential. Calcium pentothenate 2 mgs is also recommended in this diet. Hospitalisation is essential and it provides rest to the patient.

The normal diet prescription of a hypertension patient is a low calorie, low fat, low sodium diet with normal protein in it. Since obesity is common among those patients with essential hypertension, weight reduction is essential. A moderate amount of protein, that is, 1 gm of protein per kg (ideal weight) body weight is recommended. If kidney diseases cause hypertension, low protein diets of 20 to 30 gms are recommended. As a general rule 1,000 to 1,200 kcals and 50 gms of protein are recommended. Though animal protein has no direct relation in increasing the pressure, their cholesterol content and saturated fatty acid content have harmful effects in a hypertension patient.

Since atherosclerosis accompanies hypertension high intake of fat, especially animal fat and vanaspati, and coconut oil are restricted. About 30 gms of vegetable oil is recommended.

Low sodium diet is generally prescribed for a hypertension patient; 2 gms and 5 gms sodium restriction is introduced in cardiovascular renal diseases and in hypertension, respectively. Low sodium foodstuffs are to be selected for a hypertension patient. Animal foods are rich in sodium content and seafoods and canned foods are better avoided in a low sodium diet. Foods rich in sodium are beef, kidney, liver, beetroots, rye, enriched breads and cereals, salted butter, items where baking powder is used, cereal brans, kidney, liver, beetroots, cornflakes, salted butter, baking powder, riceflakes, cream, soda, egg, sardines, tuna, skimmed milk, onion, legumes and vegetables like cabbage. Cooking salt, salted preserves, and snack items and chips are not allowed in a low sodium diet.

Foods allowed in a low sodium diet are bread, chapathi, breakfast cereals or wheat, rice, millets or oats without salt, pulses, vegetable soups, vegetable salads from selected vegetables like tomato, sprouted green gram, vegetables like potato, yam, drumstick, beans, vegetable oils, sugar, jaggery, honey, desserts, dried fruits except raisins, and fresh fruits. Beverages except milk drinks are allowed.

Animal foods like meat, fish, chicken, eggs, beetroot, carrots, leafy vegetables, sweets and pastry, readymade food items where salt is used, papad, chutney, pickles and canned foods are excluded. Also milk is minimised in sodium restricted diet.

Fluid content of a hypertension diet depends on oedema in the body.

A Low Sodium Diet

Time	Meal
6 a.m.	Coffee
8 a.m.	Sweet potato stuffed chapathi Pineapple, Coffee
11 a.m.	Grape juice
12.30 p.m.	Rice or chapathi, Fish curry, Carrot kheer, Cucumber raita
4 p.m.	Banana, Toast, Mango, Coffee
8 p.m.	Rice gruel or soft chapathi, Green gram curry, Meat cutlet, Fruit cup
9 p.m.	Milk

This diet provides 62.5 gms protein, 516.6 mgms sodium, 38 gms fat and 2015 kcals.

A Sample Diet for a Hypertension Patient

(No Salt is added)

Time	Meal
6 a.m.	Coffee
8 a.m.	Soft chapathi (2 in nos), Egg curry (less oil), Plantain, Coffee
10 a.m.	Lime juice
12.30 p.m.	Potato-tomato soup, Rice or chapathi (50 gms), Bittergourd with tamarind juice, Tomato curry, Drumstick pugath, Curds, Guava
4 p.m.	Tea, Vermicelli savoury
6 p.m.	Buttermilk
8 p.m.	Chapathi, Tomato-dal mashed, Orange
10 p.m.	Milk (skimmed milk)

This diet provides 50 gms protein, 1,800 kcals and 750 mgs sodium.

Atherosclerosis

Atherosclerosis is a chronic vascular disease characterised by thickening, hardening and loss of elasticity of the arterial walls. Lipids infiltrate the arterial wall of an atherosclerosis patient which is followed by degenerative changes. One of the major causes of heart attacks is atherosclerosis. Coronary arteries, which supply blood to the heart muscles, are affected because of the deposits of plaques containing fat, especially cholesterol. Sometimes the plaque becomes very thick and the inner lining of the arteries bursts which leads to clot formation or thrombosis. This blocks the blood supply within the heart and the heart muscles suffer from lack of oxygen causing myocardial infarction. If the damage is severe the heart fails to function and death may occur immediately. Atherosclerosis of the cerebral arteries causes paralysis or stroke and in the renal arteries it leads to high blood pressure.

The raised plasma lipid level is due to heredity, age, hormones, high calorie intake, cholesterol content in the diet, triglycerides in the diet, plasma lipo protein content, total fat content, saturated and unsaturated fat content in the diet, protein content of the diet, vitamin and mineral content in the diet, and smoking and emotional stress in the person. Longstanding hypertension and diabetes predispose to atherosclerosis. This disease is common among males and among obese people.

Heredity plays an important role in coronary heart disease. Short, stock, short-necked persons are more exposed to this disease compared to tall, thin people. Dietary habits and living pattern of the family may also contribute to it.

The onset usually takes place during early adult life but symptoms are manifested only at the age of 50 or above. Myocardial infarction and ischaemic heart diseases are observed in infants and children but atherosclerosis occurs in an adult age.

Sex hormones have some influence in the occurrence of atherosclerosis. Atherosclerosis is common among male members and it occurs among women after menopause, at the same rate as in males.

Oestrogen administered to males reduces the plasma cholesterol level in coronary artery disease even though it is not practical. In hypothyroidism total blood lipid and cholesterol level are high.

The serum lipids rise with an increase in total calorie intake. Obese people are more prone to atherosclerosis and obesity is the result of high calorie intake. Studies have shown that in communities where calories and fats are consumed in large quantities the incidence of atherosclerosis is more.

The cholesterol content in the diet has high relationship with the development of atheromatous patches in the arterial walls. An excess of cholesterol and saturated fat-laden foods in the body can lead to the hardening of the arteries.

Among the Bantus in Uganda where fat consumption is very low the incidence of coronary heart disease is not seen.

Fats in food materials are mainly saturated (hard) fats which are solid at room temperature, mono-unsaturated fats and poly-unsaturated fats are soft. Saturated fats are rich in cholesterol. Egg yolk, organ meats like heart, brain, liver, kidney, shellfish like oysters, crabs, prawns, shrimps, lobsters, dairy products like butter, cream and milk and all animal products are rich in cholesterol content. Pork, mutton fat, hydrogenated oils and coconut oil and palmoil are also rich in cholesterol. Low consumption of saturated fats reduces coronary infection, sudden death and cerebral infarction. As a whole vegetarians have a low plasma cholesterol but it is elevated if animal foods are included. Plasma cholesterol is elevated in pregnancy, diabetes, nephrosis, obstructive jaundice, cirrhosis, hypothyroidism and in cholecystitis. Low plasma cholesterol level is seen in hyperthyroidism, anaemia and in acute infection.

Cholesterol is synthesised in the liver and in the intestine. Dietary cholesterol content regulates the endogenous production. But even in a cholesterol-free diet endogenous production continues. Fasting, low cholesterol diet and increased bile flow reduces the synthesis by the liver. A small quantity of cholesterol is essential as it forms an insulating sheath for nerves and raw materials for hormones. In all tissues some amount of cholesterol are present and form some chemical agents which determine our growth, energy and sexual characteristics. Bile contains cholesterol. But excess cholesterol in the blood causes artery blockage. High cholesterol or saturated fat content in the diet produces excess cholesterol in the blood. To limit the fat content in the diet poly-unsaturated fats like sunflower oil, saffola oil, corn oil, soyabean oil, groundnut oil, sesame oil, rice bran oil and other vegetable oils can be used.

Sistosterol, a vegetable sterol of cholesterol family, interferes with cholesterol absorption. If five to ten grammes of this is given to a person sistosterol combines with the cholesterol of food and bile to form unabsorbable compounds. Soyabean and cottonseeds are rich in sistosterol.

Lipo proteins are compounds of lipids attached to proteins of different densities. This makes insoluble lipids soluble for transport. Parts of cholesterol, neutral fat and phospholipids attach themselves with protein to form proteins. Alpha, beta and prebeta lipo proteins are in our blood. In coronary heart disease the pre-beta and beta lipo proteins are increased.

Dietary advice is the first thing required in the management of patients with high cholesterol and triglyceride level. Total calories should be reduced to bring down body weight to ideal weight. Latest studies have shown that ingestion of large quantities of sucrose causes an elevation of blood triglycerides because sucrose increases the intestinal synthesis of cholesterol in the body. So a moderate to low calorie diet according to weight is recommended for an atherosclerosis patient. Protein allowance of 1 gm per kg of body weight is permitted but animal proteins are not recommended for an atherosclerosis patient. Low fat, low cholesterol diet is prescribed for an atherosclerosis patient. Animal fats, organ meats, eggs and seafoods are restricted and so vitamin deficiency, especially vitamin A deficiency, may occur. Supplement of vitamin A is essential. Leafy and other vegetables can be used liberally, but since they are not palatable without salt and seasoning the patient has to develop a habit to consume it.

Foods allowed are skimmed milk, coffee and tea in limited amounts, soft drinks, non-fat cereal foods like rice, wheat, biscuits, breads, roots like potatoes, pulses, lean meat, small fish, fowl, vegetable oils, all fruits and vegetables, sugar, honey and desserts and fruit preparations where fat is not used.

Foods avoided are whole milk, cream, cereal preparations and snack items where baking soda is used, fried and baked items where cream or fats are used, bakery items, animal foods, like meat, only fish, animal fats like butter, ghee, hydrogenated fats like vanaspati fats like vanaspati, pickles, nuts, papads and preserves where fats are used.

Three or four smaller meals are suggested instead of two big meals. The evening meals must be two hours before retiring to bed. Regular exercise and relaxed mental attitude help to reduce pressure. Aggressiveness, tensions and worries increase the pressure. Dietary fibre reduces the food consumption and so a high fibre diet is recommended. Since vegetable proteins have a tendency to reduce blood cholesterol, a vegetarian diet is more appreciated for an atherosclerosis patient. The pectin in fruits also reduces the cholesterol content of blood. Heavy smokers and uncontrolled diabetics and alcoholics have a higher death rate from heart attacks.

A Sample Menu for Atherosclerosis

Time	Meal
6 a.m.	Coffee
8 a.m.	Dry chapathi, Red gram dal curry, Coffee
10 a.m.	Lime juice
12.30 Noon	Steamed vegetable pulao or chapathi, Tomato-peas salad
4 p.m.	Ragi porridge Pury plantain
6 p.m.	Buttermilk (non-fat)
8 p.m.	Chapathi, Fish curry, Potato-spinach saute

This diet provides 44 gms protein, 24 gms fat and 1,384 kcals.

49

KIDNEY DISEASES

Kidneys are the major excretory organs in our body. They are also
called as the guardians of the nutritional wealth of our body. All useful
substances and nutrients are reabsorbed by the proximal convoluted
tubules of nephrons. In renal failure excessive loss of water,
electrolytes, calcium and phosphorus and proteins take place.

The kidneys which weigh only 0.3 per cent of body weight perform
very important functions. Formation and expulsion of urine,
maintenance of normal nutrition, acid-base and electrolyte balance and
secretion of certain hormones like renin and erythroprotein are the
major functions of the kidneys.

The waste products of the body, especially the end products of
protein, metabolism, are excreted by the kidneys. Urea is the major
component of urine which is about 30 gms in urine. Urea is derived
from ingested food and from the breakdown of body tissues. If urea is
more than 4 per cent of urine, complications occur in the body. In renal
disorders urine formation is affected. A healthy person's kidney filters
about 170 litres of fluid and 1 to 2 litres of urine is produced. Acid and
basic mineral salts and other nitrogenous end products of protein
metabolism such as uric acid and creatinine are eliminated by the
kidney. Ammonia is synthesised by the kidney and excreted through
urine.

Nephritic syndrome, nephrotic syndrome and chronic renal failure
are the common disorders of the kidney.

Acute Glomerulonephritis

This disease is also known as Bright's disease. In this condition
inflammation or degeneration of the kidney takes place.

Nephritis is characterised by oliguria, hematuria, nitrogen
retention, hypertension, oedema and proteinuria. Glomeruli, tubules

and intestinal tissues are affected. Usually it occurs in children due to streptococcic infections like scarlet fever, tonsillitis, pneumonia and other respiratory infections. If children are affected 85 to 95 per cent make a complete recovery whereas if adults are affected only 50 per cent gain complete recovery. Carelessness in treatment and dietetic control leads to chronic renal failure. Renal infarction, acute polyonephritis and metallic poisoning also cause acute glomerulonephritis.

Dietary modification includes a low protein, low sodium, low potassium, high carbohydrate diet with moderate fluid content. In the acute state of illness nausea and vomiting occur and normal food consumption is impossible. At the end of the second week normal diet can be given.

Carbohydrate is included liberally to supply 1,700 kcals per day. Cereals in all forms are allowed, but no cooking salt is added.

A low protein diet is recommended so as to give rest to the kidney. Complete proteins are better to ensure maximum utilisation.

If anuria develops protein should be stopped. When urine formation is about 500 to 700 ml, about 0.5 gm protein per kg body weight is allowed.

Vitamins, especially vitamins C and B complex, are recommened in very high quantities. More than 100 mgs of vitamin C is recommended.

In acute nephritis kidney is unable to do proper filtration, therefore, sodium and potassium are not excreted and electrolyte balance and water balance are disturbed. If oedema is present, sodium is restricted. When urine formation is reduced potassium is also restricted.

Fluid intake is regulated based on urine formation. Intake and output of fluid and urine must be checked; 1,000 ml plus output of urine is the best method of calculation of fluids.

A soft, low protein, low sodium must be suggested to the patient. Animal proteins like meat, fish, eggs, liver and other flesh foods, milk in excess, excess peas, beans, pulses and all nuts are restricted in nephritis diet. Papad, chutney or pickles are avoided.

Bread, chapathis of wheat, rice, millets, breakfast cereals, 3 cups of milk and milk products, all vegetables, roots and tubers, sugar and

jaggery, boiled sweets, fresh fruits, arrowroot, cornflour and plain
biscuits are allowed.

A Sample Diet for an Actue Glomerulonephritis Patient

Time	Meal
6 a.m.	Coffee
8 a.m.	Bread, Butter (2 slices), Jam, Grape juice
11 a.m.	Orange juice
12.30 p.m.	Tomato rice or soft chapathi (2 nos.), Tomato curry, Steamed cabbage raita, Fruit cup
4 p.m.	Rava ladoo (2 nos.), Tea
7 p.m.	Sago pudding (1 cup)
8 p.m.	Soft chapathi (2) or uppuma (1-2 cup), Tomato-dal mashed, Fruit salad
10 p.m.	Milk (skimmed milk)

The diet suppplies 1,850 kcals, proteins-36 gms, fat - 32 gms.

Nephrotic Syndrome

Albuminuria, haematuria, oedema and proteinuria, hypertension and
diminished renal functions are the common symptoms of nephrotic
syndrome. Serum cholesterol levels are raised, nitrogenous waste
products are retained and gradually uraemia or renal failure occurs.
Renal excretory capacity is maintained even if only 10 per cent of
kidney tissues are in working condition. After that excretory and
regulatory functions of the kidneys are affected and the waste products
are accumulated in the blood. This condition is known as uraemia.
Chronic glomerulonephritis, vascular kidney diseases like malignant
hypertension, hypertensive arteriosclerosis, atherosclerotic
nephrosclerosis and vascular lesions produce degenerative destruction
of nephrosis. Diabetes develops nephropathy which gradually destroys
nephrons. Neglected gout and congenital abnormalities like polycystic
diseases present since birth eventually lead to renal failure.

Dietetic management includes enough calories, fat and a high
protein and high vitamin C content in the diet; 2,000 kcals, 1.5 to 2 gms
of protein and 1 gm fat/kg body weight are recommended. A high
protein diet is required to meet the heavy loss of albumin and protein

depletion of the tissues. Since proteins are lost, resistance power is reduced and the patient becomes susceptible to infection. So a high protein diet is essential.

Sodium is restricted to prevent oedema. Cooking salt is restricted and readymade foods where salt is added are also avoided. But severe sodium restriction may lead to body depletion of sodium. For a nephrotic patient 500 mgs to 800 mgs of sodium is recommended. Substitutes for sodium must be carefully selected as it may affect the potassium elimination. Fluid is restricted only when the kidney is affected in its functions accompanied by oedema.

Cereals in all forms are allowed for a nephrotic patient. Pulses, beans, fleshy foods like meat, fish, eggs are allowed. Milk is not allowed but skimmed milk can be used. Soups are excluded but vegetables, roots and tubers, cooking fat, sugar and jaggery, pastries, dessert, sweets and fruits are allowed. Condiments and spices, papads, pickles and chutney are not permitted.

Sample Diet for Nephrotic Syndrome

Time	Meal
6 a.m.	Coffee
8 a.m.	Rava porridge, Toast, Poached egg, Coffee
10 a.m.	Lime juice, Banana
12.30 p.m.	Rice or soft chapathi, Pumpkin dal curry, Meat cutlet, Vegetable salad, curd
4 p.m.	Coffee, Pancake
8 p.m.	Chappati, Tomato-dal curry, Fish molee, Spinach or amaranth saute
10 p.m.	Milk (skimmed milk)

This diet supplies 82 gms, proteins 3,200 kcals fat, 80 gms.

Since calcium and potassium deficiency may accompany severe proteinuria, bone rarefaction and hypokalemia are common in nephrosis, low sodium milk with potassium supplements is essential in the treatment of this condition. A soft bland diet is suggested. Vitamin supplements, especially vitamin C, are essential. Thus a high protein, high carbohydrate, salt free, moderate fat with restricted fluid are recommended for a nephrotic patient.

Renal Failure

Diminished renal function leads to renal failure. It can be acute or chronic in nature. Waste products are accumulated in the blood and tissues and anuria occurs in acute renal failure. Headaches, nausea, drowsiness, lethargy and coma are the symptoms. In chronic renal failure, functioning nephrons are few. Nephrons are hypertrophied. Infection or trauma creates new catabolic loads to the damaged nephrons and blood urea may rise only 10 to 15 mgs per 100 ml daily. Cardiovascular oedema, neurological changes, skin and skeletal changes are common.

Dietetic treatment aims to minimise protein catabolism, to avoid dehydration and overhydration, to control electrolytes and fluid loss through vomiting and diarrhoea, to arrest acidosis and to minimise complications. A minimum of 600 to 1,000 kcals mainly from carbohydrate and fats is recommended. Protein foods are restricted except in the case of peritoreal dialysis or haemodialysis. In this condition 40 gms of protein is recommended. Usually the protein content of the diet varies depending upon the urea content of the blood. Fluid content is calculated based on urine formation. Total loss plus 500 ml is the allotment. Sodium restriction is also judged by the physician based on sodium loss in the urine. Hyperkalaemia or potassium intoxication produce deleterious effects and potassium sources like tomato juice, coffee or tea, cocoa, and molasses are avoided. Since normal food is not given, other sources of potassium-rich vegetables or beans are not included in the diets. A planned diet is not possible because of the severe complications in uraemia. If the condition improves liberal amounts of protein can be included with a high carbohydrate content. A bland, easily digested diet with sodium restriction, if there is oedema, is recommended for uraemia.

Urinary Calculi

In urinary calculi stones are developed anywhere along the urinary tract, in the kidneys, ureters, bladder and urethra. Small foci are formed and supersaturated urinary salts are precipitated around the foci of mucoid structures. Mucopolysaccharides and mucoprotein combine with chemicals bound to form the foci. The end products of protein metabolism leaves uric acid, phosphate and oxalates, sodium, calcium and magnesium. A urine concentrated with calcium phosphate and ammonium phosphate predisposes stone formation. Abnormal colloids in the urine cements precipitated crystals around the foci, and concentration of urine due to low fluid intake helps the calculus formation.

Aetiological factors are heredity, climate, fluids, vitamin B complex deficiency, vitamin A deficiency and excessive vitamin D and calcium content, hyperthyroidism and frequent infections. People residing in hot climates are more prone to develop renal calculi compared to people of other areas. During summer calculi occurs more often as compared to in cold weather.

Due to high perspiration in tropical areas urine becomes concentrated if large quantities of fluids are not ingested daily. A high fluid intake of more than 8 to 10 glasses enables the urine to be in dilute state. This prevents stone formation. Urinary oxalate excretion is more if tryptophan content in the diet is more. B complex vitamins, especially B6, decreases the urinary oxalate excretion. Vitamin A deficiency causes roughening of the epithelial tissues in our body, thereby helping the precipitation of stones in the renal system. Vitamin D is essential for proper bone calcification and if excess vitamin D with calcium is administered as supplements it can produce urinary calculi in later course. In hyperparathyroidism the breakdown of bone matrix is more which leads to inorganic calcium and phosphorus deposits in the urinary tract. Prolonged bed rest and congenital malformation in renal pelvis, ureter or bladder, prostate enlargement and urinary infection can also produce calculi.

Renal calculi are with calcium combined to oxalates, urates, or phosphates and high oxalate content in the diet. Excessive uric acid releases high inorganic phosphates in the diet; low urinary magnesium and high calcium excretion are the direct causes for urinary calculi.

Dietary Modifications

The role of diet in the formation of stones is not clearly known. Even though formation of stones is a metabolic defect where certain chemicals are either excreted more or retained more in the urine, foods rich in such chemicals are restricted as a dietary modification for urinary calculi. Two commonest types of stones in the adult population are those made of uric acid and of calcium oxalate. In a stone-forming person, especially in oxalate stones, the patient absorbs and re-excretes a greater proportion of calcium from a normal diet compared to a non-stone-forming person. In magnesium deficiency excessive oxalate is excreted. Uric acid calculi are common in adults. Increased uric acid content in urine makes the calcium oxalate in the urine less soluble and develops stones with calcium oxalate and traces of urates. Acidification of the urine is dangerous in such patients because of the high solubility of free uric acid in acid medium. In alkaline medium uric acid combines with alkali and forms alkaline urates.

Protein is the main source of uric acid in our body. In starvation body proteins are depleted and breakdown of protein and fat helps the liberation of uric acid. If excessive fluid is ingested this can be minimised. A high fluid intake is recommended for all three types of urinary calculi. A dilute urine prevents precipitate formation around the matrix. Acidity of the urine must be regulated. Purine content in the diet has to be reduced in low uric acid diets. Organ meats like kidney, liver, brain, heart and sardines, fish, fish roe, herrings are rich in purine content. These foods are strictly prohibited in urinary calculi and in gout. Beans, peas, cauliflower, spinach, amaranthus, meat, seafoods, yeast and wholegrain cereals are moderate in its purine content. All other vegetables, fruits, milk, eggs, refined cereals and cereal products, sugar and sweets are poor in purine content.

If the stone is a calcium oxalate stone, high fluid intake reduces the concentration of calcium and oxalate iron in the urine. Acidification of the urine by taking acidifying agents keep the calcium and oxalate in solution. Calcium and oxalate intake must be avoided. Calcium-rich foods are milk and milk products, small fish with bones, canned sardines, beans, prawns, crabs, cauliflower, egg yolk, molasses, potatoes, tapioca, colocasia, ragi, gingerale, cane sugar and onion. Foods rich in oxalates are beef, coffee, cola drinks, tea, cashewnuts, chocolates, grapes, plum, leafy vegetables, beetroot, yam, gooseberries.

Even though dietary oxalates are controlled endogenous production of oxalates takes place independent of exogenous dietary supply. Often calcium phosphate stones are formed and to avoid this along with calcium, dietary phosphates also must be restricted. Milk, cheese, milk products, wholegrain, cereals, bran, oatmeal, eggs, organ meats, nuts, soyabean, meats, banana, carrot, cherry and soft drink are rich in phosphorus content. A high fluid intake, about 3 litres, is essential to prevent stone formation. Urinary infection produces complications and care must be taken to prevent it.

High intake of calcium, hypervitaminosis D, prolonged skeletal immobilisation, prolonged acidosis, postmenopausal osteoporosis and hyperparathyroidism produce hypercalcinuria. If any of these cause hypercalcinuria it must be treated first. Vegetarian diets are more appreciated for urinary calculi.

50

DIET IN GOUT AND OSTEOARTHRITIS

Gout

Gout is a hereditary disease which occurs mainly among males. This condition is characterised by disturbed purine metabolism and abnormal uric acid deposition in the joints. In the cartilages and articular cartilages of joints sodium-urate is deposited. Recurrent attacks of pain and swelling occur. Over-production or inadequate excretion of uric acid produce this condition. Certain vegetable and animal foods contain nucleo proteins which are broken down to proteins and nucleic acid. One byproduct of such a breadown is purine. Purines are oxidised to uric acid proabably in the liver. Apart from this endogenous uric acid or the exogenous uric acid from food sources, the human body can synthesise uric acid from carbon and nitrogen compounds from the metabolic pool. Animal foods and organ meats are rich in uric acid. About 200 to 500 mgs from animal foods and 300 to 600 mgs even from a purine-free diet is derived by the body. Normal serum uric acid level is 3 to 5 mgs per 1 pp ml. But in a gout patient the serum uric acid level is 6 mgs or more per 100 ml of blood from men and 5 mgs per 100 ml for women. Administration of lactose results in decreased urinary urate excretion and serum uric acid level. Fasting increases the uric acid level in normal and gout persons. Little alcohol with low purine diet decreases the urate level in serum but large quantities produce high serum uric acid level. Among vegetarians the occurrence of gout is less.

The uric acid is deposited in and around the joints, the metatarsals, knee and toe joints. In acute and chronic forms gout attacks. Acute attacks are often mentioned as gout arthritis. Monosodium urate monohydrate crystals are formed from the phagocytes during gout attacks. Thus precipitation of urate crystals and leucocytic activity are presumed responsible for gout arthritis. Since the concept of gout is changing, dietary modifications are also changing. In a gout patient's diet purine rich foods are avoided. Fish roe, sweet breads, sardines, meat extracts, soup, herring, salmon, liver, kidney, pomfret, prawns, chicken, meat, green peas, lentils, spinach, mushrooms, cauliflower, brinjals, pulses, oatmeal, custard apple are rich to moderate sources of purine which must be avoided. Coffee and tea contain methylated purines which are oxidised to methyl uric acid, but usually this is excreted through urine. Still coffee and tea are to be minimised. All vegetables and fruits except those mentioned above are allowed. An overweight person must reduce weight; therefore a low calorie diet is recommended; 1,200 to 1,500 kcals are enough.

The protein content must be moderate to low, preferably milk protein, or vegetable proteins are recommended; 40 to 60 gms are harmless. Fats enable the deposition of urates and a low fat diet is recommended. Liberal fluid intake so as to excrete 1,200 ml of urine is recommended. About 3 litres of fluid can be given. Tea or coffee has to be limited to 2 to 3 cups daily. Alcoholic beverages are to be limited because after the ingestion of alcohol gout attacks are common. Beer is very harmful.

A low purine, low fat, low protein diet with moderate calorie content is recommended for a gout or gout arthritis patient. High fluid and vitamin content are essential.

Foods allowed are bread or chapathi or wheat, rice, maize, bajra or ragi, breakfast cereals, rice, egg, milk or milk products, vegetable soups, low purine vegetables, little fat, desserts without cream or much fat, fresh fruits, and pulses (limited amount), meat or fish (permitted items only when there is no gout attack).

Condiments and spices, papad, chutney, pickles and nuts are not allowed. Milk and milk products are restricted.

Osteoarthritis

Osteoarthritis is also known as degenerative arthritis. It is a chronic progressive disorder where the weight-bearing joints are degenerated. It is common among obese people, especially the middle aged. Knees, hips, lumbar and cervical spine are the common places where degenerative changes occur. Weight reduction takes off the strain from joints. Low calorie, low purine, low fat, low protein diet with high fluid and vitamin supplements are recommended.

A Sample Diet for a Gout Patient

Time	Meal
6 a.m.	Milk (skimmed milk)
8 a.m.	Chapathi, Vegetable stew, Coffee (skimmed milk)
10 a.m.	Pineapple juice
12.30 p.m.	Rice or soft chapathi, Dal curry, Amaranth pugath, Buttermilk
2 p.m.	Barley water
4 p.m.	Vegetable cutlet, Coffee
8 p.m.	Broken wheat gruel, Plantain, Bread pudding (skimmed milk).

51

ACIDIC AND ALKALINE FOODS

The mineral element left after the combustion of food is known as ash. Ash, sodium, potassium, calcium and magnesium are alkaline radicals. Chloride, phosphate and sulphate are acid radicals. The reaction of blood is maintained slightly alkaline by kidneys. Kidneys excrete acid or alkaline urine to make the blood pH. In kidney diseases the alkali reserve of the blood may be affected. In urinary calculi especially, in calcium phosphate, for crystal formation diet has an influence.

Acid-producing foods	Alkaline foods
Whole wheat	Fruits like apple, apricots,
Bread	banana, berries, dates
Cornmeal	Grape juice
Oatmeal	Lemon juice
Puffed rice	Olive
Puffed wheat	Pumpkin
Egg	Spinach
Egg yolk	Tomato
Groundnut	Oranges
Chocolate	Peach
Fish	Pineapple
Mackerel	Raisins
Oysters	Milk
Salmon	Asparagus
Pomfret	Beetroot
Meat	Carrots
Poultry	Cabbage
Beef	Cauliflower
Kidney	Cucumber
Liver	Beans
Chicken	Lettuce

Mutton		Onion
Pork		Green peas
Rabbit		Potato

Potassium-rich Foods

Bread	Kidney	Whole
wheat	Liver	Bran
Pig	Wheat germ	Pork
Eggs	Salmon	Milk
Sardine	Apricots	Tuna
Banana	Coconut	Groundnut
Duck	Cherries	Peanut butter
Berries	Chocolate	Raisins
Soyabeans	Dates	Sweet potato
Oranges	Tomatoes	Pineapple
Plums	Strawberries	Beef
Brain	Chicken	

Sodium-rich Foods

Commercial foods made with milk, salt

Chocloate milk	Frozen limabeans
Condensed milk	Potato chips
Ice-cream	Glazed fruits
Malted milk	Dried fruits with
Greens, spinach	sodium sulfite added
Beets, carrots	Yeast bread, canned
Frozen peas with salt	foods, enriched cereals
Milk mixes	

Bakery items with baking soda, salted popcorn, salted readymade items, shell fish, crab, oysters, peanut butter, salted butter, beverages with flavoured powders, animal foods and commercial sweetened desserts.

52

DIET DURING NERVOUS DISTURBANCES

Research work in the science of nutrition has brought to light a greater relationship between nutrition and the functions of the nervous system. Glucose, B complex vitamins like thiamine, riboflavin, niacin, choline and B6 are essential for normal health of the nervous system. Choline and B6 deficiency affect the impulse-transmitting capacity and produces epilepsy and convulsions if the deficiency is prolonged. Thiamine depleted diets in experimental cases produced irritability, depression and quarrelsome nature. They were suspicious, non-cooperative and fearful in their nature. Administration of thiamine cured all these symptoms. Niacin deficiency produces pellagra. In pellagra nervous disturbances occur. Anxiety, loss of appetite, insomnia, depressions and tension status are the first symptoms of nervous disorder. Emotional instability and in later stage fearful hallucinations, mania and delerium are common. Apart from this encephalopathy may occur. In thiamine deficiency polyneuritis results. Numbness and tingling of lower extremities and burning of the toes and feet and muscle cramps are the earlier symptoms. Later on sensory and motor senses are lost from the legs.

Apart from all these deficiency symptoms dietary treatment is used for mental disorders like convulsion, anorexia nervosa, epilepsy and hysteria and in severe alcoholism.

Epilepsy

In idiopathic epilepsy the central nervous system is affected. This condition is characterised by loss of consciousness for short intervals which is accompanied by severe convulsions and spasms.

A ketogenic diet is very useful in its treatment. In such a diet complication may arise if kidney troubles are present in the patient. A very high fat diet is recommended in a ketogenic diet. The aim of including a ketogenic diet is to produce acidosis by reducing glucose content in the diet. When high fat intake is included it prevents complete combustion of fat and results in the formation of the ketone bodies, acetone, acetoacetic acid and hydroxybutyric acid. Fluid content is reduced leading to progressive dehydration and accumulation of ketone bodies. Since this disease is common among children, it is difficult to implement ketogenic diet because it is unpalatable and deficient in many nutrients. Severe pyridoxine deficiency also produces epileptic form of convulsions and abnormal electroencephalograph especially among children. Administration of high doses of pyridoxine and foods rich in pyridoxine are useful in its treatment. Ketogenic diet is recommended only when drug therapy is not effective in the treatment of epilepsy. About 1 gm of protein/kg of body weight and only 10 gms carbohydrate is allowed in a ketogenic diet. A ketogenic diet is deficient in calcium, iron and in water soluble vitamins, therefore supplements of those nutrients are essential.

Often a patient may feel nausea and vomiting on a ketogenic diet. Sudden transfer from a normal diet produces these symptoms. Gradual change from normal diet to ketogenic diet reduces these symptoms.

Egg, meat, butter, cream, fruits, vegetables, poultry, fish and all other fats are allowed. Preparations with cereals, starchy roots and tubers, sugar, fruits and vegetables rich in carbohydrates are restricted. Milk is not allowed because of its lactose and sugar content. So are desserts and puddings.

Anorexia Nervosa

Prolonged malnutrition and anxiety can produce some other psychiatric disorders and so careful planning is essential in psychoneuroses, psychosis and addiction. Anorexia nervosa is common among nervous people. Hysterical manifestation and self-imposed starvation to combat emotional conflicts are common among young people, especially in women between 15 and 40 years. Fear, anxiety, conflicting emotion in the patient and immaturity in adolescence are the causes. Rapport with the patient helps to reach the root cause of the symptoms.

Dietary treatment along with psychiatric treatment is essential. Small, hourly feeds of a high protein, high vitaminised fluid diet is recommended. If self-feeding is not possible nasal feeding is essential.

53

DIET IN ALCOHOLISM

Chronic alcoholism may be considered as a psychosomatic disease. Ethanol which is present in ethyl alcohol contains 7 calories per gramme and it acts as a drug. Ingestion of ethanol distributes in total body water and blood, body tissues and body secretions are affected. Ingested alcohol is eliminated from the body mainly by oxidation with small quantities appearing in breath and urine.

Alcoholic's metabolic pathways, especially carbohydrates and fat metabolism, are affected adversely if supplementation of other nutrients are not done. Alcoholics have an unduly high requirement of B complex vitamins. Therapeutic doses of B complex vitamins are essential. Alcoholics as a group are peptic ulcer prone and chronic alcoholism results in gastrointestinal disturbances. Alcohol intake is associated with liver changes, especially in the form of fatty liver. Ethanol has an ill-effect upon mobilisation of fatty acids from adipose tissues and often increases the level of plasma non-esterified fatty acids. Hepato toxins produced by alcohol and mainly chloroform and carbon tetrachloride reduce the ability of the liver to secrete lipo proteins. Chronic alcoholism has been associated with deficiency diseases. Prevalence of cirrhosis of liver is often due to deficiency of certain essential nutrients. Protein deficiency produces fatty liver, hypo albuminemia, hypocholesterolemia, oedema, and normocytic anaemia. Vitamin A deficiency occurs most rapidly. Thiamin deficiency is the most common vitamin deficiency which results in ophthalmoplegia, palsy, ataxia, confusion, coma and peripheral neuropathy and often cardiac failure. Cardiac muscle metabolism is affected and lower extremities are badly affected. Depressed tendon reflexes, muscle cramps and weakness, pain and discomfort in the feet also occur.

Riboflavin deficiency is seen in an alcoholic. Dermatitis, angular stomatitis, and cheilosis are common. Pyridoxine deficiency produces convulsions, irritability, insomnia, mild ataxia and skin lesions. Folic acid deficiency produces macrocytive anaemia. Magnesium deficiency is common and potassium deficiency upsets the electrolyte balance.

Dietary Modification in Alcoholism

Deficiency of protein, B complex and minerals are common among alcoholics. Therefore, a well balanced diet high in protein and water soluble vitamins improves the health of an alcoholic. Without an adequate diet the liver of the alcoholics is likely to be damaged. Alcohol stimulates secretion of gastric juice and if enough food is not taken it leads to gastritis. In an empty stomach, if alcohol is consumed, peripheral blood vessels are dilated giving a visible flushing in the skin. Iron is usually accumulated in the body as alcoholic beverages are rich in iron and the drink stimulates iron absorption. Generally the intake of food is decreased and anorexia takes place. Coupled with B vitamin deficiency toxic substances are left out on the nerves which results in alcoholic polyneuropathy. Amnesic syndromes develop gradually. Fatty liver, alcoholic hepatitis, cirrhosis and haemochromatosis, gout and pancreatitis are the diseases common to alcoholics. Dietetic treatment depends on the complication in the person.

NUTRITION IN ALLERGIES

Allergy may be defined as the reaction of tissues to specific substances. The allergen is an external substance capable of producing specific antibodies in the body of the allergic person. Clinical manifestations of allergy are bronchial asthma, hay fever, hives, oedema, gastrointestinal symptoms, headaches, dermatitis and itching.

If ingestion of specific foods produce allergy it is termed as food allergy. Nausea, vomiting, urticaria, diarrhoea, colic or spastic constipation, headache, itching, oedema, dermatitis, circulatory collapse, asthma, shock or even death occur due to allergy. Food allergy is common among infants and young children. Most allergies are protein in nature. Protein foods like egg, milk, gluten of wheat, soyabeans and certain other protein foods commonly produce allergy. Denaturation of proteins often results in loss of their allergenic capacity. Raw or pasteurised milk may produce allergy but thoroughly boiled or evaporated milk may not produce allergy.

Diagnosis of the allergic food is difficult. Case history of all foods consumed must be tested using a food diary. Scratch or patch tests are also used to detect allergy.

Dietary treatment is mainly aimed to eliminate the foods which produce allergy. Trial diets including foods known to be allergenic are given to the patient. Exclusion of the allergic food from the dietary is the only effective means to prevent allergy. If infants are born with milk allergy, substitutes must be made through goat's milk or evaporated milk. Soyabean milk is used as a substitute since soyabean is very nutritious.

A normal well balanced diet excluding the allergic item can be given.

ASSESSMENT OF NUTRITIONAL STATUS

In the world today most national governments have active nutrition programmes. The need for such programmes and their efficiency can only be determined by periodic assessments of nutritional needs and deficiencies which have never been easy and always require the exercise of considerable judgement. The methods used include:

1. Clinical examinations.
2. Biochemical and other laboratory investigations.
3. The study of vital statistics.
4. The study of anthropometric data.
5. Dietary surveys.

Clinical Examinations

The distinction between the well and poorly nourished might appear to present no difficulty. A well nourished person is strong and active with firm muscles, bright eyes and a smooth elastic skin. The pooly fed person is weak and lethargic, with feeble muscles and, perhaps, a rough dry skin. Accurate recording of the incidence of major nutritional diseases and also the lesser stigmata of malnutrition is a valuable part of a nutritional survey.

Whenever possible and particularly in the less developed countries where under and malnutrition are common the incidence of nutritional diseases should be determined by examining a satisfactory sample of the population by economic class, occupation, age and sex.

Pre-school children, their mothers and elderly people living alone are particularly liable to deficiency diseases and are overlooked by surveys of functional groups such as school children, factory workers, farmers or businessmen. The latter types of survey are easier to conduct. In times of famine or food shortage the clinical stage of people walking about in the streets may be no guide. Those weak with undernutrition may be unable to leave their homes.

A real difficulty arises in recognising minimal signs of nutritional disorders. In examining the eyes and skin, and observing and recording minor changes that are not pathological, care should be taken and the surveyor must be properly trained and should strictly follow the guideline indicated for the purpose.

Record Card	Date
No:	Date of birth or age:
Name:	Sex:
Father's name:	Weight: Height:
Mother's name:	Arm circumference:
Special conditions:	
Pregnancy	
Lactation	
Pre-school	

Hair

Depigmentation
Pluckability
Texture: Silky
             Coarse
             Rough

Mouth

Angular stomatitis, glossites
Hypertrophic gums
Pallor of buccal mucus
membranes.

Eyes

Bitot's spots
Watering eyes

Tooth

Total no. of teeth present: No. of caries teeth:

Thyroid

Goitre.

Gr:I	Palpable,	not visible
Gr:II	"	visible, small size
Gr:III	"	visible, large size nodules

Blood

Haemoglobin level (specify method).

Skin

Oedema

Follicular hyperkeratosis (symmetrical)
Posterior aspect of forearms
Pigmented areas, neck, chest, forearms, hand, feet etc.

Skeleton

Rickety rosary, widening of epiphyses of wrists.

Deformed lower limbs

Bandy legs, knock knees.

Other signs

Name of observer:

Appointment

(A tick should be marked on the card against all positive findings and the part of the body examined).

Signs of Protein Calorie Malnutrition

Hair

Sparse: The hair may become thin, fine and silky in texture and sparse, that is covering the scalp less absentedly and completely and with wider gaps between.

Discoloured: The hair shows a distinct lightening of its normal colour. Various changes of colour may be found. In subjects with normally black hair the changes usually seen are dark brown, coppery reddish and blonde. Allowance should be made in some communities like washermen, because of their practices, depigmentation may be present. It is suggested that it would be noted only when the complete scalp is affected.

Easy pluckability: In this sign a small clump or tuft of hair can be easily pulled out with a moderate force and without pain. It is usually accompanied by the other hair changes such as depigmentation; thinness and sparseness and occurs in kwashiorkor.

Moon Face

This is a peculiarly rounded prominence of the cheeks which protrude over the general level of the nasolabial folds. The mouth presents a parched appearance. The condition is encountered mostly in the pre-school child with protein calorie malnutrition of the kwashiorkor type. Pitting or pressure does not occur.

Skin changes

Flaky point dermatosis/crazy pavement dermatosis Extensive, often bilateral hyper-pigmented patches of skin or superficial ulceration often resembling a second degree burn. It can occur anywhere but characteristically on the buttocks and the back of the thighs.

Oedema

First apparent over the wrinkles and feet, it may extend to other areas of the extremities. In early stages it can be detected by firm pressure for 3 seconds with one digit on the nodial surface of the tibia. The sign is taken as positive if there is a visible and palpable pit that persists after the pressure is removed. It is recorded only if present bilaterally.

Clinical Signs as Means of Judging Nutritional Status

The nutritional status of a child may be judged by a physician either (a) on his estimate of the child's general nutritive intake, or (b) on specific evidence of nutritional deficiency symptoms. The physician's estimate of a child's nutritional status is usually based mainly on the overall appearance and bearing of the child, on the amount of his subcutaneous tissue and on his growth record. A well nourished happily adjusted child has the general appearance of vitality and well being that is a characteristic of all healthy young animals whose bodies are functioning normally and efficiently. His eyes are clear and bright with no dark circles beneath them; his hair is smooth and glossy. His skeleton is well grown and sturdy with strong straight arms and legs, well shaped head and chest. His teeth are sound and well formed and are set in well shaped jaws with room enough to prevent any crowding or overlapping. The tissues around the teeth are firm and faint and cling to the teeth closely. There are no signs of easy bleeding.

Biochemical and Other Laboratory Investigations

Data accumulated on human response to diet under controlled conditions, that is, metabolic studies, have been used to establish standards for evaluation of the nutritional status of nutrients. Just as biochemical analysis are limited primarily to blood in human metabolic studies, so are analysis for surveys limited to blood and urine. Collection of urine samples obviously presents more problems than blood. Most often a single blood sample is analysed and may be a fasting sample, collected in the morning before any food is eaten or a random sample taken at any time during the day. The techniques most commonly used in surveys are measurement of thiamine, riboflavin, and u-methyl nicotine amide in urine and haemoglobin, vitamin A, carotene and ascorbic acid in blood. Serum proteins are often determined than some other measurements. The determination of plasma amino acids appears to be useful.

The Study of Vital Statistics

Most countries keep at least some vital statistics and from them it is usually possible to draw certain inferences about the nutrition of people. The most used statistics for this purpose has been the infant mortality rate. It has been suggested that the neo-natal mortality and the still birth rate may give a more precise index of nutrition. The manifestations and effects of malnutrition are well known to be severe in toddlers (1-4 years). Death rate from infectious diseases has been used in the past as indications of nutritional status of a population. They are, however, of little practical value in most countries at the present time because of the use of specific remedies either against the diseases or their complications. In times of food scarcity, daily, weekly and monthly crude death rates may give valuable information about changes from conditions of hardship to conditions of famine.

The Study of Anthropometric Data

Heights and Weights

If children do not get sufficient food, they fail to grow properly. Similarly, adults without enough to eat lose weight and those who overeat gain weight. The weighing machine is a useful and accurate tool for investigating nutritional status. Measurements of weights of adults and of large groups of children at various ages have been used as an index of nutritional status and have proved very valuable when correctly interpreted. The weighing machine has also been widely used in school medical services and at child health clinics as a simple diagnostic tool for the purpose of screening children who may be undernourished.

It is important to realise that other factors besides food intake determine weight, notably constitutional or genetic make-up. There are tall, thin, light people and short, thickset, heavy individuals who may each be equally healthy; the weighing machine alone cannot determine their relative nutritional status. Other physical measurements and partricularly height are useful.

There are certain difficulties involved in the use of such a simple piece of apparatus as a weighing machine. Every balance needs regular checking and, if necessary, recalibration. Lever balances are very reliable and a yearly check is all that is necessary. Spring balances are most unreliable and if used regularly needs repeated checks. Indeed, they cannot be recommended for accurate work. It is seldom practical to weigh people naked. A correction is usually for the article of clothing worn. They may vary greatly from season to season.

Height should be measured against a flat surface and the subject must stand as upright as possible without raising the heels from the ground.

Standing Height

It is measured with an anthropometric rod or a wooden scale.

1. The subject will stand erect with heels together after removing his shoes.
2. He will look straight, the head held comfortably erect, the arms hanging at the side.
3. The buttocks, shoulders and back of the head will be in the same line and touching the rod.
4. The movable headpiece of the rod and wooden piece will touch the head gently and lowered by its own pressure.
5. Height is measured to the nearest millimetre.

Body Weight

1. It is usually measured at basal conditions.
2. After removing the shoes the subject will stand on the platform of the scales of level activated balance.
3. Measurement should be made to the nearest 1/10th of a kilogramme.
4. The subject will not touch anything else.
5. The subject is weighted with minimal clothing.

In cases of non-cooperation, the child's weight can be taken with an adult holding him. When adult weight is deducted from the above, the child's weight can be arrived at.

Mid-upper Arm Circumference

The weight recording is a useful method but at times is not recorded accurately by the paramedical personnel. Moreover, reliable and sturdy weighing machines are often not available for field surveys. The age of a child is not known quite often which again presents difficulty in correct assessment of the nutritional status of pre-school children by weight.

Height in addition to the inaccuracy gives a fallacious impression in genetically tall or short children.

The mid-arm circumference gives an assessment of muscle mass, subcutaneous tissue and hence indirectly to the nutritional status. It is relatively simpler to measure for a rapid community survey and varies very little with age between 1 and 4 years. The upper arm is uniformly round and free from oedema and does not vary with the height of the child. It can be measured quickly, requires no special equipment and can be measured accurately by a trained para-medical personnel.

1. It is measured at the mid-point of the upper arm.
2. Mid-point can be marked by making central point of the distance between the olecrenon of the ulna and the acronion of the scapula when the arm is fixed at the elbow.
3. It is taken on the left arm.
4. The left arm will be hanging loosely on the side with a steel tape, the circumference of the arm is measured by passing it around the arm applying firmly but without disturbing the contours of the arm.

56
DIET SURVEYS

A large majority of our people are satisfied by filling their bellies with some foodstuffs. Most of the people ignore the nutritious aspect of the food they eat. Prevalence of malnutrition is due to insufficient intake of foodstuffs. In order to assess the nutritional status dietary intake must be calculated. Diet surveys are used to collect information about the dietary intake, dietary habits, preservation methods, cooking methods and special diets for special conditions and in diseases. Diet surveys also provide information regarding the economic and social factors influencing food production and consumption patterns of families and communities.

To conduct diet surveys certain factors are to be taken into account. They are trained personnel, population sampling, various methods available for conducing diet surveys and analysis of the data and calculations of nutritive values.

The persons to be engaged in conducting diet survey must be trained in conducting such surveys. They must be trained to create rapport with the housewives and in adopting tactful methods to collect information from them. They must be aware of other principles of nutrition and dietary habits of the local community.

Population sampling must be carried out with the help of a statistician. The choice of diet survey methods depends on the purpose of the survey.

The sample size also depends on the purpose of the survey, availability of trained personnel, time and resources like money. The duration of the survey depends on the purpose and methods adopted. Normally 7 to 10 days are preferred for diet surveys.

Methods of Diet Survey

Commonly used methods in our country are: (1) oral questionnaire method, (2) food inventory or log book method, and (3) weighing of raw and cooked foods.

Oral Questionnaire Method

Oral questionnaire or interview is the most commonly used method of diet survey. The investigator has to formulate a diet survey questionnaire depending upon the purpose. After conducting a pilot study with the questionnaire changes can be made on the pattern of the questions. Then the investigator goes from door to door and collects information regarding the types and qualities of foods consumed. The data is not very perfect, only approximate amounts can be collected through this method. Therefore, this method is suitable only to collect information on the general dietary patterns or an approximate picture of dietary habits of a large section of population. General ideas like choice of foods, foods avoided in certain conditions, foods included in special conditions or in festivals, food fads and fallacies, are to be collected. The advantages of the questionnaire method are that it is not a time-consuming method, therefore a large number of families can be covered within a specific time.

Food Inventory or Log Book Method

This method can be used only with a literate group because a book with question is entrusted to the head of the family or to the housewife. The person entrusted must enter all purchases in the book. Full cooperation from the householder is essential because reliability of the data depends upon the entry. Therefore at times the data may not be authentic.

Weighing of Raw and Cooked Foods

This method is the most reliable one. But it is time-consuming and therefore it is not used for a large sample. As the investigator cannot leave the questionnaire with the householder she has to stay near and record the amount of various foods before and after cooking. The amount of food used can be recorded by weighing the leftovers after consumption. Often the housewife shows more raw foods to give a wrong impression about their food intake. Therefore the investigator must have some practical knowledge about the quantities of cooked foods of various sources.

Adult Consumption Unit

In order to find out the nutritional adequacy of a family, a group adult consumption unit is calculated. In this method, the heterogenic groups of people i.e., school going, adult, geriatric, pregnant, a uniform calculation can be applied. This makes the total requirement calculation simple. For adult consumption unit a sedentary man is taken as one adult consumption unit (ACU) and the calorie requirements of other age groups and special groups are expressed in terms of proportionate adult consumption units.

The adult consumption unit coefficient laid down by the Indian Council of Medical Research for the various groups and the type of physical activity is given below:

Adult male (Sedentary worker)		1.0
Adult male (Moderate worker)		1.2
Adult male (Heavy worker)		1.6
Adult female (Sedentary worker)		0.8
Adult female (Moderate worker)		0.9
Adult female (Heavy worker)		1.2
Adolescents	12 - 21 yrs	1.0
Children	9 - 12 yrs	0.8
Children	7 - 9 yrs	0.7
Children	5 - 7 yrs	0.6
Children	3 - 5 yrs	0.5
Children	1 - 3 yrs	0.4

Calculation of Nutritive Value of the Family Diet in Terms of Adult Consumption Unit

To find out the adult consumption unit of the family, the number of persons, their physical activities and their ages have to be recorded. Total consumption unit has to be calculated using the above table. For example, for a family of 4, the adult consumption unit is given below:

Member	Age	Occupation	A.C.U.
Father	57 yrs	Retired Teacher	1.2
Mother	55 yrs	Housewife	0.9
Daughter	23 yrs	Student	0.9
Son	17 yrs	Student	1.0
		Total	4.0

The adult consumption unit of the family is 4. The total calorie requirement of the family is calculated below.

The energy requirement for a sedentary man for 4 A.C.U.	=	2,800 kcals
	=	2,800 x 4
	=	11,200 kcals
Total cereals for the family per day	=	460 gms x 4
	=	1,040 gms

57

NUTRITION EDUCATION

Several dietary and clinical surveys carried out in different parts of our country have revealed that malnutrition is rampant. Nutrition education assumes special significance in the Indian context because the problem of malnutrition in India is mainly due to ignorance, poverty and lack of knowledge regarding the value of foods. Dietary practices, especially in children and pregnant and lactating mothers, are often governed by social taboos based on food fads. Nutrition education is the foundation for improvement in the dietary habits of this vulnerable set of population. Rigid dietary habits need correction and only systematic nutrition education programmes can bring changes in dietary habits. Nutrition awareness is essential to bring changes in dietary habits and creating nutrition awareness entirely depends on education and training.

Nutrition education requires identification of needs and collection of baseline data enables to identify the needs. It is a popular belief that young mothers or adolescents must be educated about the basic principles of health and nutrition. Studies on nutrition education in our country have proved that even elderly women need education as they are the ones who mislead the youngsters. Various topics of nutrition can be selected for nutrition education. Selection of foods and preparation of foods, feeding practices of various groups, special diets during pregnancy and lactation, infancy, pre-school age, supplementary feeding, weaning foods, low cost recipes, food sanitation, food-borne infections, food adulteration, nutrition and health, therapeutic diets, food fads and fallacies and deficiency diseases and their prevention are some common topics used for nutrition education.

Extension education methods can be utilised for nutrition education. Collection of background data, analysis of problems, plan of action, calendar of activities, selection of audio-visual aids, methods of teaching and evaluation are the various steps involved in nutrition education programme.

The various approaches suitable for nutrition education are (1) Individual contacts through home visits, consulting individual training, (2) Group contacts through simple talks, demonstrations and discussions, (3) Group demonstrations, (4) Hospital visits, and (5) Nutrition rehabilitation training. These are the methods suitable for rural groups.

Nutrition education and training can be implemented through schools and colleges. Good nutrition education, if followed effectively, can be a useful tool to bring economic development in the country as it provides good health. Better health enables people to improve their productive efficiency and it enhances the purchasing capacity and the consumption patterns of the population. Food and nutrition is thus intimately linked with production and economic development of a country.

Training in nutrition at various levels—schools, colleges, adult education centres, village level workers—is essential. Housewives are ignorant about the principles of nutrition as they are not trained anywhere. Thus the researches on these lines are wasted as the messages are not passed on to the people. Various feeding programmes and nutrition programmes which are implemented through various organisations can be used as nutrition education channels. Feeding programmes under the family and child welfare departments, school feeding programmes, the composite programme for women and pre-school children, the applied nutrition programmes, world food programmes and other state programmes can be utilised for education purposes.

Nutrition Programmes

A number of nutrition programmes were initiated by the Government of India. Most of them are functioning under the guided supervision of development department, social welfare department and voluntary agencies in various states.

Applied Nutrition Programmes

The applied nutrition programme (ANP) is evolved on the basis of the fundamental premise that though malnutrition is primarily due to mass poverty it is also due to ignorance and that appropriate choice of foods and feeding practices without involving extra cost from the family can improve the nutritional status of the people, especially young children.

Objectives

It is well known that many young children in India are undernourished. This undernourishment is dangerous. If children do not receive adequate nourishment when they are young, they will never grow to be strong, healthy and productive adults. Furthermore, undernourished children are more likely to become ill. Undernourishment is directly or indirectly responsible for illness and death.

The goal of ANP is to prevent the bad effects of undernourishment before they can occur. The ANP works at the village and family levels to improve nutrition, particularly of young children. To bring about such improvement the programme supports the local production of good and nutritious foods, consumption of such foods, especially by young children, pregnant women and nursing mothers, and education about good foods and proper feeding of young children and women who are pregnant or nursing (nutrition education).

Improvement in nutrition will not be effective unless there is also improvement in health. The ANP should be implemented with local health workers to provide health check-ups, immunisation, safe drinking water and proper sanitation. The ANP does not have enough funds to assist all the village in a block. Therefore, it is necessary to choose those villages which have a reasonable chance of success. As many ANP activities as possible should be started in the village selected.

The ANP also does not have enough funds to cover all the families in the village selected to participate in the programme. Care should be taken to reach the most disadvantaged families such as the families of the Harijans, tribal people, small cultivators and landless labourers, which have young children, pregnant women and nursing mothers.

By concentrating on these selected villages and families it should be possible to demonstrate clearly the results of the programme. This should lead to the voluntary use of beneficial practices in other villages of the blocks which is called the radiation effect.

Nutrition Education

People will not change their beliefs and habits concerning food unless they are convinced that changes will benefit them and their children. Therefore, the goal of ANP is to educate village families about the benefits of nutritious foods, good child feeding practices and improved preparation and preservation of foods.

Many traditional practices such as prolonged breastfeeding and eating roti and rice with dal are basically good. Nutrition education should emphasise such traditional practices and at the same time should teach new practices where necessary. By using nutritious local foods and good feeding practices it is possible to improve the health of undernourished children at little or no extra expense to the family.

Nutrition education should be provided in cooperation with schools, Balwadis, PHCS, sub centres, Mahila Mandals and Yuvak Mandals. It can be given by people such as school teachers, Balsevikas, Mukhya Sevikas, Gram Sevikas and medical staff to the PHC and sub-centres. Efforts should be made to bring this eduction to the poorest villagers, who may not ordinarily participate in village organisations. The education should stress on basic messages about nutritious foods, child feed and child care.

The method of practical demonstration with the participation of the villagers ought to be used as much as possible. In the demonstrations, only local food and easily available equipment should be used; charts, posters and film shows should also be used to make the information clear and interesting.

Some Main Messages

Breastfeed as long as possible. Introduce some solid food 5 to 6 times a day. Do not reduce food in illness. Use health services available. Get children immunised. Keep yourself and your surroundings clean. Drink clean water. Have no more than 2 or 3 children 2 to 3 years apart. Try to eat some green leafy vegetables every day.

Production Activities

The ANP gives many kinds of assistance for production of good nutritious foods depending on local conditions. The programme now emphasises assistance to home gardens, school gardens and community gardens. These gardens are used to grow dals, leafy vegetables and other nutritious vegetables and fruits. The products are then used to demonstrate the preparation and use of the foods.

Gardens should become as self-sufficient as possible. After the first season, seeds should be obtained either from the garden itself or from the sale of surplus products. Local manure should be used as much as possible. When available, waste water from the village should be used for irrigation.

Home gardens should be emphasized where possible, because of their importance in making nutritious foods available to the individual.

School gardens will be supported if the following conditions are met—suitable land is available close to the school and water for irrigation is available at a reasonable cost. The garden is made part of the regular school programme of the students and the students must look after the garden themselves.

Community gardens can be used both to demonstrate the proper cultivation of nutritious food and to produce food for feeding purposes. Cash crops may be grown to make the gardens self-supporting but the entire net profit of the garden must be used for demonstration feeding projects at health centres or balwadis. The garden should be run by a village organisation such as a Yuvak Mandal or Mahila Mandal.

Foods of Animal Origin

The ANP now emphasises the cultivation of nutritious dals, vegetables and fruits in home, school and community gardens rather than the production of foods of animal origin, which are much more expensive. Moreover, if local conditions are suitable, activities such as poultry, fisheries, piggeries and goat keeping can be supported.

Consumption and Supporting Activities

Feeding Projects

Feeding projects under A N P will be chiefly for the purpose of practical demonstrations for nutrition education.

Agents for Change

The ANP cannot succeed unless villagers themselves accept the need for new practices. Therefore, the cooperation of village leaders is essential in planning and running the programme in each village. The support of women and youth is also important.

Mahila Mandals

Training will be provided to members of Mahila Mandals in order to help them play a large role in the programme. Examples of appropriate activities for Mahila Mandals are: demonstrations to women of methods of cooking and storage of food, child feeding, development of nutritious recipes from local foods and running or helping in a balwadi. Many other such activities could be developed locally as well.

Yuvak Mandals

Training will also be given to members of Yuvak Mandals. Appropriate activities for Yuvak Mandals are operating a community garden, village fish tank, or poultry unit, construction for improved storage facilities, for clearing drains and improving wells and undertaking other agricultural activities and making equipments and toys for balwadis.

Combination with Health and Other Services

If it is to be effective the ANP cannot be treated as a separate programme. Only if it is combined with health education, agriculture, water and other programmes can it be of substantial impact. The medical staff in the blocks should cooperate with the Block Development Officer and others to provide the necessary health services. The medical staff will help in the preparation of the block plan, provide health check-ups and immunisation, diagnose cases of malnutrition among village children, provide treatment for malnourished children and so on. Staff of other programmes will also cooperate to provide drinking water, irrigation facilities, balwadis and other such services in the villages taken up under the ANP.

Organisation of the Programme

The Department of Rural Development (Ministry of Agriculture and Irrigation), Government of India has overall charge of the programme. The State Department of Community Development or its equivalent is in charge of the ANP in the State, the officer responsible is the State ANP coordinator. At the district level, the District Collector will have overall charge of the programme. He will be assisted by other district development officials.

At the block level, the BDO will have overall charge of the programme. He will be assisted by a coordination committee including the head of the Panchayat Samiti, the Block Agricultural Extension Officer, the Mukhya Sevika, the Doctor in charge of the PHC and other block officials.

At the village level, the gram sevika and the gram sevak will be chiefly responsible for the implementation of the programme.

Initiation of the Programme

As soon as possible, after the start of the financial years on first April, the BDO and other officials of the new ANP blocks will receive an orientation to the ANP and training in the preparation of the Block Plan. The BDO will then begin the work as the block plan is completed. He will submit copies to the State ANP coordinator and to the UNICEF field representatives, if necessary. The State Government may be asked by the Government of India to submit a modified plan or provide additional information. As soon as the block plan is approved by the Government of India, the State will ensure that all posts in the blocks including those of gram sevikas, are filled. Preparatory activities such as the digging of wells will begin and the training of block and village staff will proceed.

Block Plans

Experience has shown that the condition and needs of blocks all over India and even of villages in the same block can be quite different. It is important to the ANP to plan realistically in terms of the needs and resources of each block and of the villages of that block. The BDO and his staff will be responsible for preparing a realistic block plan based on their local knowledge of the block. The BDO and other block officials will receive special training in the preparation of a block plan. The BDO and the medical officer under the supervision of the State Nutrition Officer will conduct a survey to identify local nutritional problems. Then after consulting block and village workers as well as the villagers, the BDO will select the villages for ANP activities that will be suitable in these villages. He will write a detailed plan of action for the block. The importance of making realistic plans before ANP activities cannot be overemphasised.

Selection of Villages

To make the programme effective, it is important to introduce as many ANP activities as practical in the village simultaneously. Villages with facilities that will improve the chances for successful implementation of the programme should be given preference. Such facilities may include water for drinking and agricultural purposes, a road, bus services, proximity of a health centre or sub centre, availability of land for garden. Other government programmes or activities in the villages in a block should be selected for intensive integrated development under the

ANP. However, if other villages in the block show interest, they can also be assisted to develop particular actvities.

The ANP activities must be planned so that they continue even after the 5-year programme of assistance is finished. If activities are introduced in a village only in the third and fourth year of the programme, it is not likely that they will become established before the end of the programme. Therefore, it is better to choose all of the village in the first two years of the programme and start all activities in these villages as soon as possible.

Suitability to Local Conditions

If it is essential the ANP should be tailored to the special needs and conditions of each block and each village. In the past the practice has been to introduce ANP activities according to a standard pattern and a fixed financial limit. This is not realistic and is usually not successful. Now the needs of each village and the activities to be carried out will be used to decide what assistance and how much will be given to each block.

Nutrition education should be carried on in every village selected for ANP. Production activities must emphasise the growing of nutritious dals, vegetables and fruits. However, these actvities can be carried out in many ways, depending upon the local conditions and resources. For instance, if a community garden is not possible because village houses are scattered or because land or water is not available, it may be possible to plan on funds to increase the number of home gardens in that village. Activities such as poultry or fisheries should be started only if local conditions are suitable and such activities can be maintained. Local officials and villagers must consider carefully the local conditions, resources and needs and then decide on the best plan.

Community Participation

Unless the community itself is concerned about the usefulness of the activities of the ANP and unless the community is involved in planning and carrying them out, the programme will not succeed.

In making the block plan, the BDO should consult the villagers. He will then be able to assess the problems and resources of the villages and, together with the villagers, decide the activities to be started. The village organisation such as the Mahila Mandals and Yuvak Mandals play an important role in the ANP. Members of these organisations will receive special training. They will then be able to organise such activities as common gardens, nutrition education and balwadi training.

The ANP will not succeed unless the block staff and the villagers understand the purpose of the programme and the rules in maintaining the work. The ANP training that they will receive should explain to them their work and also that of others so that all can work together to make the ANP a success. As soon as possible, after the selection of new blocks, the BDO agricultural officer, education officers, medical officers, Mukhya Sevikas and other important block officials will receive an orientation to the programme and training in the preparation of the Block Plan.

Later, training will be given to gram sevikas, balsevikas, teachers, panchayat officials and members of Mahila and Yuvak Mandals. The training will emphasise nutrition education. Mukhya and Gram Sevikas will receive practical training in teaching and demonstration. School teachers will be given material on nutrition so that they can make nutrition a part of their regular lessons.

Fifth Plan Funds

The Government of India will contribute Rs.30,000 per year for each block. The state government will contribute Rs.51,000 per year for each block. The United Nations Children's Emergency Fund (UNICEF) will contribute supplies of equipment, cash grants and assistance for training to a maximum value of Rs.1,60,000 per block, spread over the operational period of the programme. The figure of Rs.20,000 is a ceiling the UNICEF supports and does not necessarily represent the amounts that will be provided to every block. Actual expenditure in each block will be determined by the needs and capacities of the individual blocks. The central and state funds will be placed in a common pool and disbursements will be accounted for by the state government on block by block basis.

Composite Programme for Women and Pre-school Children

The pre-school age is the most crucial period in a child's life. This is the period when the child increases the activity and is exposed to the environment outside the home. Providing a nutritious and wholesome diet and immunising the child against diseases common during childhood are of utmost importance. Equally important is providing education to this age group through balwadis. Mere distribution of food to the children will not have a substantial effect unless the economic status of the mother is also simultaneously improved. For the successful implementation of programmes aimed at the overall development of the child, associate organisations like Mahila Samajams have to be fully involved in such programmes. After taking all the above aspects into consideration the Composite Programme for Women and Pre-school (CPWP) children was evolved and put into operation as part of the Applied Nutrition Programme in all the blocks in the state from the year 1975-76 in a phased manner with the following objectives:

1. To improve the health of the children (both physical and mental).

2. To inculcate a sense of discipline and equality among the children.

3. To promote healthy living habits.

4. To create a desire among the children to go to school and acquire knowledge.

5. To impart nutrition and health education to mothers.

6. To provide additional income for the mother for giving special attention to the needs of the children.

The main features of the regular ANP are found in the CPWP also. The CPWP has the following important aspects additionally:

   (i) Education to the children.
   (ii) Health check-up and immunisation of pre-school and pregnant and nursing mothers.

7. The medical officer of the Public Health Centre is expected to visit the balwadi at least once a month and the Auxilliary Nurse-Midwife once a week, for health check-up and immunisation. Growth charts for the children are maintained in duplicate—one kept by the balwadi teacher and the other by the mother. Growth charts to record the health status of the children and one DDS (Diet Drug Supplement) set costing Rs.400 is given by the UNICEF to every balwadi.

8. The target group consists of economically, socially and nutritionally backward children within the age group of 0 to 5 years and pregnant and nursing mothers. In each regular ANP centre 70 children and 30 mothers are enrolled. In a CPWP centre 100 children and 30 mothers are enrolled. The beneficiaries are selected by a committee consisting of the Block Development Officer or his representative, the Medical Officer of the Public Health Centre or his representative, the

president of the Panchayat and the president of the Mahila Samajam. The socio-economic and nutritional status of the family will be the basic criterion for selection.

9. The feeding programme under both ANP and CPWP is implemented through organised Mahila Samajams. In the case of CPWP, Samajams having at least five cents of land with a building are chosen as implementing agencies. While sanctioning centres it is ensured that there is no other feeding centre within a radius of one kilometre. In the regular ANP feeding centre feeding is conducted only once a day. In the case of the CPWP, children attending balwadi classes are fed a second time. In specially recommended cases of severe malnutrition, there is provision for one more feeding. In the regular ANP centres feeding is done 25 days in a month. In the CPWP centres feeding is conducted 26 days a month.

10. The nutritive value of the feed is 14 grammes protein and about 280 calories. The composition of the diet is as follows:

(i)	Regular ANP	grain	80 gms
(ii)	CPWP first feeding:	grain	80 gms
		oil	07 gms
		milk powder	30 gms
	Second feeding:	grain	30 gms

11. The cost of the feed, at subsidised rate, works out to 40 paise and 50 paise on an average in the regular ANP and CPWP centres, respectively.

12. In the CPWP centres the balwadi teachers are given an allowance of rupees 100 per month. In all other centres the conveners are paid a monthly allowance of 25. No separate preparation charges are paid. The fuel requirements are met out of voluntary contributions in kind collected by the Mahila Samajams. In fact, the whole programme revolves around the Mahila Samajams.

13. The programme is guided and supervised by the personnel of the Development Department. At the village level, lady Village Extension Officers are in charge of the programme. Their work is supervised by the Block Development Officer and the Extension Officer (women's welfare) at the block level. At the district level, the Assistant Development Commissioner and the District Women's Welfare Officer, under the guidance of the Collector, control and supervise the implementation of the programme.

14. Apart from feeding, nutrition education, health check-up and immunisation, there is also the production component of the programme consisting of financial assistance and technical advice for goat rearing, backyard poultry, kitchen gardening, a building for balwadi, environmental sanitation and training of balwadi teachers. This is a critical component of the ANP, in so far as the objective is to include and inculcate among the vulnerable sections in the rural areas, the habit of producing and consuming with very little additional strain, foods of high nutritional value. The basic concept behind the package of services and activities under the ANP is itself one of extension, that is, to train and educate the rural poor about the various aspects of nutrition and production of essential food items of nutritive value so that in course of time the people themselves would look after their own nutrition requirements balanced.

One-meal-a-day Programme

15. In 1979, the International Year of the Child, the government decided that supplementary nutrition programme should cover all undernourished pre-school children in the state. Towards the realisation of this objective, the one-meal-a-day programme was introduced in 1979-80. During that year the programme covered 4.13 lakhs of pre-school chidren through 4,825 feeding centres. The programme is being contributed with the same number of feeding centres. The target group under this programme is children under five years and feeding is conducted 300 days in a year, that is, an average of 25 days in a month.

16. The quantity of food materials supplied under this programme to each beneficiary is as follows:

1.	CSM/Bulgar Wheat	40 gms
2.	Pulses	10 gms
3.	Rice	40 gms
4.	Oil	10 gms

This meal costs 12.5 paise at subsidised rates.

17. In rural areas, the District Collector is empowered to administer this scheme through the staff of the Development Department. In urban areas this task is entrusted to the Social Welfare Department. The feeding programme is actually carried out by voluntary organisations. In the rural areas the beneficiary children are selected by a committee consisting of the Block Development Officer, the Medical Officer of the Primary Health Centre, the president of the

Panchayat and the president of the local Mahila Samaj. In urban areas the Committee consists of the municipal commissioner, the municipal health officer or medical officer and the president of the voluntary agency concerned.

Special Nutrition Programme (SNP)

18. The Special Nutrition Programme was launched as a nationwide programme in 1971, to combat the incidence of malnutrition among the vulnerable groups like children below 6 years, pregnant women and lactating mothers. It was first introduced in the urban slums and tribal areas. Subsequently, it was extended to other areas like poverty-stricken nutritionally-deficient pockets.

19. The objective of the scheme is to supplement the diet of selected beneficiaries with additional protein and calories to make up the deficiency in their daily food intake. Under this programme special sweet bread from Modern Bakeries, special milk bread from private bakeries, milk from Milma or cooperative societies, locally available food consisting of rice and pulses, are supplied. The quantity of food supplied contains an average of 5 to 6 gms of protein and 250 to 300 kcals. In addition Adexeline capsules containing vitamins A and D are also being supplied.

20. Originally the number of beneficaries in most of the feeding centres sanctioned during 1979 and 1980 was fixed at 100 per centre. Ten per cent of the beneficiaries in the SNP feeding centres will be pregnant women and lactating mothers and the rest will be children below the age of six years.

21. While introducing the scheme the per capita rate per beneficiary per day was fixed at 23.5 paise consisting of 18 paise for food, 2 paise for transportation of food materials and 3.5 paise for administrative charges. During 1974 the per capita unit cost of food was enhanced from 18 paise to 20 paise per beneficiary per day. Subsequently, the per capita rate was enhanced to 30 paise per head per day (i.e., food charges 24.5 paise, transportation 2 paise and administrative expenses 3.5 paise).

Integrated Child Development Services (ICDS)

22. The latest approach to nutrition is to provide a package of services comprising nutrition, medical check-up, immunisation, referral services, day-care services, education for mothers and

functional literacy for adult women. These services are extended with the Anganwadi as the focal point. There will be one Anganwadi for every thousand population. The entire population in a block will be covered by setting up the requisite number of Anganwadis. This scheme is known as the ICDS and is evolved along the lines of the national pattern. As soon as the ICDS starts functioning in a block, the Special Nutrition Centres are merged into it.

23. The ICDS, as a centrally sponsored scheme, has been introduced through blocks in states. Central assistance is obtained for administrative charges. Equipment is donated by the UNICEF. Only the nutrition component of the scheme is financed out of the state plan outlay. Besides the above, there are ICDS blocks sponsored and financed by the state governments.

24. The food usually being supplied to the beneficiaries under the ICDS are gruel and green gram. The diet costs 30 paise per child below 3 years and 50 paise per child above 3 years. The target group under the ICDS is the same as in the case of the Special Nutrition Programme. The number of feedings in a year is also the same. Of the beneficiaries 10 per cent will be pregnant women and lactating mothers and the rest will be pre-school children.

World Food Programme (WFP)

25. During the Fifth Plan, the Government of India introduced a new scheme, the "World Food Programme" (WFP), as a part of the Special Nutrition Programme. During this period 2,000 feeding centres started functioning under this scheme. During 1979-80 another 300 feeding centres were also started. In each centre, there are 100 beneficiaries out of which 12.5 per cent will be pregnant women and lactating mothers and the rest will be children below the age of 6 years. At present WFP covers nearly 2,30,000 beneficiaries spread over 2,300 feeding centres.

26. Uppuma made out of soya fortified Bulgar wheat and butter oil/salad oil are being distributed to the beneficiaries under WFP as detailed below:

Soya-fortified Bulgar wheat is given to pre-school children (0-6 years) 80 gms per day per head and to pregnant women and lactating mothers 125 gms per day per head.

Butter oil/salad oil is given 10 gms each to all beneficiaries.

Organisational Arrangement—Social Welfare Department

27. The feeding centres under SNP and WFP in the State are run by the local bodies like municipalities, corporations, panchayats and voluntary organisations like Bharat Sevak Samaj, Gandhi Smarak Nidhi and Mahila Samajams. In the case of SNP feeding centres there is one organiser and one helper to distribute the food materials to the beneficiaries. An amount of Rs. 20 and Rs.10 per month respectively is being paid to them as honorarium. The transportation of food materials to the SNP feeding centres is being arranged by the Government through the contractors. Under the ICDS the Anganwadi worker gets an honorarium of Rs. 175 per month and the helper gets Rs.50 per month. In the case of WFP feeding centres, an allowance of Rs.40 per month is being paid to the voluntary organisations as grant. In addition to this the local bodies like panchayats are given financial assistance for the purchase of cooking vessels to the feeding centres. The transportation of food materials from the Warehousing Corporation Depot to the feeding centres is being done by the voluntary organisations themselves. They are also permitted to sell the empty containers and to utilise the amount for meeting the transportation cost.

28. The Health Services Department operates with this department to provide health services in the nutrition programme. Medical check-up and immunisation to the beneficiaries in the centres in urban areas are being conducted by the health staff of the corporations and municipalities and those in the rural and tribal areas by the Medical Officers in Primary Health Centres. Government has accorded sanction to meet the additional expenses towards petrol charges in connection with the visit of Medical Officers of the Primary Health Centre to the nearby feeding centres of WFP for the conduct of Health Education, Nutrition Survey and Immunisation.

29. The organisers and helpers are the nominees of the voluntary organisation responsible for implementing the nutrition programme. In every centre, there is an organiser and a helper. The organisers are responsible for the proper maintenance of printed records such as admission register, attendance register, stock register and medical check-up register. They are also vested with the responsibility of receiving the food supplies, their proper preservation, storage and distribution to the beneficiaries. The helpers are responsible for the preparation of food articles for distribution. They also render assistance to the organiser for spot feeding of children.

30. There are two officers, one in the gazetted cadre (District Social Welfare Officer) and the other in the non-gazetted cadre (Inspector) for each district for the supervision of the feeding centres. Four inspectors in the non-gazetted cadre are appointed in the directorate for attending to the scrutiny of the bills of the SNP. The supervisors are entrusted with the work of supervision of feeding centres, arrangement of Nutrition Education Camps, selection of location of feeding centres, payment of honorarium to the organisers and helpers of feeding centres, allotment of food materials consistent with the number of beneficiaries in each feeding centre, allocation of cost of food materials and transportation charges.

31. One-day training camps at the rate of two camps in each district are being conducted by the department for giving nutrition education and training to the organisers of the feeding centres and to the mothers of the beneficiaries. The importance of nutrition, child care and family planning are being taught by the Medical Officer and Block Development Officer, in the camp in the feeding centres given to the supervisor-inspectors by the professors of medical colleges.

32. Some feeding centres in the States have now become defunct for various reasons such as non-availability of special bread, practical difficulties in serving cooked food made out of rice and pulse and irregularities noticed in the supply of food articles.

The recommendation of the District Committee is therefore necessary for allotting and cancelling and redistributing the centres to voluntary agencies. These committees are not being convened at regular intervals. Hence, much difficulty is being experienced in the matter of starting, cancelling and redistributing the centres.

Health-Based Nutrition Programme

33. The Department of Health Services implements mainly three nutrition programmes of which two are meant for prophylaxis against nutritional anaemia among mothers and children and against blindness in children caused by vitamin A deficiency. Under these two programmes only iron and vitamins are supplied to the beneficiaries. Feeding is conducted only under the Integrated Health Package Programme. A brief description of the above programme follows:

Prophylaxis against Nutritional Anaemia among Mothers and Children

34. This programme was started in the year 1970-71. The family

welfare programme supplies the cost of drugs as grant to the state government. Expectant and breastfeeding mothers, acceptors of family planning methods like IUD, tubectomy and pre-school children receive the benefit of this scheme. Tablets containing iron and folic acid are distributed through AN clinics, PH clinics and paediatric clinics of hospitals, PHCs and FW centres under the guidance of Medical Officers.

35. Haemoglobin percentage is obtained before starting the programme and at 3 months interval wherever facilities are available. The drugs are issued for a week at a time. Each beneficiary gets 100 tablets.

Adult: 60 gms iron   0.5 mgs folic acid.
Child: 20 gms iron   0.1 mgs folic acid.

Difficulties experienced are irregular supply and lack of motivation to come to the centre. The most deserving beneficiaries often do not come to the centre or do not come regularly.

Prophylaxis against Blindness in Children by Vitamin A Deficiency

36. Blindness due to vitamin A deficiency is more prevalent in the pre-school age group. Studies have shown that vitamin A in oil given orally is readily absorbed and stored in the liver from where it is gradually released for utilisation in the tissues. Vitamin A is procured by the Department of Family Planning and distributed to the State Health Department.

37. The vitamin A capsules are administered to children in the age group of 1 to 5 years in homes, personally by peripheral workers like AIM and EPHA. Two lakhs of IU/60,000 microgrammes of vitamin A is given at an interval of 6 months till the children attain 5 years of age. In view of the limited financial resources the programme is restricted to areas where there is maximum prevalence of vitamin A deficiency.

Proforma for Use in Diet Surveys

Interviewer: Family No.:
Date: Address:

General Information

1. Head of the family:
   Caste: Religion:
2. Composition of family:

Sl. No.	Name	Sex	Age	Education	Occupation*	Income	Relation to head
1.							
2.							
3.							
4.							
5.							
6.							
7.							
8.							
9.							
10.							

*Include subsidiary occupations

3. (a) Information on married women:
   Number of children born:
   Number of children surviving:
   Miscarriages:
   Still births:

   (b)

	Present family	Father's family	Mother's family
Number of children born			
Number of children surviving			

(c) Record of deceased family members:

Sl. No.	Name	When occurred	Relation to head	Age at death	Cause of death
1.					
2.					
3.					
4.					
5.					
6.					
7.					
8.					
9.					
10.					

4. Approximate monthly expenditure on:
   (a) Milk and milk products
   (b) Vegetables and fruits
   (c) Groceries
   (d) Fuel
   (e) Rent

Dietary Survey

1. *Food Habits*
   (a) Vegetarian/non-vegetarian/non-vegetarian but usually takes vegetarian food
   (b) Common dietary pattern:

Morning	1st day	2nd day	3rd day	4th day	5th day	6th day	7th day
Mid-day							
Afternoon							
Evening							
Others							

2. *Special Foods*
   (a) For different groups

Groups	Foods recommended	Foods avoided
1. Adults		
2. Infants		
3. Pregnant women		
4. Lactating women		
5. Invalids		

   (b) During illness

Illness	Foods recommended	Foods avoided
1. Cold		
2. Fever		
3. Diarrhoea		
4. Dysentery		
5. Other conditions		

   (c) During different seasons

Seasons	Foods recommended	Foods avoided
Summer		
Winter		
Monsoon		

(d) For religious or other reasons (include data on 'fasts' under-taken by family members and foods taken during 'fasting')

Occasion	Foods permitted	Foods avoided

(e) (i) Foods consumed by previous generation and not consumed now:

(ii) Foods consumed now and not consumed by previous generation:

3. Methods of Cooking

Foods	Boiling	Steaming	Frying	Baking	Pressure Cooking
(a) Roti					
(b) Rice					
(c) Dal					
(d) Vegetables					

4. *Food Sharing Practices:*

5. *Members Eating Out:*

Member	Type of food taken outside
(a) Regularly	
(b) Occasionally	

6. Foods consumed at home

Foodstuff	Amount consumed (gm)**	Source from which obtained
1. *Cereals and millets**		
(a) Rice		
(b) Wheat		
(c) Other grains		
(d) Other cereal or starchy foods		
(e) Processed cereal foods		
2. *Pulses and nuts*		
(a) Dals		
(b) Whole legumes		
(c) Groundnut, til etc.		
(d) Other nuts		
(e) Parched legumes		
3. *Vegetables*		
(a) Leafy vegetables		
(b) Roots and tubers		
(c) Others		
4. *Animal foods*		
(a) Fish, meat and chicken		
(b) Egg		
5. *Milk and milk products*		
(a) Whole milk		
(b) Toned milk		
(c) Milk powder		
(d) Curd		
(e) Baby food		
(f) Cheese		
(g) Mava		
(h) Milk sweets		
(i) Ice-cream		
(j) Other milk products		

* Specify the type of rice used, parboiled, milled or handpounded; for (c) specify grains used; for (d) include macaroni, sago, suji, poha etc.; for (e) include bread, biscuit, cakes, cornflakes, parched grains etc.
** Specify per day, week or month.

Foodstuff	*Amount consumed (gm)***	*Source from which obtained*
6. *Fats and oils*		
(a) Butter		
(b) Dalda		
(c) Groundnut oil		
(d) Ghee		
(e) Refined oil		
(f) Other oils (specify)		
7. *Sugar*		
(a) Refined sugar		
(b) Jaggery		
(c) Others (honey, molasses etc.)		
8. *Condiments*		
(a) Tamarind		
(b) Cocum		
(c) Chillies		
(d) Mango slices		
(e) Other spices		
9. *Preserved and processed foods*		
(a) Pickles		
(b) Papad		
(c) Jams and jellies		
(d) Other canned or bottled foods		
10. *Beverages*		
(a) Tea		
(b) Coffee		
(c) Cocoa		
(d) Malted foods		
(e) Carbonated drinks		
11. *Miscellaneous*		
(a) Betelnut		
(b) Betel leaves		
(c) Chewing tobacco		
(d) Smoking tobacco		

	Amount consumed per day (gm) *		
	Per family	*Per capita*	*Per consumption unit*
Foodstuffs			
Cereals			
(rice+other grains)			
Pulses			
Leafy vegetables			
Root vegetable			
Other vegetables			
Meat			
Fats and oils			
Milk			
Sugar and jaggery			
Nutrients			
Calories			
Protein			
Fat			
Carbohydrate			
Calcium (mg)			
Phosphorus (mg)			
Iron (mg)			
Vitamin A as:			
Carotene (i.u.)			
Pre-formed			
vitamin (i.u.)			
Thiamine (mg)			
Riboflavin (mg)			
Niacin (mg)			
Vitamin C (mg)			

* unless otherwise specified

APPENDIX - III

Physical and Clinical Status

| | | | | Family No. | |
Name	Sex	Age	Height	Weight	Deficiency symptoms